THE MILLER'S
ANGEL BABY

THE MILLER'S ANGEL BABY

A Memoir of My Alcoholic Father's Secret Life

A.R. MILLER

To my beloved dog, Teddy: you have been by my side through it all. Thank you for your loyalty and for always knowing when I needed your company the most. I love you.

"The longer I live, the more I realize the impact of attitude on life. Attitude, to me, is more important than facts. It is more important than the past, than education, than money, than circumstances, than failures, than successes, than what other people think or say or do. It is more important than appearance, giftedness or skill. It will make or break a company...a church...a home. The remarkable thing is, we have a choice every day regarding the attitude we will embrace for that day. We cannot change our past...we cannot change the fact that people will act in a certain way. We cannot change the inevitable. The only thing we can do is play on the one string we have, and that is our attitude. I am convinced that life is 10% what happens to me and 90% how I react to it. And so it is with you...we are in charge of our attitudes."

- Charles R. Swindoll

GET YOUR FREE GIFT

As a thank you for buying my book,
I'm offering a copy of my life-changing Daily Affirmations!
Just visit my website to get your copy today.

Get your free gift by visiting:
AlexisRoseBooks.com

Author's Note

Throughout my book, I mention ways I learned to successfully cope with all the difficulties thrown my way, including meditation and prayer. At the back of my book, I've included resources to help you on your own journey. My goal is to inspire hope and encourage others during difficult times.

PROLOGUE

"Just tell them the baby's dead and leave that hussy. It's time you came back home, Alec," said his mom, Thelma, in a bossy, cold tone of voice. She continued, "There's nothing for you there in Idaho. I bet you that first child isn't even yours. That hussy was probably pregnant when she met you, and she was just looking for a shiny, new gullible GI like you, fresh out of boot camp, to sink her claws into. And now, eleven months after her first baby was born, you two newlyweds have welcomed a crippled child into the world! It serves your dumb ass, right! Didn't I tell you something like this would happen? When you lay down with dogs, you get fleas!"

This was not the warm welcome he was expecting from his mom when he sent his letter to her last week announcing that he and his wife, Cassandra, were the proud parents of another baby girl. Her name was Melissa, and he was careful to note in the letter that this sweet angel would need extra care and attention because of her handicap. Alec loved kids, and he was up for the challenge. He decided to tune his wretched mother out as she droned on.

As he moved the phone receiver farther from his ear, he could still hear her shouting. "No son of mine would do this. I raised you better, Alec!! I *know* that you know better!! You grew up on military bases your entire life, boy. How could you be so dumb to fall for some local piece of ass hanging round the base? They're all just looking for health insurance and child support. Didn't you learn anything from your dad's Army buddies, Wilson and Carter? Both their lives were ruined by wicked women like the one you married!" his mom yelled into the phone, between quick drags on her cigarette. The more she talked, the faster and louder her words spilled out, like marbles from a bag—and the farther he held the phone receiver from his ear. Finally, there was a moment of silence, and he guessed she was stopping to come up for air and take a long drag on one of her precious cigarettes.

Alec brought the phone closer to his ear just as his mom began speaking in a hushed, cold voice, like a low growl, "Like I said, just tell everyone the baby was born crippled and died of complications. No one will be the wiser."

Alec could just see her lips curled under as she uttered every word. She called this her "mean mouth," and he knew it all too well, for she was quite adept at using it on him and his older sister, Vicky, or Vicks, for short. Their mom's mean streak and controlling nature were exactly why Vicks cut ties with her and didn't even bother coming to their dad's funeral. Or, as he and Vicks lovingly liked to call him, "the Old Man." But that's a different story for another day.

Alec refocused, collected his thoughts, and steadied his nerves before calmly saying, "But, Mom, you don't understand; as far as I'm concerned, both kids are mine, and I love Cassandra. We'll be fine. We can move back to Philadelphia and live in your duplex. You don't have an upstairs tenant; we can move in! You'll see. That way, I'll be close to you. Right upstairs, literally, as your tenant. I know you've been struggling to do it all since the funeral last year. You and the Old Man had a great marriage, and I know this must be hard on you. With me there, I can easily help you and take care of my family. It doesn't have to be either-or. I can be there for you and my family. The Air Force has been good to me. I have good skills and can get a good engineering tech job, probably down at the naval shipyards." As Alec finished, he tried to keep a light, hopeful tone.

"Look, Alec," she shouted, "Now's your chance to fix your situation and clean this all up, like it never happened, then get on with your life!"

In truth, Alec knew she was just trying to manipulate him into coming home—purely for her own self-interests.

As if on cue, she said, "Now that your father's passed away, I need your help here full-time. You're all I've got, Alec," her tone was pleading. "Your sister's as good as gone; I can't depend on her for shit. She's visiting me now, but I'm sure she only showed up on my doorstep because she's broke and wants money. After all the Old Man and I did for her. We paid for her nursing school, and she threw it all away and got knocked up by a loser. All I wanted was for her to keep her legs shut and become a nurse. Was that too much to ask? That good-for-nothing hussy can go to hell, too," she finished with a bitter tone full of regret and remorse.

Alec knew that Vicks' decision to quit nursing school had crushed Mom and the Old Man. They put so much pressure on Vicks to be the first girl in the family to become a nurse. That was Mom's greatest desire, to have her daughter become a nurse. The pressure was too much for his sister. She made Alec promise not to tell Mom and the Old Man that she was dropping out and eloping. They'd covered for each other their whole lives, and he wasn't about to stop now. He loved his sister and would always have her back.

There was a pause, as his mom took a long drag on her cigarette. Then, without missing a beat, she went back on her tirade, "You don't have time to raise a family and help me. And mark my words;

a crippled child will bleed you dry in medical bills. The obstetrician should have told you two idiots that it was stillborn and secretly put that pitiful child in a home. How are two 22-year-old kids like you going to raise a 12-month-old baby *and* a crippled 1-month-old baby? Alec, let me remind you, this is 1964, you're a Negro, and your wife's a Mexican. You're living on a military base in Idaho, literally in the middle of nowhere, surrounded by mountains, almost an hour outside of Boise. The odds are stacked against you, son. A light-skinned Negro like you and a dark-skinned Mexican woman like her are just asking for trouble the minute you step foot off that base. What happens if you have to take that baby to specialists in Boise and your car breaks down in the middle of nowhere? The Old Man is dead and gone, and I'm in Philadelphia; what good does that do you? It's best for you to put this behind you and come back home," she spoke as if she were going to have the final say.

At this point, Alec lost his mind. He had been doing his best to remain calm, but that comment pushed him over the edge; he was furious and decided to let her have it. "I've listened to this crap long enough. Those are my daughters and wife you're talking about, and I won't have it! Stop calling my daughter pitiful and crippled. Do you hear me? Stop it! Her name is MELISSA. Did you get that, *Mom*? Her name is MELISSA!"

This was the first time Alec had ever stood up to his mother in his entire life; every cell in him was tingling, and his body was hot and trembling with rage. This act symbolized the first time he had ever respected himself and put his needs ahead of his mother's. He truly felt seen, respected, and alive for the first time, and he was on a roll. Years of hurt and pent-up rage colored his words. He yelled out, "I'm not your damn Momma's Boy. I'm not your doormat. I'm not your slave. I'm not your puppet. I don't answer to you. I don't need your damn help; I don't need your approval, and I don't need you!"

"Oh, well, well, now, is that so? You won't have it!" she screamed. "Well, son, you *owe* me. Remember all the times I covered for your drunken ass when you were in *high school*, running wild in Germany? Remember when that girl showed up at our front door saying she was pregnant with your child? I told her and her folks to get lost and that if they didn't get off our property, I'd have the MPs drag their asses off it. I slammed the front door in their lying faces! And who picked your ass up at the police station and covered it all up so the Old Man wouldn't find out that you were in a *whorehouse* at 15? I did!" she continued screaming, her voice raising in volume and octaves. "You. Owe. Me." There was a long pause between each of those last three words, and Alec was sure his mom was lighting another cigarette to calm her nerves.

He retorted, "Leave the past in the past, Mom; I don't owe you anything, and I'm not going to be manipulated or threatened by you. That ship has sailed. Drop it."

Mom flatly stated, "Well, if that's how you want it, then I'm done sending you money every month to help your sorry ass pay the bills. Consider yourself cut off. See how long you last without me. Mark my words, you'll be crawling back home to your momma with your tail between your legs. So, like I said, finish your tour, divorce Cassandra, and go your separate ways. When you come back home, tell everyone the baby died and the marriage ended. It's quite believable, especially since she was born with so many complications. If you want to give Cassandra child support, that's on you. As far as I'm concerned, Cassandra and her kids are dead to us. She can take care of herself and HER mess."

Alec nonchalantly replied, "Well, I guess this is where we part ways, then. I'm sick of your games, and I'm done caving into you. Goodbye, Mom," Alec slammed down the receiver, sighed, and felt the weight of the world fall off of his 22-year-old shoulders. He was finally free of his mother's death grip on his life. He had put his foot down that day and decided to own up to the consequences of his actions for the first time. Finally, he was truly on his own, and he knew the Old Man would be proud. The ripple effect of his decision would be felt for decades, long after his eyes had closed.

What a story; I could almost smell my grandmother's coffee and cigarette smoke as I listened to my Aunt Vicks recount that horrific telephone conversation. Little did my grandmom know, on that fateful 1964 day, that Vicks had been upstairs eavesdropping on the entire conversation from the bedroom telephone. My head was spinning, and I thought I would be ill.

TABLE OF CONTENTS

CHAPTER 1

The first day of school started off like any other first day of school we'd ever known, except this time, I couldn't shake the nagging feeling in my gut that my dad's increasingly bizarre behavior was going to come to a head soon, and it wasn't going to be pretty.

I pushed the feeling down, put on a happy face, and gleefully shouted to my kids, "Come on, let's go; you don't want to be late for your first day of school, kids!" To my surprise, they turned off the TV, hopped off the sofa, and quickly ran from the family room and into the mudroom, where I was waiting for them.

Before I could even tell Chad and Arianna to put their shoes on, they had already started doing it. "Whose kids are these? Clearly, these aren't my kids," I joked playfully. Thank God they cooperated easily because I truly didn't have the emotional bandwidth to deal with first-day jitters and emotional meltdowns. To be honest, I was trying desperately to hold myself together and juggling way too many proverbial plates of responsibility as it was; I was about an inch away from a complete emotional breakdown. Thankfully, the morning routine went smoothly.

To encourage their good behavior, I thanked them both heartily for coming the first time they were called and proceeded to stoop down and help Arianna tie her shoelaces. As I bent down to tie the fresh, white laces in her Topsiders, she patted my head and said, "I get to go to school with Chad today; I'm big like him now, and I get to ride the bus!"

I finished tying her shoes, beamed at them, and said, "You're right, Arianna, you are starting kindergarten today, and Chad is starting fifth grade!" They both smiled as I gathered up their book bags and lunch boxes from the nearby wooden bench in the mudroom. Then, just like a mother duck with two little ducklings in tow, they followed me from the mudroom and out into the garage.

Oh, how I wish every school morning could be this nice and easy. But I knew this was a rare blip in the order of things and chose to savor the momentary calm and cooperation. And then, I thought of their father, *How I wish my husband were here to see the kids off for the first day of school.*

Being a military wife and mom had its highs and lows, and this was definitely one of the lows. It seemed like Michael was often away for the major milestone moments in our children's lives. When we met in college, he had finished serving his four years in the Army to pay for college and was enrolled in ROTC during those years. *I had no intention of being an Army wife.* My entire family was ex-military, and I had heard enough stories to know I wanted no part of that life.

Michael assured me he was finished with the military. He was going to college to become a schoolteacher, and that's who I thought I was marrying—a schoolteacher. I never dreamed in a million years that his teaching career would flop, and he'd enlist with the Pennsylvania Army National Guard less than two years into our marriage. I did not sign on to be a military wife, but I chose to make the best of it. At least he was only stationed to work in Pennsylvania. There was no way I was leaving my hometown and the life I knew. So, we made it work.

Unfortunately, he was not immune to overseas deployments. They were infrequent, but even one was one too many. At the time, he was deployed in the Middle East for a six-month tour of duty. Thankfully, his desk job was out of harm's way. He was about seven hours ahead of us, so our early mornings were his late afternoons. The kids didn't understand what a time change meant. As I dialed his number, I explained it for the umpteenth time, "Daddy is on the other side of the world, so the sun and moon can't shine in the same place at the same time. It's 7:15 in the morning here, but where Daddy is living, it's 2:15 in the afternoon. He's already had breakfast and lunch."

They stared at me blankly, and I just chuckled. After a few rings, Michael picked up, and it was so good to see his face on the video chat. We chatted about first-day jitters, and he asked the kids to text him photos of any pictures they drew today. I savored this sacred time with him. When he wasn't deployed, he left for work before dawn, and he has always made it a point to call the kids before they left for daycare or school.

It was a sacred little morning ritual that we all looked forward to. I was grateful that we could still keep that tradition alive during his deployment. It truly was the little things like this that made all the difference. It eased my pangs of loneliness and worry. Also, the semblance of normalcy and routine helped ease the kids' anxiety and lifted their spirits about Michael being gone.

After hanging up, we marked off today's date, Monday, August 26th, 2016, on the kitchen calendar and counted down the days until he came home. He left in May and would be back home on November 16th, 2016. We had three months left; we had a special celebration planned this weekend to commemorate the halfway mark. This deployment wasn't our family's first rodeo. Thankfully, this one was only six months and not a year. And on the plus side, he was in a relatively "peaceful" area doing a "desk job," safely out of harm's way.

After a round of high-fives and happy dancing, we made a bee-line for the garage, and I drove the kids down to the bus stop. We lived in a small development, and I could see the kids gathered at the bus stop, all wearing loafers, white polos, and either maroon pants for the boys or maroon plaid skirts for the girls. As I drove, the kids chatted back and forth nervously; I could tell they both had first-day jitters. They'd been such good sports about going to private school. Arianna should be fine; this would be all she'd ever know. On the other hand, Chad had been in public school since kindergarten. I prayed he adjusted well and made new friends. At least a handful of the neighborhood kids he grew up with also attended.

I remember he and his father had both pitched a fit when I initially announced last winter that I wanted the kids to start private school in the fall. With me working again, I finally had the means to put them both through school. Truth be told, I had really wanted them to attend the local Waldorf School, but my husband, Michael, felt the school was too alternative for his comfort level. Christian school was the only private school we could both agree on. And even that was a stretch.

In Michael's opinion, the local public school was just fine; it was a good school district, and our taxes paid for it, so the kids should attend it. Thank God I was able to persuade him to see things my way. I really wanted the best education possible for them and an education rooted in faith was the cherry on top. I loved attending private school as a child and wouldn't be the person I am today without that foundational education. I always wanted this for our children, and now it was finally going to happen. I just wished they started school after Labor Day instead of the week before. I wanted to milk every last day of summer!

As we drove down to the cul-de-sac and parked, we reviewed one last time what our street address was, and that they were to ride bus number 39 in the morning, but in the afternoon, they would ride bus 50, which would take them to aftercare. I hoped to drill this information into their little heads. Fingers crossed, they both remembered to get on the correct bus and off at the correct stop this afternoon. I reminded them of one last thing: "And remember kids, Grandmom will pick you up from aftercare at Whole Child Prep today, not me; I will meet you at the house when I get home from work."

They nodded, and that was that; I prepared to release my babies into the care of new people for the next school year by saying a quick prayer, as I turned the ignition off.

When we got out of the car, I could see my neighbor, Tina, walking toward the bus stop with a basket of cookies and her brood of kids. She is the sweetest mom and a dear friend, and every year she baked cookies for the kids on the first day of school as a little send-off treat. This year she baked and decorated school-bus-shaped cookies that were individually bagged for all ten kids at the bus stop. I got body-wide chills just imagining myself trying to plan and coordinate getting the ingredients and making the cut-out shapes, let alone successfully baking them, decorating them, and having them bagged and ready for the 7:30 a.m. bus. Within seconds, all the cookies were gobbled up, the bus arrived, and we said our goodbyes.

Off to work I went, feeling a mix of remorse, guilt, shame, and joy. As I drove, I wrestled with the doubts in my head. I wondered if I had made the correct choice when I decided to work outside the home. I wondered if I even liked being a mom well enough to be around my kids 24/7. I wondered if the other moms were judging me when I went off to work, since I was the only woman in our small development who worked outside the home. My thoughts spiraled out of control as I mindlessly drove to work.

Thankfully, I became aware of my racing thoughts about half-way through my commute. I practiced the mindfulness techniques I learned in my new yoga class; I just lovingly observed the thoughts and thanked my mind for showing me this story. Then, I decided to choose something better-feeling to think about.

I cranked up the car's AC and auto-dialed my mom. During our call, I recounted the morning in great detail for her since she couldn't be there today. As we talked, she asked me how I was feeling; I responded wistfully, "You know, Mom, I used to feel guilty on the first day of school. I was the only mom at the bus stop dressed for work and rushing off to a job or grad school. The rest of the moms are homemakers. I've always wondered if I'm shortchanging myself and my kids by going to work and putting them in childcare. But I realize now that I do not like being home with my children 24/7. And I'm fine saying that. I love them dearly and enjoy spending time with them. However, at this point, I'm more concerned with the quality of my time with them, not the quantity of time."

My mom was always guilt-tripping me about one thing or another when it came to my parenting skills and how much time Michael and I spent with them. I was kicking myself for starting this conversation with her. True to form, good old Carla gave her two cents, "Look, Alexis, those kids need you home. You've got the rest of your life to play dress-up and drive to an office looking cute. Right now, your behind needs to be home raising the children you birthed."

I shot back, "That's all fine and good; however, you're not the one who has to spend all day with them, and you're not the one with a deployed husband. I know myself, and I am not cut out to be a stay-at-home mom. I have career aspirations and dreams I want to live out now, not twenty years from now, after my kids have sucked the life out of me. I've busted my butt for the last three years as a returning adult student to earn a second master's degree. I am proud of what I accomplished, and my children are just fine. I am married to a good man, and we are raising our children as we see fit."

I could hear her sigh on the other end of the line. And lucky for me, my commute was short, and I was pulling into the parking lot at work. I quickly said, "Listen, Mom, I know you care about the kids and want the best for them. And I know you were a single working mom and did your best with me. But now it's my turn to raise my family as my husband and I see fit. I've got to go to work now; I love you and will talk to you tonight when you come over." Before she could utter a retort, I said, "Bye," and quickly hung up.

CHAPTER 2

Oh, how I love my job! I made my way to the interior design department and greeted my team of sales reps, project managers, and fellow designers as I got settled at my desk. I'd been working at RMK Interiors for nine months, and so far, I'd been given increasingly challenging tasks to do, that were really putting my new master's degree to use.

This firm worked on commercial, education, and healthcare projects worldwide. I was working under an amazing senior interior designer, Shannon Rawlings; she was showing me the ropes. She knew a lot of people in the industry, and I was so grateful to be working under her. I was helping her select all the fabrics and finishes for the office furniture in a tech company in DC. It was my largest project yet, with two floors and 60,000 square feet! The owners wanted to keep it sleek and modern, with pops of color tied to their company logo colors, which were teal and orange. They chose sleek, all-white finishes with bold pops of color in the lounge areas, conference rooms, and breakrooms.

The conference rooms would have tables that convert to ping-pong tables! The credenzas were customized to chill the owner's favorite wines. On that fateful day, I was to select new samples for the solid surface counters, wall tile, and floor tile for all the bathrooms and break rooms. Apparently, the client changed her mind at the last minute and wanted to have an entirely new color palette. Shannon showed me the updated look the client was going for in each space, and it was my job to select products that were in stock and met the performance criteria, price point, lead time, and aesthetics she was looking for. My appointment was booked at the top local tile show-room, and I planned to drive there after our morning project status meeting. I had roughly two hours to find the products and bring them back for Shannon to review. She'd keep what she liked and present it to the client tomorrow, along with the rest of the furniture and finishes we had been curating.

Tile Envy was about a thirty-minute drive from the office, so I decided to listen to a business podcast on founders and their business failures. Halfway through the podcast, my cell phone rang. It was Dad. A chill ran down my spine. He had been acting more and more bizarre the past two months following my father-in-law's death. I think the death may have stirred up memories of my grandmother's death.

Normally, I saw Dad for holidays and birthdays, and we spoke once or twice a month. Now, he was calling my home phone 4–5 times per week. I was coming home to find multiple messages on my voicemail from him. They never mentioned anything important, just random things he forgot to tell me the last time we talked. He'd talk, and I'd listen to him tell me random stories about a vacation he took thirty years ago, a movie he saw twenty years ago, or about how high he was on pot one time. About fifteen minutes into the conversation, I'd tell him I had to get off the call and go get ready for bed.

More times than not, when we talked, he was under the influence. At first, it was sweet to speak with him. I thought he was checking in on us because Michael was deployed. But then, it became sour really quickly when he started calling me half-drunk at 10 and 11 o'clock at night, waking the kids and me up from a dead sleep. Something had triggered his relapse, and I had to get to the bottom of it because my job performance, marriage, and, quite frankly, my sanity depended on it. I was Alec's only daughter and living relative around for miles, so that meant he called me for help. And like a dutiful, loving daughter, I rose to the occasion and helped. But was I really helping him?

This was the first time he had ever called my cell during the day, so I decided to answer. *Maybe he's sober, and we can have a real conversation?* I was using hands-free, and the podcast turned off when I answered the call. "Hi, Dad, how are you? Is everything okay?" I asked with a note of concern in my voice.

What came next was not expected. He sounded completely *wasted* at 11 o'clock in the morning, his words were half-slurred, and he was talking gibberish.

To give Dad the benefit of the doubt, I asked him, "Dad, are you okay? Do you need to go to the doctor?"

He hiccupped and slurred, "No, I don't need to go see any docs; all's good here with me. What's up with you? How come you don't call me more? Oh, let me tell you about when I saw Bigfoot on the highway." And with that statement, I knew he was drunk; he only mentioned his "Bigfoot sighting," on a North Dakota highway, when he was drunk.

I was almost to the tile showroom and had to wrap this call up fast. I cut Dad off quickly and said, "Listen, thanks for the call, Dad. I will call later to check on you. Bye." And with that, I hung up.

It pained me to hang up on my father, but what other choice did I have? He was drunk!! Normally, he paced his drinking throughout the day and didn't hit the hard liquor hard until nightfall. That had been his daily routine for as long as I could remember. He had always been able to hold his liquor and go on about his day, buzzed. Whatever the trigger was, he had decided to silence it with his favorite numbing agent.

Finally, I shook my head and said a little prayer for him before turning the podcast back on. I made a mental note to myself, "Do not get wrapped up in his mess, Alexis; you have a family who needs you and a life of your own." As far as I was concerned, *it was his mess.* But not getting involved was easier said than done. As the only child and only living relative for miles, I felt guilty about not helping my father. But I also didn't want to inherit his mess or bring it into my home and compromise my marriage and the safety and welfare of my family.

Maybe the recent death of my father-in-law is hitting Dad harder than I thought? They weren't that close, but *maybe* it had stirred up painful memories for Dad that he just had no other way to process.

In a couple of minutes, my phone rang again, and I decided to let it go to voicemail. I would be at the tile showroom in 5 minutes. I could check my voicemail then. I pulled my racing mind back to reality and quickly accelerated forward. A few minutes later, I saw the strip mall ahead and recognized the sleek green and white signage for Tile Envy.

After parking in the lot, I had ten minutes to spare before my appointment and decided to check my voicemail. As I swiped across the screen and scrolled down quickly, my suspicion was confirmed—a message from Dad. I listened to it, and it was just more drunken babble. I deleted it, put my phone on vibrate, and gathered my tote bag and purse. *I do not have the time, energy, or desire to deal with Dad's BS; I have building finishes to select!*

No sooner than I crossed the street, he called again. I thought, "Why is this happening to me? What did I ever do to anyone? It's not fair! Why couldn't I have been born to a set of average, well-adjusted, wealthy, loving parents and lived happily ever after, *the end?*" I ignored the call and proceeded to Tile Envy, all the while deep breathing to clear my head and calm my nerves. There was no time to process his BS; I had a job to do.

I was meeting Becca Dunn, Creative Concierge, in 5 minutes; that gave me a quick second or two to quickly scan the showroom's eye candy. I gazed at the array of backsplashes and stopped at a beautiful kitchen display with Carrera marble counters, a white farmhouse sink; and my favorite brushed stainless-steel, single-handle, high-arc faucet, with a pull-down knurled spout. It was such an industrial chic-looking faucet! We specified it on so many projects; it was in all the shelter magazines, pinned on practically every trendy Pinterest board, and I had it installed in my own kitchen. Tile Envy's finishes and creativity never ceased to amaze me, and in moments like this, I really loved my job.

I quickly took my phone out to snap some selfies and posted them on Instagram. I noticed Dad had called me *six more times* since I'd walked into the showroom. *What is going on!?* I was losing my cool and needed to pull myself together before my meeting.

The entire appointment, I was in a fog; my head was elsewhere, thinking about Dad. I just remember heels clicking across the store floor, big clawfoot bathtubs, sparkly backsplashes, twinkling chandeliers, the smell of coffee and chai tea, dramatic walls of rectangular subway tile with aqua and gold mosaic tiles, marble slabs displayed in rows like soldiers, and Becca's melodious voice singing the praises and durability of product after product. It was sensory overload, and it all swirled together like colorful sprinkles being quickly blended into cake batter.

Luckily, Becca's keen eye for style complemented the look we were going for with this project, and her samples were just what I was looking for. I quickly curated a great selection to show my boss, based on the tile samples she pulled ahead of time for me. The price points, durability level, and in-stock availability were all acceptable, and this was going to be a fast and easy process. It was all a blur, but I did my best to focus, despite my mounting anxiety about Dad. I put on a happy, interested-looking face, nodded along, acted like I gave a shit, and scanned and selected four of each: floor, subway, and accent tiles. *Done!*

We chose my favorite brushed stainless-steel, single-handle high-arc faucet, with a pull-down knurled spout for all break rooms and the matching hands-free, high-arc faucet for the bathrooms. *Too easy!*

I was ready to head back to the office on time and on budget. I knew Shannon would just love these samples. I said my goodbyes, signed off on the paperwork, and carried the samples back to the car. On the ride back, I couldn't reach Dad. His phone just went to voicemail. I was getting more nervous by the minute. I felt helpless and distraught.

I arrived back at the office with time to spare; I sat in my car to collect myself, and as I nervously ran my fingers through my hair, what looked like a clump of hair fell out onto my lap. I was ready to start bawling like a baby. I couldn't ignore it anymore. My hair had been shedding at an alarming rate for the past three months, and I had to face the facts—I was losing my hair and needed to find out why.

I had worked so hard to grow my hair, and it pained me to see it falling out. I speed-dialed my hairdresser and booked the next available time she had, which wasn't until mid-September, about three weeks away. I don't know why I had waited so long to make this appointment. Honestly, my hair was starting to look and feel like a Brillo™ pot-scrubbing pad. I sighed deeply, gathered the samples, and trudged back into the office after pasting another fake smile on my face.

CHAPTER 3

The afternoon did not go as expected. After seeing the samples, in the middle of the open office, Shannon literally reamed me out in front of everyone. She yelled at the top of her lungs, "What is this shit? This isn't what I told you to get! How could you screw this up so badly? I gave you one simple task: select the solid surface counters, wall tile, and floor tile for all the bathrooms and break rooms. I showed you the exact style I wanted and specifically said, 'NO brushed steel tiles.' Yet, every single backsplash sample you have here has brushed steel tiles. Are you blind!? We are down to the wire on this project, and a change order this late in the game could delay the whole project. I needed these finishes selected *today*, and over-nighted to the client for her review tomorrow. There was no room for error."

I was completely aghast. Unbeknownst to me, I brought the wrong samples back to the office. Shannon wanted glass tile mosaic with NO brushed steel tiles; unfortunately, every backsplash sample I brought back had brushed steel tiles interspersed between the mosaic glass tiles. She took one look at the samples I set out on the table and became irate, to say the least.

Before I could get a word in, she continued on, "A first-year intern could have done a better job than this. You will be going back on your lunch break to fix this. No, better yet, I'll have the intern do it. I need these samples finalized today and in the client's hands tomorrow. This is your third screw-up in a month. Screw up again, Alexis, and I *will* see to it that you're canned, and you can kiss your interior design career goodbye." She said this with her hands on her hips and a sneer on her face. It was such an unbecoming look on her attractive face.

I apologized and felt every eye in the office boring a hole into my skull, like a laser beam focused on burning a hole into a piece of metal.

She acknowledged my apology with a sneer and a disappointed, "Hmph."

The look of disdain and disappointment on her face was what got to me the most. I thought, "So much for looking up to her and having a mentor in the industry. She's nothing but a condescending wench. It's people like her who give this industry a bad rap. There are better, more constructive, and professional ways to speak to someone and counsel them on their performance. We all make mistakes." As I thought this, she cocked one eyebrow, looked me up and down, and said dismissively, "That will be all, Alexis. Finish your work on the floor plans for this project and have them to me by the end of the week for final review." She turned on her heels, walked over to the intern's desk, and proceeded to give the intern her afternoon marching orders.

It was bad enough the intern was fetching Shannon's coffee, lunch, and dry cleaning; now, she had to drop everything to fix my mistake. Some would call this "paying your dues" in the industry. I called it bullying in a toxic work environment. I shook off the shock, walked down the long hall as best I could without crying, and focused on making it to the exit. I avoided making eye contact with the slew of curious eyes peering at me over the cubicle walls that lined each side of the painfully long aisle.

After what felt like an eon, I made it to the glass door, swung it open, and practically ran to the bathroom. Once inside the safety of the last stall, the waterworks began. I couldn't keep my emotions bottled up anymore. I cried tears for my father and the cascade of disturbing calls I'd been getting from him. I cried tears for my family and how truly disconnected I felt from my kids as a working mom. I cried tears for my marriage, which was feeling the strain of my husband being deployed. I cried tears for the mess I'd just gotten myself into at yet another dead-end, toxic job.

Shannon was an influential person in the local design circles in the city, and I had really wanted to nurture a connection with her. It looked like I could kiss that dream goodbye. *What will I do if I lose my job? I'm still paying off the last of the credit card debt for the new clothes, shoes, and purses I brought to build my work wardrobe!* Clothes that I might end up wearing to the unemployment office if Shannon got her way. *How did I end up in another crummy, dead-end job with a crummy supervisor and little room for advancement and growth?*

It was bittersweet to realize that I had just graduated with a new degree and $100,000 of debt to follow my dream of becoming an interior designer. Yet, I ended up in another soul-crushing, dead-end job, where I was bullied and harassed. I grabbed a wad of toilet paper, dabbed my eyes, and blew my nose. I had lost track of time and needed to get back to my desk. I left the stall, splashed some water on my face, dabbed some lip gloss on my lips, prayed to God for strength, and read the positive affirmations saved in my iPhone notes. That was how I spent my lunch break. *What an epic day. This is the job I love?*

I squared my shoulders back, gave one last look in the mirror, and noticed a clump of my hair on the counter. My eyes bulged as I looked up at the top of my scalp and noticed a pale gaping hole in the center of my dark hair. I exclaimed out loud, "What the hell! I can't win!" I gently ran my fingers through my hair and tried in vain to make a new part that would hide the bald spot. To my dismay, nothing worked, and I had to fish a hair tie out of my pants pocket and pull my hair up into a messy bun.

I gathered up what courage I had left, squared my shoulders again, forced a smile, and walked back to my desk. As I reached the door to my department, I saw the other designers crowded around Shannon's desk, and they were all talking up a storm. I guessed they were talking about me. As I opened the door, I faked a cough, and they all scattered like roaches, fleeing from the light that pierced their dark intentions and exposed their misdeeds. I ignored them as they scurried past me, sat down at my desk, and began working on the floor plans for Shannon's project, as if nothing had happened. No time to wallow in my misery, I ignored the awkward silence and began typing away at my computer; it was time to produce good results.

The afternoon hours slowly dragged by, and I did my best to keep my chin up and hold a stiff upper lip. As soon as the clock struck 5:00 p.m., I logged off my computer, gathered my things, and told everyone, "Goodnight." Most people were still sitting at their desks plugging away, but I had no interest in working one second beyond my assigned work hours. As soon as the exit door closed behind me, and I felt the hot summer air on my skin, I breathed a sigh of relief and thanked God for getting me out of that place. I hurried to my car, sped out of the parking lot, and raced home.

How quickly things had changed since this morning. I should have trusted my gut and never accepted that wretched position in the first place. I should have kept the faith and held out for a more worthwhile job. To be honest, I knew the moment I clicked through a couple of links on their website, this was no company I wanted to work for. Yet, I applied for the job anyway, out of desperation. Against my better judgment, I went on the interview, and despite the red flags raised, I came back for a second interview and accepted the position. I've been lying to myself and everyone else ever since, telling everyone how great my job was just to save face. *I changed careers for this?*

I vowed to never again settle for less in any area of my life. I would go without, before I settled for something that didn't meet my list of expectations. I vowed to get clear on what I wanted in my next job and start putting out feelers.

As I drove home, reminiscing, I vowed out loud to myself, "From this day forward, as long as I am alive, I promise I will never sell myself short again for another crummy job. I am worth better and will no longer settle, suffer, sacrifice, or struggle. I will hold out for the best." Chills ran down my spine, and the hair on my arms rose on end when I exclaimed this vow. I felt like something had shifted in me, and a weight was unloaded.

Hot tears streamed down my face the entire ride home, and I honestly don't know how I made it home safely. I sat in my driveway for a good ten minutes and blasted the cold A/C on my face. I hoped in vain that it would dry my tears and reduce my puffy eyelids. I felt cornered and just didn't know what else to do, so I prayed. I let the car idle and just prayed. I prayed to God for strength, energy, and patience for the start of my second shift as a single parent. I gave thanks that my mom had picked the kids up from daycare and picked up a pizza for dinner. I prayed over Michael's safety and that my father would sober up. I missed "sober" Dad. I could really use his company right about now, with Michael gone.

The alone time did wonders for my soul. I could feel my tense shoulders drop as the details of the day faded away, thank God. I breathed deeply and exhaled. My eyes looked better when I looked in the rearview mirror—time to go in and be with the kids for the night. I pulled into the garage and let the second shift begin.

Thank God they didn't know I had been sitting in the driveway recharging and steeling myself for the nightly tasks. My kids happily regaled me with the tales of their first day when I walked in the door. Arianna loved her kindergarten teacher, and it turned out, she did know a classmate! I sent God another quick prayer of thanks that things were off to a good start for the school year. I had enough on my plate and was grateful to have something go smoothly today.

We ate pizza with my mom and made plans for the weekend to celebrate reaching the halfway mark of their dad's deployment. On nights like this, I wished I wasn't a military wife; I wished my husband earned a great salary working a regular 9–5, came home every night, and had weekends off. It seemed like he was always gone when something important happened or when the crap hit the fan, and life went off the rails. The last thing I wanted to do was burden Michael with bad news, but I really needed to get the day's events off my chest and talk with him; he was my best friend and confidant. I could always bounce ideas off him, and he always gave me sound advice and wise counsel. I really valued his opinion.

With the seven-hour time difference, it was too late to call him now; he was already in bed for the night. I had decided to text him, just to let him know that I needed some work advice and to ask whether he was free tomorrow night around seven his time, which was 1 p.m. my time. I could FaceTime him over my lunch break. Surprisingly, he was still up and texted me back right away with a single word, "Yes."

That was all I needed to know. I was grateful and looked forward to tomorrow.

Work was much better the next day; Shannon was in a better mood. I guessed it was because her precious samples made it to the client by 10 a.m., and the client approved all the new finishes. Shannon thanked us all for our hard work and even apologized to me for her behavior.

I accepted her apology and wondered if I should tell her the backstory about my family problems. *Is it wise to mix personal and professional business? Or will it muddy the waters and tarnish my professional reputation?* I decided she needed an explanation for my erratic behavior.

When she stopped by my cubicle to apologize, I briefly summarized what was going on with Dad's drinking relapse and my husband's deployment. In an instant, her whole demeanor towards me changed. She pulled up a chair, sat next to me at my desk, and talked in a hushed voice, "Alexis, I am so sorry for my behavior. First of all, I'd like to extend a thank you to your husband for his service. I am grateful for the sacrifices he has made, the sacrifices you and your family have made for me and countless others in this great country, and the freedoms we hold dear. I did not know you had so much on your plate."

She paused for a moment, looked me square in the eye, and then continued, "Regardless of how much you have on your plate, that was no excuse for my behavior. Truth be told, I'm struggling with my own personal issues, and I overreacted yesterday. And I have been overreacting for quite some time. I'm afraid I'm the one who's going to be canned. But thank you for telling me. My father was also an alcoholic, so I can kind of relate to some of what you are going through. After my mom passed, I was his caregiver. Anytime you need to talk, please don't hesitate to reach out. I am happy to give you my cell phone number."

"Have you talked to your supervisor about this? I've noticed a decline in your performance; I am sure she has too. I highly recommend scheduling a time to explain the situation to her. I've talked to my boss about what I'm going through, and he's been very supportive. I didn't go into the gory details, but he knows what's going on; if I have to leave suddenly or come in late, there's a valid reason why." As she said this, she reached into the chest pocket of her navy wool blazer and handed me one of her business cards.

I accepted it and thanked her. My mind was racing, but I was able to manage a few words. "Boy, am I glad we had this talk. I'm sorry to hear that you are going through things, too. I appreciate your candor, professional advice, and offer of assistance. Thank you, I appreciate it. It's been a challenge to see Dad go downhill. I hadn't thought of talking to my supervisor about this; it makes sense to let her know. I will email Bryanna and schedule a time to talk with her. Thank you."

And with that, Shannon smiled and said, "Good, I'm glad we talked. And please, I mean what I said, call me anytime. I've been through a lot and can point you in the direction of resources and support groups, if that's something you're interested in. Have a good day, and be sure to prioritize taking care of yourself." She rose from her chair and walked back over to her cubicle.

I was so thankful for the conversation and glad I let my guard down and talked about my family situation and what I was struggling with. She felt more like a big sister in that moment than a co-worker. *God, how I wish I actually had sisters.* I hated being an only child. I was one of twenty-two first cousins, and they all had siblings. I was always the odd ball out. Ever since I was a child, I wanted older sisters to take me under their wing, take me places, protect me, dote on me, and love me. I longed for the sibling bond I saw among my cousins. *But as a grown woman, I can forget that.*

Darn if I didn't marry an only child with only four first cousins in Michigan! At least my kids had each other. I prayed they would always stay close and on good terms long after my eyes close forever.

My lunch break rolled around, and I was in a much better frame of mind to talk to Michael about my dad and work. I drove to a nearby park and parked under a shady tree with the A/C on full blast. The FaceTime started as usual; we said our hellos, and I updated him on the kids. He asked what was wrong, and I burst into tears telling him about my dad and his increased erratic drunk calls during the night and day. I told him about my problems at work, and how I felt the whole world was crashing in at times.

Michael sighed and, after a long pause, asked me what I needed from him. "I know I'm on the other side of the globe, but I'll help you any way I can, babe. You mean the world to me, and I want you to be happy and feel loved. I am sorry I can't be there to take you in my arms and hold you. I wish I could make this all just go away. I love you." At that moment, that was really all I needed to hear to fill my cup.

I breathed a sigh of relief and said, "I'm sorry to burden you. Please pray for me. I need wisdom. I need to know how to help my dad without taking on his problems or enabling him. I also need herculean strength to keep up with home and work responsibilities.

I feel like I'm juggling too many plates, and I need a lot of helping hands to take over tasks before I self-implode."

Michael thought for a minute and then suggested I talk to Dad when he came to our house for the annual Labor Day party. We normally held a combined annual event to celebrate not only Labor Day, but also all of our summer birthdays. My immediate family members all have an August birthday, as does my mother-in-law. I told Michael that I really didn't feel much like celebrating this year with him gone, my father-in-law, Gil, passing in the spring, and now Dad relapsing. I said, "Honestly, babe, at this point, I was thinking Labor Day 2016 might get skipped this year. I'm not sure how that news will go over with my mom or yours, and the kids would prob- ably freak over not getting presents and birthday cake…but I just don't feel like celebrating right now."

Michael listened and paused before carefully phrasing the next words he spoke. "Well, it's not written in stone that we have to host an annual Labor Day party. I also don't know of any official "Good Wife" guidebooks on the market. So, if some make-believe standards of domesticity are draining you, don't play that game. It's not a big deal. They'll all get over it. Then again, maybe you'll feel differently after a good night's rest. Maybe the annual get-together will be good for everyone, and I can always FaceTime with you guys. The sense of normalcy and honoring of tradition might ease everyone's anxiety levels. And then again, maybe you decide to cater the whole event, so you're not cooking anything. It's August 26th, so you still have time to plan a menu and call in a food order with Antonio's Gourmet Deli for delivery and set up. It's up to you, whatever you want."

I thought about what he said and told him I'd sleep on it. As if on cue, Michael said, "In the grand scheme of things, with both of us working full-time, our parents getting older by the minute, your dad relapsing, and me being deployed, would you ever consider a nanny, a housekeeper, and a meal delivery service? The nanny could be at the house to welcome the kids, help with their homework and prepare dinner, so all you have to do is walk in the door. How about a housekeeper coming in once a week to help with laundry and clean the house? I know you like gardening, but how about we start having landscapers do the heavy weeding, mulching, and shrub and tree pruning instead of you trying to do it all? I think that would take a fair amount of stress off your shoulders. What do you think, Love?"

I raised my eyebrows at all of this and took it all in; he had a point. I didn't have to do everything myself. I was raised to *think* I needed to do it all to be a good wife and mom, but my cup was empty, and I needed a break. The last thing I wanted to do was harbor resentment and bitterness towards my family. I was exhausted and needed to put my pride aside and drop the good wife/bad wife drama. It was time to acknowledge and accept that I am a human being, not a robot. My current schedule and demands were not sustainable. I was burning myself out in the process of over-caring for my family and maintaining a dust-free, squeaky-clean home. I exclaimed, "You're right, forget being Superwoman flying solo; I need the entire Justice League! I like your suggestions, and we can afford it, so why not? I'm down with that! Thanks, babe. I'll see if any of our neighbors have references. And on second thought, I'll most likely go ahead with the party and cater it. Speaking of parties, we'll be seeing you soon for the halfway-day celebration this weekend!!"

Michael smiled and said, "Glad to help, babe. I'm glad I could be of use across the miles. Hold off contacting the neighbors. Instead, shoot me a list of qualities you're looking for, and I'll go online and create a profile for us on one of those home-helpers' websites. I've got some time to kill and this will fill in that time. Plus, the military gives a great discount on those websites for their nanny and housecleaning services. I'll send you the password, and you can start setting up the services you want and screen the applicants. I love you and will talk to you tomorrow morning with the kids. I'm looking forward to our halfway-day celebration this weekend. Have a safe drive back to work, and know that I think about you all the time. I'm counting down the days, babe. Three months to go! We've got this."

My time was running short, so we said our goodbyes quickly—so much for a romantic moment, alone without the kids. At least the reception was good.

CHAPTER 4

I hadn't heard from Dad in a few days and decided to call him on Sunday afternoon to invite him to my annual family Labor Day party. Labor Day was still over a week away; if I could get in touch with him now, it would give him time to sober up. The phone rang a few times, and on the sixth ring, he picked up. We had a family joke about being at the far end of the house when the phone rang and rang before finally picking up. Without fail I said, "Hi Dad, were you at the far end of the house?"

He laughed and said, "Yes."

Thank God he sounded sober when we began talking. I invited him to the family Labor Day party, and he agreed to come. While I sat there at my kitchen island, stirring my bowl of watermelon gazpacho, I decided to use this opportunity to ask him what was going on and why he was calling me during the work day sounding half-drunk. There was a long pause, and he just let the words fall out of his mouth like marbles dumped out of a bag.

He began spilling the details with a quick sigh, "Well, Alexis, it's a long story. Remember, I told you I found a renter for Mom's Conlyn Street duplex? Well, the renter I was referring to was Doolie Pine, Trina's son, who lived up Conlyn Street, in our old neighborhood."

My jaw dropped, all gazpacho stirring stopped, and I interrupted him, "Wait, let me get this straight; you rented my grandmother's house to Doolie Pine? The guy who's the neighborhood trouble maker, hoodlum, drug head, and gang banger? *That* Doolie Pine? Are you *serious?*"

I remembered the day when we were kids, and Doolie had caused a mess of trouble. Old, Mr. Washington came out to his front stoop to see what the ruckus was all about. When he found out Doolie was the cause, he said, "Doolie, trouble sticks to you like sap to a pine tree."

We all laughed, and the name stuck with Doolie ever since.

My mouth was ajar, my eyes were bulging, and I could *hear* my lids blinking. There was a long pause before Dad replied, "As I was saying, yes, *that* Doolie Pine. He was clean last year, and for the longest time, he was making the rent payments on time. I had tenants upstairs in the duplex too. A nice, African couple and their toddler had moved into the upstairs apartment. Things were great, and the steady income was a big help, now that I'm on Social Security. But, about four months ago, Doolie Pine got mixed up in the wrong crowd again, and things went downhill fast. He lost his job, started robbing people, doing drugs, and running with his old gang in the streets. I'm in a world of trouble."

I breathed deeply and took all this in. My mind was swirling. My grandmom must be rolling over in her grave right now. She had lived in that duplex for over fifty years and lovingly maintained it. We had created many great family memories in that old, West Oak Lane house. I would have loved to know why she left her house to her screw-up son instead of to me, her responsible granddaughter. I would not trust Dad to handle any finances, let alone a house. He was like a train wreck with money and property. She knew I was responsible, and honestly, a part of me always resented my grandmother for leaving her property to my dad. I knew he'd screw it up. I guess she knew I could take care of myself and thought she'd better leave her son with a ton of cash and a guaranteed roof over his head. *Well, I bet she never saw this coming.*

I snapped back to reality and prayed silently that this was just a dream I'd be waking up from in a second. Sadly, it wasn't, and my father droned on. Sadly, he admitted, "I haven't been getting checks from Doolie Pine or the upstairs tenants, the Bozemans, for several months. I can't even *find* Doolie Pine. I called the upstairs tenants and got no answer. I wrote them a letter instead. Luckily, the Bozemans replied to my letter and told me they were paying their rent to Doolie Pine. Apparently, he told them the house was *his* now, and he was their landlord, not me. They said he threatened to report them as illegals if they caused him any trouble. They've been paying him for months, not me."

My eyes blinked and nearly bugged out again. As I shook my head in disbelief, I blurted out, "*What?* He told them what? Are you kidding me? And they believed him? Did you go down there and talk to Doolie Pine?"

My father hesitantly replied, "Ah, about that, well, um, oh, it's not exactly safe for me to drive down there and be seen on Conlyn Street, um, you know, the old neighborhood isn't what it used to be, and I kind of got myself into a bit of a mess down there. I never really told you the full story about why I moved out of Mom's house in such a rush in the first place and got a hotel out in Bristol last year."

There was a pause, and with great effort and restraint, I calmly said, "Please, Dad, go on; I'm all ears."

He spoke with great hesitation, "You see, um, well, I got mixed up with some fast women when Mom died, and I collected my inheritance." He let out a chuckle and a short whistle before speaking in a bittersweet tone tinged with a hint of delight, "My dear, let me tell you, after years of taking care of Dear Old Mom, I needed to let off *steam!* After she died, Conlyn Street became my long-awaited bachelor pad. I was doing a lot of partying with fast women and letting *off* that steam. When I wasn't at Conlyn Street, I was down the shore partying in Atlantic City at the casinos. At that time, I was helping one of the young women out; she was down on her luck and took a liking to me. We were with each other for a while; we'd stay down in AC for weeks."

After that shocking recap, his tone of voice changed and became more serious as the other shoe dropped, "Well, the problem was, I didn't know she had a boyfriend in jail. But he knew about me, and as soon as he made bail, he came to the house on Conlyn Street to find me and beat the living daylights out of me." There was a pause, and then Dad quickly blurted out the rest, "I woke up one night to him banging on my front door and shouting, 'I'll kill you, old man, for messing with my woman. I'll kill you; show your face around here again, and I'll kill you.'" He threw a rock through one of the front windows; he damned near bent the metal storm door off the hinges. I was sleeping upstairs in the front bedroom, right below all the commotion. I had my cell on the nightstand and called 9-1-1, then crept out of bed, crawled over to the closet, got my shotgun, and loaded it. I backed myself against the wall, facing my bedroom doorway. If that mf'er broke in and came up my stairs, I'd have something for his black ass when he walked in the room. I also loaded my big, hollow-point bullets in my 9mm pistol and was ready to take down anyone who dared step foot into my home. Those bullets would drop a bear, so I knew they'd drop his sorry ass."

By that point, I was blinking back tears and was beside myself. I kept praying it was a dream I'd wake up from. Yet, no matter how many times I shook my head and blinked my eyes, I kept coming back to the sound of his voice recounting his sad state of affairs. I seriously just wanted to run upstairs to my bedroom, lock the door, and hide under the covers forever.

He continued on, "So, long story short, it was a close call; he didn't get into the house, and by the time the cops showed up, he had fled the scene. I knew who he was and where to find him, and several neighbors had already called the police to report the crime and identified him by name. I filed a report, and that didn't go over too well with the guy's parole officer. He earned himself more time in jail. I didn't know how long it would take him to make bail, so once I secured the front door, I threw some clothes in a suitcase and high-tailed it out of there. I stayed at a motel for a week. He couldn't make bail, which gave me time to move out. I didn't want to burden you, so I lived in the motel until I found the house for sale in Bristol. I used what was left of my inheritance from Mom to buy it in cash. It needs some work, but I'm handy and have a handyman."

I was shocked. I didn't know what part shocked me more. The thought of my 74-year-old father partying and having sex made me want to gag. The thought of him fleeing from my grandmother's house for his life because of a jilted, jealous ex-con with a score to settle made me feel faint. I could kind of live with the thought of him staying in an extended-stay hotel, but the fact that he never told me about any of this saddened me beyond words and took my breath away. It was more than I could process at the moment. I was stressed and frustrated, and I could practically feel the remaining strands of hair on my head falling out by the second.

Dad was a talker, and he talked on, "I had planned on using the $250,000 inheritance from Mom to buy a restaurant and run it; that was always one of my dreams. But, after my partying, there was only about half left. When I needed to get out of town for my own safety, I thought it was best to buy a house. I never called you because I knew you were busy with your career and family and all. I didn't want to trouble you. Now you know the story about Doolie Pine and why I moved out to Bristol. I heard he needed a place to stay, so I offered him the first floor of the duplex and put an ad in the paper to rent out the second floor of the duplex. Once things went off the rails, I started drinking more to calm my nerves."

There was a pause, and I managed to choke out, "I'm so sorry this has happened to you, Dad. I can't even imagine what this past year has been like for you. I wish you had said something sooner. What are you going to do?" I asked with concern.

He paused and said that he had called City Hall to find out his rights as a landlord and how to evict Doolie Pine. He added, "The African family already moved out; not only were they afraid of Doolie Pine, but his loud parties kept waking up their baby. I just got their letter. We've kept in touch, and they were nice people. They found a place in Mount Airy, close to their jobs at Chestnut Hill College. They were nice enough to pay me two months of back rent. But Alexis, I need your help with Doolie Pine. He owes me back rent, he stopped paying the utilities, and I want him out of that house. He's got to go."

After talking some more, it turned out he had no written contract with Doolie Pine, just a handshake and a verbal gentleman's agreement. I agreed to research information for him and would have it ready when he came to my annual Labor Day party. Just when I thought things couldn't get any worse, he saved the best for last and hit me with an even bigger blow. He cleared his throat and said, "I've also got some problems at my new house in Bristol. I am essentially squatting here."

This stopped me dead in my tracks. I was so shocked and bewildered I could have taken the half-eaten bowl of gazpacho and chucked it across the kitchen. My mind was racing, and I was only halfway taking in what he was saying; the bits and pieces I heard sounded something like, "...the Bristol house...I'm the one squatting...can't live there yet...water not hooked up...house is under construction and not cleared for occupancy with the township, so I'm keeping most things in boxes, so it looks like I'm not moved in. I simply can't stay in hotels anymore. I found a good contractor; he comes over, and we sit and talk and drink beers."

I don't recall what else he said. For my sanity's sake, I had to tune most of it out. I just wanted to scream. I just couldn't hear any more of this madness. I wanted to hang the phone up and pretend like I was just a normal woman having a normal dinner at home on a Friday night, sitting in my beautiful kitchen scrolling Instagram. I just wanted all this mess to go away. I just wanted a normal life.

I pushed my chair away from the island and walked outside to get a breath of fresh air. As I paced back and forth across my flagstone paver patio, I did my best to repeat everything back to him. "So, let me get this straight, Dad. Are you telling me that you've been living in that house for almost a year and have no permit from the township to occupy it legally?"

"Yes."

I continued on, "And are you telling me that the handyman, I mean *contractor*, working on your home is a *friend* of the lady whose ex-convict boyfriend was banging on your front door, threatening to kill you?"

There was a long pause before I heard him say, "Um, yes. That's right. You heard right. He and I are best buds. His name is Dan, and he's done a great job at the Bristol house. He's finished the basement and added a full bath down there with a nice sink, toilet, and shower. He's even given me a used fridge for my garage. He knows I like to stock up on meat when Acme is having a sale. Everything was going fine until Dan ran into some health issues and couldn't come back to finish the work on the upstairs, which I technically need to have completed before I can live there."

I blinked and asked him why he didn't just hire a new contractor, vetted through a reputable source, this time.

He sighed and said, "Well, that's where the trouble lies. You see, Dan had been in the hospital with kidney and liver failure from all the beer and soda he'd been drinking. And with him being out of work and all, he couldn't support his family. We spoke man-to-man, and he asked me if I'd give him a cash advance for the work he was going to do in the rest of my house. You see, he needed to pay for his daughter's college tuition. And his work truck had gotten repossessed. He's my friend, so I said 'yes.' I felt bad for the guy and gave him an advance on the work to help him out. Shortly after getting the money, he left town to get treatment in a special clinic in Arizona, and I haven't been able to track him down since."

There was a long, awkward pause. I gently scratched my head and did my best to paraphrase everything back to him before jumping to conclusions and getting ticked off. "So, let me get this straight, Dad. Are you telling me that you gave your buddy, Don, Dan, whatever his name is, the guy who's a friend of *the lady whose ex-con ex-boyfriend wanted to kill you,* you gave *him* a cash advance, and now he's mysteriously M.I.A.? And just how much money did you give him, might I ask?"

I could hear Dad's audible gulp as he swallowed air and said, "I gave him $50,000 in good faith. He's my buddy and he needed help. I trusted him. He seemed legit. He wrote out a nice estimate, and I put a third down. At first, things went great. He showed up on time. He was upbeat and updated me on the construction. And if more money was needed to continue to do the job, he told me. It was just an estimate, so I was fine with that."

I nodded along.

He continued on, recounting the events, "The job took longer than expected. When I'd ask 'why,' he'd say that he ran into some unexpected setbacks; it was an older house, and it needed more work once he started getting into the electrical and plumbing. He always thanked me for my patience and asked for more money. I was supposed to pay in thirds, but I trusted him. Then I started getting angry, and my patience wore thin. I told him he needed to finish up, or else I was cutting him off and firing him. He said he didn't have permits, and if I cut him off, I'd never be able to find a legitimate contractor to come in and finish the work, and it could raise suspicion with the township, and I could be fined. Then he just stopped showing up altogether. For weeks, I couldn't track him down, and he didn't answer his phone."

It all sounded very suspicious to me, and I was sure he was just scammed by Dan and possibly that lady friend and ex-con. I kept my suspicions to myself and said, "Oh, wow, Dad, that sounds horrible. I wish you had said something to me sooner. So, what happened after that?"

He continued, "I finally reached him on the phone and told him I was going to press charges and report him to the Better Business Bureau. He sounded like crap and said he was in the hospital dying of kidney failure, his work truck got repossessed, and he sold his car to help pay for his daughter's college tuition. He asked me if I'd lend him money, man-to-man, and said that when he got out of the hospital, he'd be back to finish the job. The basement was done, but he needed to remodel the kitchen and hall bath. I spent all my savings to help him. And then he went M.I.A. I guessed maybe he died. I didn't want to bother his family, and I sure as hell wasn't going to call that psycho ex-girlfriend. So here we are, and now I'm squatting in the house. The kitchen and hall bath are still in their original state; they aren't pretty, but they work."

I was flabbergasted. I swore my hair started falling out in more and more clumps the longer I listened to this conversation. Finally, I couldn't listen to the insanity anymore and blurted out, "Did you even know this man's last name? Did you even meet his daughter? Does he even have a daughter, for that matter? Did you actually visit him in the hospital??"

All Dad could muster was the word, "No."

I didn't miss a beat and said, "Well, you can kiss that money goodbye and don't hold your breath on ever seeing your buddy Dan again. Seriously, Dad, you just got scammed. That fridge was probably stolen. I hope your basement is in good working order. So where will you live? Does the township send out inspectors?"

There was a pause, and Dad spoke up, "Well, I don't think Dan ever let the township know he was doing any work on my house. I never saw any permits. I'm not really sure if an inspector will come out. I've never seen one to date, now that you mention it. I guess I'm *not* squatting! I don't know; I'm going to start unpacking my stuff and fix up the kitchen plumbing myself, and when I get ready to remodel the kitchen and master bathroom, I'll find someone else to do it. But that won't be for some time. I have to get my money right first."

Well, that was the smartest thing my father had said in the last hour and a half of conversation. *What a relief; he does have an ounce of sense left in him!* I breathed a sigh of relief and said, "Well, that sounds like a solid plan, Dad. It sounds wise to get settled in and get your finances straight. I'm happy to come over and help you unpack and get settled in. When Michael gets back from deployment, I'm sure he can help you with any plumbing that still needs to be finished."

We talked some more, and I mustered the courage to ask Dad just how much he had given Dan. I was shocked and chilled to the bone; Dad gave this man a total of $75,000. Correction, my dad was *scammed* out of $75,000.

He laughed, breathed a sigh of relief, and said, "Thanks for understanding; this has really had my nerves wound up, and I've been out of sorts. I should be good on money for the day-to-day. I'll be living low for a while and may not be able to make the drive up to see you as often as I'd like. The gas and toll prices are really high, and I probably won't be able to get the kids big gifts for a while."

I bowed my head in a silent prayer before speaking. My words were soft, and my heart was breaking, "Aw, Dad, that's the least of my concerns about gifts for the kids. We can come up and see you and bring the kids' toys with us. Plus, the kids really don't need any big fancy presents. Spending time with you is more than perfect. I love you."

He sniffed and said, "I love you too, Lexis."

I beamed and said, "Great; then it's settled. We'll see you next week for Labor Day, and I'll mail you a prepaid Visa Card to fuel up your van. Let me know if you want EZ-pass as well. I'll set it up for you and pay for it; then, you don't have to worry about paying for the tolls when you come see us or drive anywhere, for that matter."

There was a long pause; my dad didn't take handouts, and this was the first time in *my 43 years of life* that I had ever offered to pay for *anything* for my father. I stared at my rose garden in the hiatus of the long silence. *I love the pink flowers.*

Finally, he spoke, and with a deep booming voice coming from the depths of his belly, he powerfully shot the following words out of his mouth, "Sure, send me the card! Thanks. Don't you worry about the EZ-pass; I'll take care of that myself."

The line in the sand was drawn, and Dad had said how much help he was willing to accept. Just like that, the conversation ended, and we turned the topic to what time the Labor Day party would be on Sunday. Then we said our goodbyes and hung up the phone. That was that—the end.

I ran my hand through my hair, and a handful of coarse, brittle hair came out with it. I was at my wit's end and couldn't handle another problem being dolloped on my plate.

CHAPTER 5

Labor Day weekend 2016 was one to remember. First, Michael was deployed, and this was the first time ever in the history of our marriage that he wouldn't be home to celebrate our family's collective summer birthdays on Labor Day. Second, this was the first year my father-in-law, Gil, would not be there to celebrate either. Instead, we'd be honoring his memory. Last, this was the first time I'd seen my father in months, and his appearance was more than I could put into words. I decided to put on a happy face and do my best to make the most of our time together. Gil might not have been there physically, but he was there in spirit.

Carolyn and my mom arrived on time. Dad was late, as usual. We munched on dip, chips, and nuts 'til he arrived. I was glad I had decided to cater the meal. I could relax and actually enjoy the day, instead of stressing over the food. The grandkids put on a show and tried to peek inside their gift bags and shake the large, brightly wrapped birthday presents in boxes. Around 1 p.m., I could hear the loud, revving, V8-turbocharged racing engine chugging up the driveway. That was my dad, always making a late, grand entrance. He was driving his rusted-out, faded, orange, 1979 Ford Econoline van, outfitted with a high-performance, racing engine. It's loud, chugging engine vibrated the whole house; it sounded more like a tug boat than a truck. He had hood locks and everything! God only knows how much money he had poured into that rusted heap of junk.

When I went to the side door to greet him, my jaw dropped. I was stunned to see a frail, reed-thin little man with skin hanging off him. This was not the dad I knew and loved. Who was this imposter? He moved at the pace of a snail and looked like he weighed 90 pounds soaking wet. As I watched him walk closer, I thought, "What in the heck happened to him?"

It was the end of summer, and he had on slacks, loafers, a flannel shirt, and a leather vest. I knew he was short on cash and wasn't bringing birthday presents, but he failed to mention that he had no funds for food and was *starving to death*. This was more than I could take. First, Michael not being home and possibly in harm's way, mourning Gil's absence, and now this? My heart couldn't bear another blow.

I forced back the tears and swung the door open for Dad. He grabbed the door, slowly walked up the two steps, and walked into the mudroom. He was stooped over and looked up over his gold-rimmed, VA-issued eyeglasses to make eye contact with me. He was so stooped over that he appeared to be shorter than me. He said his customary, *"Hello, hello!"* in his loud booming voice that carried. Thank God his voice still sounded the same, and he appeared to be sober.

I said, "Wow, Dad, you look really thin. Are you okay?"

He said, "Yes," and we continued into the kitchen, where everyone greeted him and acted as if everything was perfectly normal. *Why didn't anyone comment on how reed thin he is and how his winter clothes are hanging off him on this hot summer day?*

We enjoyed the catered barbecue and opened the birthday presents right after dessert. The kids were happily playing with the new toys from both grandmas, and they didn't even notice that Pop-Pop Miller had entered empty-handed. We laughed, reminisced, and enjoyed a lot of good food—especially my mom's apple pie, with its cream cheese, flaky crust. Eating her pie was a sweet measure of comfort for all of us. Any time something monumental, special, or sad was going on, my mom arrived on the scene with her delicious apple pie. Today was no different.

She spent many a weekend chatting with Carolyn and Gil during his later stages of Alzheimer's, and she'd always arrived with apple pie in hand. He may not have remembered who she was, but he sure didn't forget how to fork that apple pie into his mouth.

Today, we ate for the memories, ate for the moment, looked at my young children playing in the adjacent playroom, and ate for their future. Bittersweet indeed.

Carolyn was the first to leave. My mom was next to go. She may come with apple pie, but she always made sure to leave with leftovers. Today was no exception. Burgers, dip, veggies, and coleslaw were loaded into containers for her. I hugged them both goodbye and went back into the kitchen to sit with Dad. He was still sitting at the kitchen table, picking away at his apple pie. He was never one for sweets.

We made small talk for a bit. He made no mention of his weight. I cut to the chase and broached the topic of the house on Conlyn Street. "So, Dad, what's going on with Doolie Pine? Can you evict him? I googled Philadelphia squatter's rights, and it doesn't sound like it's going to be an easy process."

He nodded and said, "You're right. It's not going to be an easy process. I talked with my lawyer, Stacey, and he gave me the contact information of a lawyer friend of his. We had a free, one-hour consult about the situation, and he explained Philadelphia squatter's rights and the eviction process. He helped me draft the eviction notice paperwork, and I mailed it to Doolie last month. Doolie was initially my tenant, even though all we had was a verbal agreement. Nonetheless, I was his landlord, and he paid me monthly rent for the first year. Then he stopped paying rent and utilities. I've been trying to deal with him on my own for the past year. During that time, he also scammed the upstairs tenants, and they stopped paying me rent, too. He told them he was their landlord, and they were paying him money. The nerve of him!"

I nodded along, and he continued the update. "Once I gave him a thirty-day written eviction notice, and he refused to vacate the property, he became a 'holdover tenant.' Thirty days was more than generous, considering how long the jerk has been squatting. He destroyed my property, scared off the upstairs tenants, and I don't have the energy to clean up the second unit and rent it out to new tenants—not with Doolie living downstairs wreaking havoc."

I listened sympathetically. I didn't have the heart to tell him that he brought this all on himself when he foolishly chose to rent the house out to Doolie in the first place. Doolie has always been nothing but trouble as far back as I can remember. But Dad was looking for a quick, easy buck, instead of taking the time to list the duplex properly and fully vet his tenants.

As I looked at my dad and listened to him, it stirred up many mixed emotions as I sized him up. He looked so frail, dangerously thin, almost emaciated; it was like he had been sucked dry and was just a walking sack of skin and bones. I was scared, sickened, alarmed, and saddened all at the same time. I wanted my parents to live forever; I had given up on them ever remarrying, but I just knew they'd always be around when I needed them. Mortality was smacking me right in the face—theirs and my own!

Technically speaking, any of us could kick the bucket at any time. So, I needed to face my life and resolve unspoken hopes, hurts, and desires. I needed to get my affairs in order and start living my life to the fullest, while I still had vigor. Witnessing Dad's circumstances was a key motivation for me to keep exercising, eating healthy, minimizing stress, managing my finances, and staying connected with my values, faith, family, and friends.

In that moment, I vowed that old age was not going to rob me of my vitality, beauty, creativity, wealth, and health. Aging did not have to feel like walking through a long hallway towards the light, with doors of opportunity swiftly closing behind me with every step. I silently declared to myself that I was *not* going out of this world like my dad.

It was good to see him sober and spend time with him. I'd missed him, problems and all; he was still my dad. And I was happy to see him.

He continued, "Now that the thirty days has expired, if I wanted to take him to court, I'd have to file a complaint with the Philadelphia Landlord-Tenant Court. Then, within about ten business days, they'd mail the complaint notice to Doolie with the appointed date and time for him to appear in court and the reasons why. The judgment would be made on either the day of or up to a week after the hearing. Doolie would have the right to appeal. If he were to appeal, then it could take up to a year to get a new court date. But if Doolie fails to appear for that hearing at the specified location, date, and exact time, he would automatically lose the case, and a default judgment would be entered against him! Woo-hoo! Even if he arrived just a couple minutes late, it's a win for me!"

That sounded very positive. I congratulated him. It sounded like he had a way to get Doolie out and get the property rehabbed and rentable. Having the duplex rentable again would generate two passive income streams for him. The neighborhood is up and coming, and he could easily get $2,500/month per unit in the duplex. I was really happy for my dad. But then the other shoe fell.

Dad said, "But Lexis, even if the judge rules in my favor, I'd still have to file another request with the court, called a 'Writ of Possession.' This basically notifies the tenant that an eviction will take place on or after eleven days from the day the Writ of Possession is served. Then I'd have to go back to court *again* to file a second Writ of Possession called an 'Alias Writ of Possession.' The sheriff would deliver this to Doolie and physically evict him from the house. The locks would be changed, or the door would be padlocked. He wouldn't be legally able to enter the property without contacting me first and getting permission. If he's not home, the notice would be posted on the door, the locks would be changed, and he couldn't enter without contacting me first. The furniture was all mine, but I don't want it anymore, now that it's infested with bedbugs."

I took all that information in and said, "So, that being said, in a perfect world where it all went smoothly, it could take up to four months from eviction notice to tenant removal?"

Dad nodded and said, "Yes, in a perfect world, that's how it would work. But life has a way of not working out perfectly for me. I'm not driving into the city and dealing with government officials and red tape. Forget that mess; just thinking about it works my nerves. I need to sell this house fast and get out from under it. I'm settled in at my new place; those inspectors never came to check out the house. So, I've unpacked and settled in. Now I want this mess on Conlyn Street off my plate, so I can finally rest easy and enjoy my old age. Let someone else handle that mess; the sooner I can get out from under that burden, the better. I want to focus on what I've got going on at my new house. I've unpacked the boxes I had stored in the garage, and I'm happy to tell you that I'm officially moved into my new home."

He smiled and continued, "The basement looks great. You'll have to come see it. Meanwhile, I need to unload Conlyn Street ASAP. Dealing with Doolie is too much, and all the stress is wearing on me. I can't eat, I can't sleep. Look at me. I'm practically skin and bones," he pointed to his midsection and then used his left hand to grasp his right wrist. He let his right wrist go floppy and shook it like a rag doll.

I looked at him and smiled, "Yes, Dad, I noticed how thin you looked the moment I set eyes on you. Thanks for telling me what's going on. Now, how are you going to unload the house?"

"I contacted one of those 1-800-house-market home buyer numbers you see advertised on highway billboards. They have been fast, responsive, and professional, so far. They specialize in buying properties regardless of their condition, including vacant properties, properties with squatters, and properties with liens on them. They will buy as is—no agent, no legal work, no inspections, no closing costs, and no headaches. And it's on my timeline. I will have a guaranteed offer within 48 hours of contacting them. I called them for an initial consultation. They gathered my information, and once they determine the costs to settle all outstanding debts, they'll give me a cash buyout offer. This could really help me out of a jam. I've seen their ads everywhere, so I thought, why the heck not?" Dad sounded hopeful.

He continued on, "The real estate attorney recommended I battle it out in court; of course, he would, he'd be getting paid. I want money in my pockets, not an attorney's."

It sounded too good to be true to me, but from the sound of Dad's voice, I could tell he had his mind made up, and there was nothing I could say to change it. "Well, Dad, it sounds like you made the best choice for yourself. Let me know if there's anything I can help you with."

He looked at me with a small smile on his face, thanked me, and told me he'd take me up on that offer in a couple of months, once he got his paperwork squared away and decided what he was going to do about the house on Conlyn Street. We talked some more; then, the kids monopolized the rest of our time together. We were up to our eyeballs in new toys, boxes, and wrapping paper.

Despite it all, I loved my dad and was glad he was sober and here with us. If all went well, maybe, just maybe, this would all work out, my stress level would go down, and I'd have more than a couple of strands of hair left on my head.

CHAPTER 6

Labor Day came and went like a blur, and the days were flying by. The nights were cooling down; the days felt like they were getting shorter by the minute, and the trees were starting to turn colors as if on cue. Fall was quickly setting in, and it was barely late September. Michael would be home from deployment in November, and the kids and I were eagerly counting down the days. Work was humming along nicely. My productivity and performance were back to optimal levels, and I felt like I was doing well.

Saturday couldn't get here fast enough. The kids were peeling my brain like a banana, and my hair was falling out in clumps. I was losing options for what to do with my thinning, steel-wool hair and needed help. My self-esteem was shriveling by the minute. This Leo babe needed help ASAP. Pulling my hair back in a bun was the best I could do these days. There were bald spots on the top of my head, and what little hair was left looked like straggly, dark-brown strands of pipe cleaner and dark-brown ringlets of steel wool. I'd always had thick, soft, brown hair—a true lion's mane in thickness and volume.

The big day finally arrived. It was time to face the inevitable and do something about my hair situation. I hated going out in public with my hair in a bun, but I couldn't cover up the balding spots on the top of my head anymore. I couldn't wear hats at the office, and

I wasn't really a wig or weave kind of person. I needed help. I woke early, dressed and fed the kids, then made the drive down to Exton to drop the kids off at my mom's house.

Just getting the kids out of my hair for a day was a breath of fresh air. I felt a hundred pounds lighter when I dropped them off, kissed them goodbye, and backed out of my mom's driveway sans kids! *Freedom!* Finally, I could play my music as loudly as I wanted. I could finish a complete thought. I felt like I could go anywhere I wanted and do whatever I wanted. It felt like heaven to this tired momma. I hopped on the PA Turnpike and made the 45-minute drive down to Chestnut Hill to meet my date with destiny.

I grew up near Chestnut Hill, and it was always so nostalgic to drive through the old neighborhoods. I always felt a pang of bittersweet remorse as I drove over the bumpy cobblestones of Germantown Avenue and craned my head to rubberneck and get a good, long look at all the interesting stores and their lovely window displays. I marveled at the new stores on the avenue since I was there last. I visited the area three or four times a year to get my hair relaxed at my favorite salon. Truly, it was the only place I trusted to do my hair. I'd been seeing the same Paul Mitchell-trained stylist, Jeanette, for the last ten years, and I wasn't stopping any time soon.

Moving to Chester County had its share of difficulties, and finding a new salon had been one of them. I vividly remember searching online in vain for a salon that met my standards *and* knew how to care for ethnic hair. I was used to living in a diverse city with a plethora of salon options at my fingertips. That was *not* the case in my rural region of Chester County. I felt like the one and only black person in a thirty-mile radius, and finding a salon proved quite difficult in a sleepy, little, rural town. I thought there'd be better options on the Main Line.

I found a couple of salons near Villanova and Saint David's, but once I sat in the chair for the initial consultations, and they saw my hair, I was told they don't relax ethnic hair. They only provided keratin treatments for wavy hair. After wasting three afternoons hearing the same pathetic rejection, the third time was the charm. I vowed to always return to Chestnut hill and stay true to my salon and the rapport I'd built with Jeanette.

Driving past the brick-front row houses and trees aglow in their red and orange fall splendor along Germantown Avenue hit differently on this balmy, sunny, Saturday morning. Usually, at the salon, Jeanette and I laughed and caught up like old friends. We usually swapped stories about the books or movies we were infatuated with and talked about our families and what's been going on in life. This time was different. I was under stress, and it showed in my hair. I'd been doing my best to hide it, but I knew there was no fooling Jeanette. She'd been doing my hair every three months for the last ten years. She knew me. No amount of side parts or updos would be able to fool her.

I was fifteen minutes early and sat in the parking lot, steeling myself for what was to come. I knew something drastic was needed to salvage what was left of my hair. *Can I hold myself together when Jeanette asks me what happened to my hair?*

Before getting out of the car, I closed my eyes and prayed to God for strength. No more stalling; it was time to get out and face the inevitable. I walked across the parking lot and stepped up to the large, brick Cape Cod that had been subdivided and converted into businesses. I walked up to the salon side, faced the white, covered patio, proceeded across the flagstone pavers to the beautiful, wooden, double doors, and pushed down on the antique, brass, lever handle. I swung the door open towards me and stepped inside. The flagstone pavers continued inside into the reception area leading up to the receptionist's desk.

I was greeted by the familiar sights, sounds, and comforts. The salon was like a home away from home for me. A sanctuary, a shelter; it was like a sacred safe space to come and bare your soul in the chair as your stylist transformed more than just your hair. I took in the surroundings on my way to the receptionist's counter. The smell of hair products, permanent processing, hairspray, shampoos, and conditioners was familiar and comforting. The salon's interior was a far cry from the traditional brick-clad exterior. The inside was a mix of urban-industrial, exposed brick meets summer beach house, with a dash of white-washed, exposed-beam ceilings and ornately carved, light pine bookcases draped with colorful scarves and stocked with colorful, beauty potions. I was tempted by the rainbow assortment of nail shellacs and the tempting variety of impulse purchase brushes, combs, and hair clips strategically placed at eye level on polished, wood shelves attached to vintage water pipes.

As I walked over to the white-washed shiplap-clad receptionist counter, I couldn't help but notice a display of clip-in hair extensions in various shades and colors. Oh boy, was that a sign! I checked in for my 11:00 appointment and grabbed a spot by the window in the cozy, waiting area tucked off to the side. I sunk into the plush, overstuffed, leather club chair, selected a beauty magazine from the stack on the coffee table, and settled down to gaze out of the floor-to-ceiling, walk-in bow windows. As I sat and flipped through the magazine, I noticed a lot of short hairstyles that were actually cute.

I had flipped through the pages to gather ideas when I felt her eyes on me. I looked up, and sure enough, Jeanette was walking over to greet me. She was a petite woman with a mega-watt personality. She had stunning, brown skin, killer fashion sense, and a heart of solid gold. Normally she'd greet me by saying, "Hi Alexis!! Look how long your hair's gotten!" followed by a hug and kiss as we walked back to her station to confirm the salon services that I was receiving that day. She'd offer me a drink and ask me if there was anything else she could get for me.

But on this day, her greeting was different. She never took her eyes off my head as we walked back to the chair. She had her arm around my shoulder. She told me to please have a seat, and her assistant, Alec, quickly rushed over to cover my neck with a towel and drape a silky, waterproof cape around me. As he gently fastened the cape around my neck at the base of my head, Jeanette rolled a small stool over and sat next to me. She leaned close to me and gently said in a whispered tone, "Girl, please don't take this the wrong way; I can tell your hair has changed. I'm not trying to pry or pass judgment. This comes from a place of concern and love. What's been happening in your life since I last saw you? Are you okay?"

Before I could say anything, I could feel my eyes welling up. As if on cue, she passed me a box of Kleenex from her station. As I blotted my eyes, I let it all out. I briefly told her what was going on with my dad, Michael's deployment, the kids starting school, and my crappy job. It truly felt like a dark night of the soul for me.

She sympathized with me and asked about my hair and when I had started noticing the changes.

I told her about the progressive shedding over the past six months, the breakage, and the change in texture. There was literally more hair caught up in my Swiffer floor duster than on my head. No matter how often I replaced the dust cloth, the Swiffer looked more like a brown wig on a stick trailing across the white-tiled, bathroom floor. I told her I was pulling clumps of my hair out of my comb and dropping them into the trash every time I combed my hair. I hated even combing it. I was easily shedding 100 strands of hair on a daily basis.

She asked if I had changed anything else in my routine: eating, sleeping, medicine, vitamins, cleaning products, or any other family dynamics.

It all really pointed back to the mounting pressures at work. It was like that was the straw that broke the camel's back, and my body just couldn't take anymore. Michael being gone, the kids, and my dad were all that I could handle. The job drama was just too much to take on, and it was showing.

She asked me what I had been doing to my hair to care for it and how I was wearing it these days.

I told her that I was still washing, deep-conditioning, blow drying, and flat ironing it twice a week. I slept on my silk pillowcase and wrapped my hair in a silk scarf when showering. At that point, buns were the only feasible option to disguise the bald spots and mix of strand lengths and textures.

She looked as sad as I did. We had been growing my hair out for the past five years. I undid my hair from the elastic hair band, so she could see all that was left of my former, thick, shoulder-length, brown hair. She took it all in with her eyes, then gently ran her fingers through my hair. After assessing my hair, she finally spoke with care and concern, "There's a lot of damage here; since I saw you last. Your texture has completely changed in a couple of months, to a coarse, brittle texture, with uneven length from breakage, and thinning from hair loss. I am so sorry, but we will have to cut a lot off to create a style. I recommend a layered bob with a tapered neck."

Then she felt at my roots and said, "They feel weak. You'll need to strengthen them from the inside out, and due to the shedding and breaking, I recommend we keep cutting off the damaged hair every time you come back."

I nodded in agreement and held back the tears.

Jeanette continued on, "It's time to really baby your hair and rebuild its strength. Please stop stressing your hair with frequent washing, blow drying, and straightening. It's time to protect and restore these tresses; okay, my friend? We need to address the hair loss and promote healthy hair growth. Patience is key. You know how long we've been growing your hair! We need to take really good care of what you have left and promote new growth."

Just the thought of cutting off what was left of my hair gave me chills. I nodded my head and asked, "Is there anything else I can do to reverse the damage and grow my hair back?"

Jeanette replied, "Of course, I have tricks up my sleeve to help you, girl! For starters, only wash your hair once a week. Let it air dry, use silk or satin scrunchies to pull your hair up, no cotton scarves, only silk or satin head coverings, no twirling or excessively playing or tugging at your hair, and keep your flat iron as low as possible to smooth out the wave and only flat iron it once or twice a week. I know you aren't a big fan of wrapping your head at night or sleeping in a bonnet, but I highly recommend it. If you are open to wearing wigs, that would be a great heat-protective alternative, so you can have style *without* putting the heat stress on your own hair to achieve it."

I took all this in, nodded, and she continued, "The salon also carries Minoxidil™. I recommend it to all my clients, and they've all gotten great results. I used it after I stopped nursing my second baby. Girl, let me tell you, when those hormones dipped, my hair was falling out faster than change from a slot machine. That Minoxidil™ was a lifesaver for me. I can show you it before you check out and answer any questions you might have. We also carry gummy vitamins with Biotin infusion."

I thanked her and asked for other more natural, minimally processed, clean, beauty options.

Jeanette nodded, "Oh, that's right, girl. I forgot you're into that wellness stuff and clean beauty. Okay, so we have an all-natural, Vegan product too that I think you'll like. It's a hair serum, non-oily, and plant-based. And it's infused with CBD, guaranteed to get results in a hundred and twenty days. Fuller hair, less shedding, and more growth are promised. I'll show all the products to you before you leave today. I'll also share my home remedies. Take out your phone and write this down; it's my tried-and-true, deep-conditioning hair treatment to soften your hair and add shine."

I reached under the protective cape covering my body and quickly grabbed my phone. I started typing away as Jeanette spilled her salon secrets.

"You'll need the following: one avocado, one egg, and olive oil. Depending on your hair thickness, you might want to use three-fourths a cup of olive oil; play around with how much . Start with putting the avocado in a bowl and mash it up, then add in the egg and olive oil. Pour in a little bit at a time and mix thoroughly before pouring in more olive oil. You want it to be thick like conditioner or body lotion, but not runny like dish soap. It will look lumpy and disgusting; you could blend it in a food blender if you want. I don't mind it clumpy. It's your choice."

"Have some plastic grocery bags on hand and towels you don't care about. Drape a towel around your shoulders and look in the mirror to make sure you thoroughly apply this goopy mixture all over your dry hair. Slather it on really thick and massage it into your scalp; it will be cold. Start at the back of your head and do it over the sink. Work your way up to the top of your head, and have your plastic bag handy. Secure it on your head, then wrap a towel around your head and leave this on for an hour; your body heat gives you a deep conditioning. Do this one time a week. I recommend making it your Sunday hair-care routine." She stopped midway through this home remedy conversation to talk to her assistant, who came over to Jeanette's station to ask her a question.

"Where was I? Oh yeah, as I was saying, make sure to rinse with warm water, NOT hot, or you'll cook the egg!! Girl do not make that mistake, or you'll be picking egg bits out of your hair all night and cursing me out. Ok!" I nodded, and she continued on, "Then, shampoo one time with your favorite moisturizing shampoo, followed by a sulfate-free moisturizing conditioner. You will only wash your hair one time a week and do this deep treatment beforehand every time. Keep doing this until your hair improves. This is such a healthy, luxurious treatment full of good fats and proteins."

I was so grateful for this information. I was feeling a shred of hope for my hair situation. This might actually work! Jeanette continued, "You'll see improvements in texture from day one. Next, you'll need some serious hair oil to nourish your scalp, fight bacteria, and moisturize your hair. My trifecta is one part melted coconut oil, one-part argan oil, and two drops of rosemary essential oil. I gently heat the coconut oil in the microwave and add the rest to it. Then gently massage this mixture into your scalp every day and run some through your hair. Do this at night and use it sparingly because the rosemary has a very strong herbal Christmas pine tree smell to it. This will help stimulate circulation to your scalp and condition and protect your hair, which means less breakage and more growth! Send me a photo update of your hair once a week. You can just text it to me. Okay?"

I nodded and tried to take in all this information. I was so grateful for her help and overwhelmed at the same time. Was my hair ever going to be restored?

Jeanette continued, "Keep eating your healthy diet, packed with nutrient-dense foods that are good for your hair. Lastly, and most importantly, nourish your *life*. Your hair is literally speaking about your lifestyle and the toll it's taking on you. It is an outward reflection of all the stress you have been enduring and possibly the misalignment of your actions versus your true calling in life. Whew, I didn't know I was going to be preaching today, girl. But here I go! Is there something else that you want to be doing with your life? Are you satisfied with where you are at, or are you staying someplace or doing something that you really don't want to be doing? Don't answer me; those are questions for you to sit with and really get clear on."

I just looked at her reflection in the mirror and tried to blink back the tears.

As she assessed my hair, she continued, "What's working? What's not working? What do you know in your heart to be true? What are you running away from? What do you need to stand and face once and for all? What are you going to do about it, to make things right? It's like you are at a breaking point, and your hair's screaming out loud that it's time to take action. Take courage girl, have faith, and pray to God for discernment. Once you make the necessary changes, I have a feeling your hair will improve, product or no product. Buy what you like; try the recipes if you like. But I've seen this before with clients, and I'm willing to bet that once you address what's eating away at you, your hair will grow back to the way it was and be healthy and strong. In the meantime, do your best to stay positive, no hyper-focusing on your hair falling out. Be solution-oriented and just keep visualizing your hair filling in and growing long and strong. Pray on that! How's that for clean beauty? Are we good?"

I nodded, too shaken up for words.

Jeanette smiled her warm smile, squeezed my shoulder, and blinked back her own tears. "So, let's get started with your relaxer and tell me about the hairstyles you've picked out in the magazine."

Her assistant had mixed the chemicals in a plastic bowl and left it at Jeanette's station. She parted my hair and used the long-handled, plastic comb to slather the thick, white, lotion-like potion onto my roots. It was an organic brand from France and was super mild for my hair type. She didn't leave it on for as long as she normally does; we went right to the bowl, rinsed, neutralized, rinsed, washed, and deep-conditioned. Before I knew it, I was at her finishing station for blow-drying and styling.

As she ran her fingers through my brittle hair, she remarked, "Yes, indeed, stress is written all over your hair, and it has taken its toll. I've never seen it like this in all the years we've known each other. There's a lot of damage here, uneven length from breakage, and thinning from hair loss; we are going to have to cut a lot off to create a style. So, have you decided on the bob with a tapered neck? Like I said before, due to the shedding and breaking, we will have to keep cutting it every time you come back. And please come every five to six weeks for trims. We'll do relaxer touch-ups as needed."

I looked at her reflection in the mirror and nodded. I was trying to avoid looking at myself with my hair standing all over my head like a lunatic in a black cape. It was bad; I was extremely depressed. It had taken me the past five years to grow my hair out. Prior to starting my current job, my hair reached the middle of my back. After a lifetime of trying to grow my hair that long, I finally succeeded during the most stressful time of life as a returning-adult student in grad school, running on empty, pulling all-nighters, juggling two young children, and a hubby in the military.

And now this!!

I agreed to the layered bob hairstyle, and she trimmed away; chunks of rough hair fell all over the black cape I was wearing and tumbled onto the floor. I sat there and wept silently, hidden under the shroud of my hair. I couldn't bring myself to look in the mirror. I heard her say, "Good, it's looking better already, your hair tolerated the relaxer well, and it feels healthier already."

I was relieved, overwhelmed, and distracted all at once. As Jeanette was cutting my hair, she prattled on about haircare products the entire time. I was trying to pay attention to her *and* monitor just *how much* hair she was chopping off. I could hear her, but she sounded way off in the distance…It was all getting to be just too much. Hair was falling all over my shoulders and the floor, her silver scissors were swishing all around me, she was talking, the nearby stylists were whizzing their blow dryers, and it was all starting to swirl in my head like a cacophony. Smells of perms, relaxers, conditioners, nail services, and skin-care treatments were assaulting my nose, and major overwhelm and anxiety were sinking in.

I could feel my throat constricting as spasms started in my lower throat, and my heart was beating like mad. My palms were sweaty, and I wasn't breathing. I was spiraling into a full-on *panic attack* in the chair. I was sinking fast, and it was taking all my willpower not to get up and run out the door, shrieking.

I started deep breathing through my nostrils and counted the window panes in the floor-to-ceiling windows spanning the front of the salon. Counting a monotonous, repeating, architectural element like this always helped to center me, bring me back to reality, and calm my nerves. I don't know how long I was zoned out, frozen like a deer in headlights.

Finally, Jeanette came back into focus and her words made sense. I could hear what was going on around me, and I was back on track. I tried to nod along and act like nothing had happened. The next thing I knew, she spun me around and said, "Take a look; what do you think?"

I looked up at myself in the mirror and shuddered. I thought my hair looked like Marcie's from Charlie Brown. All I needed was the eyeglasses. My neck and ears felt so exposed. I put my hands up to touch my hair; at least it felt soft, and the back was all one length, albeit short. I tried to be optimistic—at least it was all one length, and I could brush the bangs over to the side. She gave me a hand-held mirror and spun my chair around, so I could see the back. I smiled a small smile and touched the back of my hair. The nape was super short. I missed having long hair.

As if on cue, Jeanette said, "I kept as much length as I could; it will grow out from here, back to the length you had. We will taper your bangs as they grow out. The top was where you had the most loss and texture change; cutting bangs was really the best option. This, too, shall pass, my darling. I know this is a lot to take in; I'm proud of you, and I thank you for trusting me with your hair. You know what they say; when a woman radically changes her hair, she's about to change her life. I meant it when I said to marinate on what's eating you and to text me your progress." She fussed over my bangs and said, "Is this okay, or is there anything else I can do for you?"

I smiled gratefully and looked in the mirror at the new me. She was right, stuff was eating at me, and it was time to do something about it. So that's exactly what I decided to do. I turned to her and said, "This is perfect; here's to new beginnings." My smile grew as I gave her the mirror back.

The session was longer than normal, and unbeknownst to me, she had rescheduled her afternoon appointments to make this time for me. I purchased some of the clean hair-care products she recommended and booked out several months' worth of appointments. I promised to send Jeanette text updates about my life and my hair. We hugged goodbye, and I left the salon with $200 worth of miracle hair potions.

On the drive home, I glanced at myself in the rear-view mirror every chance I could. The new hairstyle was growing on me. As soon as I walked in the door at my mom's house, the kids both ran up to me to hug me and said my hair looked great. My mom must have coached them. There's no way they'd say that or even notice my hair on their own.

My mom walked over to me and looked me up and down. She took a step back and, with gleaming eyes, said, "You look beautiful, my darling girl."

I took both of her hands in mine and gratefully, with tears in my eyes, said, "Thanks, Mom." Then, we laughed our inside-joke laugh and released hands.

As we walked into her kitchen, she said, "Now, sit and have some apple pie. We baked it while you were at the salon. Arianna did a great job adding cinnamon, sugar, and butter to the apples, and Chad was a master at rolling out the dough and making the crust."

I looked at the kids with wonder, and they both puffed out their chests with pride and nodded their little heads. Then, we all laughed and sat down to eat Grand-mommy's delicious blue-ribbon-worthy apple pie.

CHAPTER 7

I was excited to get to work on Monday and show off my new hairstyle to match my new fall wardrobe. I was so happy that my hair actually looked good for a change. *No more bun!*

The day was off to a great start; I was having a really productive morning, looking forward to Michael's homecoming in two weeks and celebrating the Christmas holidays with him home. I was lost in those thoughts when I received an email to meet the vice president in the conference room in fifteen minutes. *What is happening?* I was certain this wasn't going to be good.

My one-year review wasn't for another month. Everyone was busy typing away at their keyboards as I walked past the rows of cubicles towards the door. I crossed the threshold of no return and walked down the long, gray-carpeted, white-walled hallway to my destiny. Before I knew it, I was sitting in the office with the VP and someone from HR. I knew what was coming. This was it. The moment I had secretly been waiting for, since the moment I dismissed my intuition's screams of "Hell, no" and accepted this job. This job taught me the hard way that I will never again wait until a situation comes to fruition *before* I trust my intuition.

The actual termination was short and sweet and ended on good terms—no hard feelings. Words were being spoken, and I had no idea what was being said; it was like a blur. I signed some papers, said "yes" when it seemed appropriate, and that was that. In a nutshell, the large project I was working on had ended; the contract was up, and they couldn't afford to keep me on anymore. As it turns out, their existing staff could divide my workload amongst themselves, now that Shannon had left and wasn't bringing in the big projects anymore. They wished me the best.

I recall saying to them both, "I kind of had a sense this moment was coming; it was blatantly obvious to me that no more big projects were in the pipeline anytime soon. It's actually a relief to be let go versus sitting around feeling like a bump on a log. Thanks for the opportunity to work on the projects and sharpen my design skills. It's a small world; I'm sure our paths will cross again."

I was secretly giddy with delight and tried to look serious as I got up, shook their hands, and bid adieu. I was giddy and relieved—no more stealing trade secrets from other manufacturers. No more guilt, no more dread. *No more stress. Thank God!*

I practically floated back to my department; leaving this place resonated like a "hell, yes" in the depths of my gut. I didn't care about the pay or the career impact. I was tired of trying to override my intuition and force myself to stay in a toxic situation. I was glad they let me go when they did. One more day there, and I might have gone bald from the stress.

As I reached the door to my office, fear gripped me, *how do I pack up without my office mates seeing me? Ugh, how embarrassing!* I took a deep breath, turned the knob, and walked in with my head held high. My boss, Bryanna, turned to look at me and smiled; I smiled back and waved goodbye in passing. She smiled and waved back. It was finished. No hard feelings. The end.

Based on my rough calculations, I had to make at least three trips to clear out my belongings. I tried to do it as quietly as possible. Note to self, don't ever bring so many grad school textbooks to the office again! I waved goodbye to people who cared to look up from their screens and sent a farewell email to everyone before logging off my computer for the last time.

After the three trips back and forth to the car, I was finished clearing out my desk. I put the last milk crate in the trunk, got in my car, and looked at the clock; it was 10:00 a.m. Thank God I was out of there. Now, since I didn't have to worry about how to break it to the boss that I was not going to steal a furniture company's trade secrets, I immediately texted the rep from that company and scheduled a lunch date; my plan was to come clean, tell her what I had been assigned to do, and clear my conscience once and for all.

After sending the text, I vowed never again to ignore my intuition and settle for a soul-crushing, dead-end job. No more settling for crap; I was going to hold out for the best life had to offer. No substitutions. No making do. No settling, just for the time being. *Screw that crap.* I wanted better for myself. I didn't come this far to come *this* far.

I turned the car on and drove out of that parking lot as fast as I could, so grateful that I'd never have to see the insides of that repurposed, drafty, domed Quonset hut again. I put my favorite music on and reveled in having the entire day to myself. Who would have ever guessed that it would be my last day! *Well, thank God my hair looked good!*

My mind raced to the future as I drove home. What would Michael say? What would I do for money? Would I reinvent myself or stick with interior design? I was so grateful for this forced hiatus. Between my dad's mess, Michael's deployment, and that dead-end job, I was exasperated and needed this break. I prayed the hair treatments I was faithfully doing would work their magic. I hoped that once Michael came home and life calmed down, my hair would return to its normal texture and grow back. I decided to see this work separation as a blessing in disguise. I just had a feeling it happened at the right time, and something big was on the horizon. I decided to embrace this as an opportunity and drove home in a state of positive, expectant bliss.

When I arrived home and settled in with a cup of tea, I called Michael and surprised him with an impromptu FaceTime. It was earlier than I usually called him, and he happened to be on a break. He could tell from my camera background that I was home; of course, he wanted to know why. I told him what happened at work, and surprisingly, he took it in stride. I told him, "Technically, I wasn't fired, so I might as well file for unemployment next week and see what happens."

He agreed and added, "Something will turn up, and if it doesn't happen right away, we will still be fine. We did just fine on my salary when you left your physical therapy career and attended grad school full-time to study interior design. I have faith that we'll get through this and come out stronger than before. Love you, Lex."

I was so grateful for his support. Our marriage was nowhere near perfect, but in moments like this, he really came through for me and walked alongside me with compassion and unconditional love.

After that, we talked about the kids, and he told me about the month-long process he'd have to go through to officially end his tour in the Middle East and fly back to the states. The out-processing would start in October in Fort Hood, Texas. He'd be there a couple of weeks. This time typically entailed a weapon turn-in, a release from active duty physical, or REFRAD as Michael called it, and lots of debriefings. Once all that was finished, he'd get to fly home! The current plan was for me and the kids to drive down to Philly on November 16th and pick him up at the Philadelphia International Airport.

We worked out some of those logistics and chatted some more about the kids. Michael said he was looking forward to being home in his own bed with his wife. It had been a long six months, and the end was finally in sight. We were both excited for this to be behind us.

I knew Michael wasn't big on pomp and circumstance. He didn't like to call a lot of attention to himself, so there would be no huge welcome home party for him, just a small gathering at home with immediate family. The local Army Unit he reported to duty at was hosting a welcome home ceremony the first weekend in December. The governor was due to stop by to welcome the troops home, and the local press would be covering it: a true Hometown Hero's homecoming. That would be the extent of his celebrating. When I asked him several weeks ago why he didn't want a huge welcome home party, he confided that at the end of the day, he was just doing his duty and didn't want any extra special attention. So that was that.

After talking to Michael, I filed for unemployment online and started that process. I qualified, and there was no shame in taking a hand up. I was grateful for the income as I sorted out my life. My next call was to my mentor, Maria. She picked up right away. I knew I could count on her for good advice, and she did not disappoint; she also didn't mince any words. She said, "Alexis, I'm sorry this happened to you; perhaps this is a blessing in disguise for you. This could be an opportunity to recalibrate and figure out your true north. In my twenty-five years in this industry, I've had my fair share of curve balls. I find that when crap hits the fan, it really doesn't matter where you start. So long as you start somewhere and don't just sit around wallowing in misery."

I nodded into the phone and gave a perfunctory, "Mm-hmm."

She acknowledged and kept going, "When my first business was an epic disaster, and I had to declare bankruptcy, I was mortified. What would people think of me? I was living on the Main Line with a big mortgage. I felt like a failure, with three kids and one on the way. My husband worked at a small non-profit, which meant I was the breadwinner. I decided to be open to the experience and the lessons I could learn from it. No shame in being unemployed, no fear about money, no pressure to rush out and find a dead-end job. Instead, I decided to release my death grip on the steering wheel of life, take a step back, take a deep breath, and think about the silver lining. Because as hard as it might be, I knew deep down there always was one. I had no choice but to pick myself up, dust myself off and begin again. That much I've learned from life. I'm not going to lie to you; it was painful to go through the experience, and it cost me my life savings at the time, some sanity, and my arrogance. But I rebuilt, and I've been in business for twenty years and going strong."

I was in awe and commended Maria for her strong comeback.

"Alexis, the important thing is to find your way, to gain your footing either back to baseline or bounce forward and land in an entirely new level of existing and perceiving the world more differently than you ever have before. And you might like it better there! This is an opportunity to move forward with a new perspective on life in a new direction of your choosing. I'm happy for you to have this opportunity. I know far too many people who've languished for decades in dead-end jobs. It's like they've got one foot in the coffin and the other on a banana peel. I don't want that for you. Seize this opportunity."

She continued on with an authoritative expert tone, like a doctor prescribing a course of action to a patient, "Alexis, take action in some direction, keep going and let yourself keep changing directions until you are on the best-feeling path that lights *you* up. It's where you finish, not where you started, that truly matters. Humble beginnings and setbacks are nothing to be ashamed of. They are stepping stones that help you determine how to pivot and course correct. They teach you valuable life lessons and hone your skills for what's to come. And, from my experience, no experience is a failure *unless* I fail to learn a lesson from it and recalibrate to a better version of myself. No matter what life throws at me, I can turn it all into gold. Heck, pardon my French; I can even turn *shit* into gold. And I know you'll do the same. Let's talk again in three months, the end of January. Let me know where you're at with things. I'm happy to be a reference for you."

After we said our goodbyes, I thought long and hard and decided to give up on rigidly following the 5-year life plan I had created for myself to climb the corporate ladder in the commercial design industry. My health and happiness meant more to me than a title and paycheck. Life had forced my hand and gave me no choice but to leave the job I hated. I was going to see it as a blessing in disguise—no more playing victim and no more settling for less. I chose to see this as an opportunity to re-assess my life and essentially take this time to rest, reflect, and redefine what success meant to me, how I wanted to live out my days, and how I wanted to earn money in exchange for the value I delivered.

The next week was like heaven. The kids were in school, and I had the whole house to myself for hours on end. I cleaned and organized. It was the perfect time to get everything in tip-top shape before Michael's homecoming. I liked to have everything neat, clean, and orderly, and the kitchen stocked with his favorite snacks and meals when he came home from long deployments.

In my fifteen years as an Army wife, I knew his nerves would be shot when he came back from deployment, and he'd need a good month to transition out of military mentality and back into civilian mentality. It was like he had to reboot and remember he wasn't barking out orders to soldiers, but simply playing with his kids and talking with his wife. At times in the past, he'd bark out orders to me and the kids like he half-expected us to say, "Sir, yes, sir," like some GI. Keeping the house neat, clean, and orderly helped make Michael feel like he was a king coming home to his castle after months of sleeping in barracks. It sounded cheesy, but it worked to calm his nerves and ease him back into domesticity.

My dad's drunk calls started up again. He'd call my cell and home phone daily. I felt bad screening his calls, but it was obvious that he was hitting the bottle hard again and not stopping anytime soon. I knew better than to invite him into my home; I had heard way too many horror stories from friends and family about taking in addicted family members and trying to support them. I wanted no part of that mess.

After the fourth day, I called him, and he appeared sober. I told him he had to stop calling my house when he was drunk. Michael would be home soon, and I didn't want him bombarded with these calls. He needed to rest and settle back into domestic life at home with the kids and me. It was an awkward conversation to be having with one's parent, but it needed to be done. I hated adulting some days. *Why is this happening to me?*

The drunk calls stopped for *one day*, then picked right back up again. We were old school and still had a home phone with a digital answering machine. I let the calls go to the machine and kept the volume on low, so the kids wouldn't hear any messages he left. Thankfully, they appeared to be pretty pre-occupied with their imaginary play, homework, and planning for their dad's return home.

I was religiously taking my daily supplements and massaging the hair growth products into my scalp and hair every morning. I was praying I'd have more hair on my head by the time he returned home. I didn't want him to see me like this.

The days appeared to meld, and the passage of time became irrelevant as I became lost in the moment. It was a much-needed respite to recalibrate my mindset, improve my health, prepare myself and the kids for my husband's return, help my dad, and last but not least, restore my hair!

CHAPTER 8

Michael's homecoming was finally drawing near. In less than 24 hours, he'd be home. The kids had been checking the days off on the kitchen calendar for the last six months. Their mounting energy was contagious. To help burn off some of that energy, we prepped the car after dinner. They loaded the car's back seat with their hand-drawn banners and red, white, and blue balloons. While they did that, I unloaded most of the roadside emergency supplies from my trunk to make room for Michael's luggage. He'd be bringing home three, huge, green, military duffel bags, plus any gifts he had for the kids and me.

We packed snacks for the car ride down, FaceTimed with Dad for the last time, and went to bed early. It felt like the night before Christmas at our house! As I lay in the huge king-size bed by myself, I thanked God that this would be the last night I'd spend alone in it. I tossed and turned and mulled over the past six months. All the prayers, lonely nights, FaceTime chats, missed family events, date nights, single-parenting drama, virtual hugs and kisses, and explaining to the kids why Dad wasn't here were coming to an end. I was tired of running this household by myself, keeping a stiff, upper lip, and persevering. I was grateful beyond measure to have my husband back home. After six, long months, the big day was finally drawing near; November 16th couldn't get here fast enough. I drifted off to sleep with gratitude in my heart and hope for the coming dawn.

The kids and I were up and dressed by 8 a.m. We practically paced the floors with our collective nervous energy. We watched a movie to kill time. Michael texted us an update, his flight out of Houston had been changed to American Airlines. No biggie; the change meant he landed at Terminal F at 2:15 instead of 3:42. *Score!*

We had an early lunch and left around 12:30; the drive was typically one hour, but we gave ourselves extra time, just in case of traffic. I had never seen the kids scramble so fast to leave the house and get into the car. The drive to Philadelphia International was pretty uneventful and fast. Thankfully, there was no rush-hour traffic or road construction to contend with at 1:00 in the afternoon, on a Wednesday. As I navigated the maze of on and off ramps surrounding the airport, the kids counted all the planes that landed and took off. I found a spot in short-term parking, close to the passenger pickup and baggage claim entrance for American, terminal F.

First time-check, I made good time; it was only 1:40 p.m. I managed to safely cross the multi-lane road with two kids, a bunch of balloons, snacks, and a welcome banner in tow, while dodging oncoming cars and shuttle buses. I wished we could have met him as soon as he walked off the plane into the terminal, but our only option was to wait at the baggage claim area. Finding a spot for all three of us to sit together was a challenge. The airport was like a huge, steel-gray labyrinth; luckily, we found a bench close to the baggage claim. The second time-check, it was 1:50 p.m. Michael was due to land at 2 p.m. I guesstimated that we'd spot him around 2:20 p.m., and he'd have his baggage by 2:30 p.m.

As we were waiting for his flight to land, the kids paced the red, terrazzo, accent lines on the floor and pretended that the adjacent grey terrazzo was quicksand. The goal was to stay on the red and not fall off into the quicksand. While they busied themselves with that game, I kept checking my text messages.

The third time-check, it was 2:00 p.m. As the kids paced back and forth on the red, terrazzo floor, they talked excitedly about all the news Dad just *had* to know about their school projects, sports, and favorite toys. They tried listening in vain for planes flying overhead and guessed what time Dad would arrive. "Is he here yet?" was their number one question on repeat. I probably checked my text messages about a thousand times, but the only ones I received were from my mom and Michael's mom asking, "Is he there yet?" The wait was almost excruciating.

To spend six months apart and have all that time boil down to a mere, thirty minutes of time separating us felt like cruel and unusual punishment. To be killing time in a drab, chilly, busy airport terminal waiting for the love of my life to arrive home safely was nerve-racking. The kids and I prayed for his safety every day of his deployment. I covered him in prayer as he flew back to the States; I prayed fervently to myself during our entire drive to the airport for our protection and his.

He was so close, yet still so far away. The minutes dragged on like hours as he traveled this last leg home. I tried to distract myself by keeping the kids occupied, but my mind was doing somersaults, and my nerves were shot. My feelings were mixed with excitement and dread.

I thought, "Will he be the same person who left six months ago? Will he have PTSD? Will he be short-tempered with the kids after not being a 'dad' for months? Will he have depression or anxiety? Would he seek help if he *did* have depression or anxiety? How long will it take him to decompress and come back to normal dad/hubby mode? Will he want to have sex tonight? Will he still find me attractive? Will he even notice my hair? Will he like my new hairdo if he does notice? Will I still find him attractive? Is the flame still there? How will the holidays go? How long before he starts in on me about my job? So much for hiring a house cleaner! What does he want for Christmas? Would he be in the mood for hosting holidays at our house? How will he do with the frequent drunken calls from Dad?"

As all these thoughts were swimming around in my head, I said a silent prayer to God to cleanse my thoughts, calm my nerves, bless my marriage, bless our reunion, bless our time together as family, and give me strength and patience to see this man with love, grace and compassion.

Oh, how I wish this was over already, and we were back home just living our regular lives. I wanted to avoid the awkward reunion and reintegration process. I wanted to skip to the good part, where Michael was used to being home and had transitioned back to domestic life as a dad and husband. I prayed it wouldn't be too awkward and drawn out. My layoff and my dad going off the deep end were more than enough emotional baggage for me to carry.

The moment we had been waiting for finally approached. My worried thoughts quickly vanished as the kids yanked on my sleeves and pointed to the American Air luggage conveyor belt. It had started rolling out luggage! The fourth time-check, it was 2:10 p.m. and the kids yapped away about all the planes they'd seen.

The fifth time-check, it was only 2:12 p.m. I willed myself *not* to look at my watch again for *at least* another ten minutes. I killed time by noting the suitcases being pulled off the baggage carrousel: big suitcases, small suitcases, hard sides, duffel bags, bright colors, grey colors, and every shade in between. As I was counting the luggage on the moving luggage conveyor belt, at that moment, a crowd of people was making their way down the hall. My heart swelled as I watched families and friends greet each other.

Will he be in this crowd of people? Would the moment I've been longing for finally happen? Would we have a moment to connect without the kids competing for his attention and affection? People passed by either self-absorbed on their cell phones or they looked around for their baggage and the exit. I loved seeing strangers' eyes light up when they reunited with a loved-one, embraced, and walked off together.

The sixth time-check, it was 2:25 p.m. I looked through the crowd one last time. Nothing.

Finally, I heard Michael's distinct cough and throat clearing before I saw him. Then, I saw his tall frame above the crowd and our eyes locked into a gaze. My heart jumped in my chest, and it felt like a lightning bolt had shot through it. We smiled with our eyes, and I broke my gaze to get the kids' attention. Several other people were reuniting with arriving passengers and gathering their luggage. The kids squealed with delight when they realized what was happening.

Words escaped me when it came to the actual reunion. It all happened so fast. Space and time flew out the window. The balloons were long gone; several had escaped the car the moment the kids opened the door, and the rest had floated away in the terminal. All we had left was the banner that the kids had made, and it took three of us to hold it. Our plan was to stand in a row holding the banner with the kids standing on a chair, so they would be my height. But that idea never saw the light of day. As soon as they spotted Dad's face through the crowds of people making their way toward the baggage claim, the kids left the banner on the chair and ran to him.

I followed quickly behind them, and we made our way to him as he made his way toward us. Luckily, there weren't that many people for us to mill through. The crowd thinned, people parted to the left and right towards different baggage claims, and Michael appeared before us, dressed in civilians and wearing his favorite, faded, red, Temple baseball cap. The kids screamed, "Daddy!!" He scooped both up in his arms and held them tight, turning his head left and right to take in the smell of their skin and hair. They tightly clung to him like there was no tomorrow.

I walked up to him and put my arms around all of them, and he kissed me. The embrace felt as familiar and cozy as wrapping up in my favorite, oversized, chunky, knit cardigan. It was like the past six months melted away, and he had never left. It was a simple, yet profound greeting. I was able to get a photo of the kids running up to him. We held up the greeting sign for him, and a friendly passerby snapped a photo of the four of us.

The kids talked a mile a minute as we made our way to the baggage claim. Michael held Chad's hand and carried Arianna in his left arm. I walked beside Chad and looked at Michael. He mentioned that he was shocked by how grown the kids had gotten. The kids had a million-and-one things to tell him. They wanted to be all over him but had to let go, so Dad could grab his duffel bags when he spotted them on the carousel.

Chad ran to get the nearest wheeled luggage caddy, and Arianna followed behind him and rode it back as Chad pushed it. We easily spotted Michael's luggage, thanks to the large black-stenciled initials and the last four of his social, boldly printed on his duffel bags. A small handful of other soldiers had made their way down to the baggage carrousel, greeted their families, and picked up their duffels to depart into the fray of traffic coming and going in the airport. We could easily spot the fellow soldiers from a mile away with their drab, olive-green duffel bags and standard GI-issued buzz cuts.

Just like that, we were back to life as a family of four. I prayed the transition would be a smooth one. I gently reminded the kids to give Dad some space and let him put the duffel bags on the dolly. Chad helped Michael push the luggage. Arianna sat on the duffels, and I was next to Michael as we walked outside towards the car. It was like any other airport pick-up. No one looking at us would have ever guessed that we had just reunited after six long months of being apart. We made our way back across the multi-lane road as a complete family.

My heart leaped when Michael casually asked, "Do you want me to drive?" Of course, I wanted him to. It had been a long time since I'd heard those words, and I savored every syllable. It's the little things like that, that I really missed when he was gone. This chapter of our lives, as a family separated, had come to a close, and it was time to pick up where we left off and begin a new chapter as a united family of four. We loaded the luggage, hopped in the car, and made our way back home.

Michael usually wasn't one for talking much in the car; he generally focused on the road. But today, he chattered away with the kids and me as he drove. It was a long day for Arianna, and her eyes had grown heavy; as she drifted off in the back seat, she murmured softly, "I missed you, Daddy; good to see you." Michael and I glanced at each other, and he squeezed my hand.

Chad was starting to nod off, too. Michael and I would have a moment's peace with each other for the last 45 minutes of the trip. As usual, all the fears that had been swirling around in my head at the airport proved to be unfounded.

I looked at him as he drove home; I had missed the familiar curve of his jawline, his buzz cut, and broad shoulders. I missed being able to sit in the passenger seat while he did all the driving. I had missed seeing his lean, muscular arms and strong hands gently holding the steering wheel. Those little things meant so much, and deployments reminded me not to take them for granted. I was blessed to have him home in one piece. The transition back to regular life proved to be uneventful. I worried for nothing. It was like the last six months apart never happened, and we were back to the daily rhythms of life: sleep, sex, food, sunshine, rain, work, church, school, homework, arguments, chores, laughter, movies, soccer practice, tummy tickles, bath time, evening prayers, holidays, and family vacations. Rinse and repeat.

We hosted a small, casual, welcome-home dinner with our parents that weekend. Despite me leaving several voice messages on his cell phone, Dad never showed up for the dinner. Whatever, his loss. Within a few short weeks, Michael was back to his usual self, my dad was no longer drunk-calling me, and it was life as usual for our family.

CHAPTER 9

I was due to see Jeanette for another hair appointment. I had a lot of good news to share with her. What a difference the drive down to Chestnut Hill was this time around; my head was much clearer. What a difference two months could make. I wasn't at that dead-end job anymore, Michael was home from deployment, and my dad had found a buyer for my grandmom's house! I was in a better frame of mind about so many things. It felt like the worst was finally behind me in terms of my dad, work, and Michael. It honestly felt like my luck had finally changed for the better. *Thank God.*

As I stepped out of the brisk, November air into the cozy salon, I was immediately greeted by the familiar sound of blow dryers whizzing, hair foils crinkling, and women happily chatting away. I looked around and noticed that they already had their holiday decorations up. Beautiful, twinkling, multi-color string lights were strung across the exposed-wood, ceiling beams. Cute, little Santa hats were placed on the tables, and small bunches of ivory poinsettia plants, in gold containers, were sitting on the product display shelves. There was jewelry on fancy, carved, wooden shelves. Brushes, scrunchies, pretty bobby pins, hair ties, and clips were practically dripping from every display rack and square surface. Christmas was right around the corner, and the salon was decked out in all its glory. If there was any last-minute shopping you needed to do, they had you covered!

As I walked towards the reception counter, Jeanette greeted me. Her low-cut afro was dyed burgundy, and she had on black tights, a long, black shirt, and black boots. She added a pop of color to her all-black ensemble with a funky, pink-, grey-, and lavender-striped cardigan, with faux-tortoise shell buttons and fluorescent yellow trim. The bright color looked amazing against her dark complexion.

We greeted each other warmly with a smile, leaned in, and gave each other a slight peck on both cheeks, French-style with a quick *la bise*. We'd known each other for over fifteen years and were long past the formality of handshakes. We walked over to her station, and I sat down. She gently ran her hand through my hair on each side of my head. "Your hair looks great; it's getting longer, and the layers are growing out nicely. It feels softer and looks good. It looks like you've been doing the weekly deep-conditioning treatments with the avocado!"

I nodded in agreement.

She continued on, "How's it been going with your job and your dad? Is your husband home?" I could hear the concern and curiosity in her voice and see it written across her face.

I quickly replied, "Well, Jeanette, I'm happy to report that my job is no longer a problem; I was let go about a month ago, and it's made all the difference in the world! Michael came home a couple of weeks ago! He loves my new hairstyle, by the way. My dad has stopped drunk calling me, and he's getting his life back in order, now that the Conlyn Street house was sold."

The rest of the appointment felt like old times as we chatted away, and she styled my hair. It was good to catch up and see her during the holidays. My hair had grown several inches, baby hairs were coming in strong, and the texture was starting to soften. Thankfully, Michael hadn't noticed the bald spots. I prayed that they would fill in soon, now that I'd alleviated the two biggest stressors in my life, my toxic job and my husband's deployment. I left the salon with my hair styled in a short bob and was under strict orders to continue to deep condition my hair once a week with the homemade avocado treatment and avoid heat styling tools.

On the drive home, Dad called, and I decided to pick up. He sounded sober and coherent for a change. We made some small talk for a bit, and he asked about Michael and the kids. He had completely forgotten about Michael's deployment ending and the welcome-home dinner. I gave him a quick recap, and he apologized for not remembering; he said he had a lot on his mind. My dad cleared his throat and, for the first time ever, asked me for help.

I was both shocked and relieved. It was about time he dropped the stoic, go-it-alone, stiff-upper-lip BS. Everyone could see he was struggling. I was so glad he plucked up the courage to be vulnerable and ask for help. I was grateful and honored that he asked me. He had finally sold my grandmother's house on Conlyn Street to one of those "We Buy Houses" businesses, and he needed me to take him to City Hall next week to handle some paperwork. Thankfully, I wasn't working, so I was available to help him. My heart swelled at the thought of being able to *be* there for my dad in his time of need.

Michael was away for training for the next two weeks, and I gave him a recap of the day's events over the phone. Michael wanted assurance that I wasn't signing any papers or giving my dad any large sums of money.

I snapped back, "Well, of course I'm not signing anything or giving him any money. What kind of fool do you take me for? I assure you, I only agreed to help my dad get to Center City to sign some papers that finalized the house sale. He never said what the papers were, and I never asked."

Michael was happy with that answer. Then, I told him the rest of the plans for the day. We'd be taking the train down to avoid driving and parking in the city. Since he had no train station near him, we both agreed the best option was for him to come to our house the night before, and we'd catch the 9:10 express from Exton to Philadelphia in the morning. That would put us down there by 9:40, and it was about a ten-minute walk from there to City Hall. *Too easy; it would be a piece of cake.* I couldn't have been further from the truth.

Michael didn't seem convinced that it was a good idea, but none-theless, he kindly suggested I ask his mom to come over to watch the kids and get them ready for school.

The week passed in a blink of an eye. The kids were excited to have dinner with Grandpa and breakfast the next day with Grandma! It also wasn't lost on them that he came bearing gifts for them. He was never one to arrive empty-handed; he had toys and candy for them when he walked in the door. He looked skinnier than ever; he was stooped over and walked as slow as molasses. Mind you, he pulled up in his 1995 cherry-red, Dodge Stealth R/T! Those two mental images just did not go together in my brain.

I shuddered to imagine how slow his reaction time must be these days and wondered just how fast and safely he was actually driving. I kept my concerns to myself for the moment and ushered him inside. We did our best to stuff his belly with good food and warm his heart with good cheer. After dinner, the kids opened their presents. My dad had given them vintage, Fisher-Price Little People toys. I don't know where he found this stuff! It was like a flashback to the 1960s.

As the kids were playing with their toys on the floor in the family room, Dad and I sat at the kitchen table and watched them. I took a sip of my chai tea, turned to Dad, and asked in a curious tone, "Thanks for the toys, Dad…where on earth do you find these vintage-looking reproductions? I remember playing with a schoolhouse like this when I was a kid! I love the fact that they have no batteries, no parts to put together, and they cultivate exploration and imagination!"

His whole face lit up as he smiled his huge, Cheshire-cat grin and replied, "Target™ has an aisle full of toys like this; it reminds me of when you and your cousins were little, and I would go shopping for toys for you all!" He chuckled, smiled, and sipped on one of the cold beers he had brought along in his mini-cooler.

I noticed that his hand shook as he lifted the beer can from the coaster and brought it to his mouth. His skin looked so papery thin on his skeletal-like hands. They looked more like the hands of a 95-year-old than a 74-year-old. I casually stole glances at him as the two of us looked at the kids playing and talked about the good old days. I thought he looked old as *dirt*. I wondered if he was eating regularly. I couldn't get over how thin and frail he looked. I guess people age differently? Maybe all the years of drinking, late nights binging on junk food, and driving cross-country as a truck driver had taken their toll on him? I wondered if it was partly because of all the stress of dealing with Mom's house on Conlyn Street and Doolie Pine.

My thoughts had started spiraling out of control. Thankfully, I had the presence of mind to distract myself with something more productive to dwell on. I made some more small talk with Dad before asking him about the details of our visit to City Hall. "So, Dad, I'm happy to hear that you found a buyer for the house. What do you need to do at City Hall tomorrow? Is the closing being held there, or something like that, with the buyer? How long will we be in the city?"

He sipped on his beer as I talked to him and then slowly lowered it with deliberation, to control the shaking in his hand. I pretended not to notice his labored effort to set the can down. He looked at me and sighed before speaking. My Dad gave me a vague answer; the buyer wouldn't be there. The purpose of tomorrow's trip, according to Dad, was for him to sign some papers at City Hall. After that, the house was no longer his to worry about.

At least, that's all he chose to be forthcoming about. I was just glad he finally found a buyer for the house! Thank God he found a house-flipper willing to take that albatross from around his neck. My dad would finally have peace of mind. The buyer agreed to handle Doolie Pine's eviction, clean up the bedbugs, pay all the past due taxes and utilities, and repair all the property damage. I left it at that and continued to drink my chai tea. We confirmed the train times for tomorrow. My mother-in-law, Carolyn, lived nearby and was going to come to our house at 8 a.m. to watch the kids and get them on the school bus. With all that arranged, we talked and watched silly kid movies the rest of the day and into the night. My dad was usually a night owl, but we both turned in for the night by 10 p.m.

Morning came quickly. The smell of coffee brewing at 6 a.m. let me know Dad was up. By the time I went downstairs to greet him and eat breakfast, he was sitting at the kitchen table, sipping the last of his coffee. As I walked toward the fridge, I said, "Dad, do you want anything quick for breakfast before we go? I'm making myself avocado toast if you want some. If not, we have oatmeal, cold cereal, yogurt, hard-boiled eggs, bananas, and apples."

He shook his head, folded his napkin, and said, "No thanks, I'm not a breakfast person."

We chatted briefly as I ate my avocado toast and drank a small glass of hibiscus berry kombucha. As I was loading the dishes into the dishwasher, I heard Carolyn's car pull up in the driveway. Right on cue, it was 7:55 a.m. I finished up in the kitchen, washed my hands, and liberally rubbed some fragrant, all-natural, lavender hand cream on my hands. It was brisk out, so I quickly grabbed a jacket from the mudroom closet before going out the side door to meet her.

Carolyn was the best mother-in-law a girl could ask for. She was super sweet, gave big warm hugs, and was the kind of neighbor who'd bring you a hot pot of chicken noodle soup if you weren't feeling well. She was always willing to lend a hand or a shoulder to cry on. But she didn't meddle in our business. She lived less than a mile away and thoroughly enjoyed herself as a retired widower. She had her group of silver-haired besties and a ton of hobbies to keep busy. She was the kind of person who baked pounds of Chex Mix each Christmas and placed it in decorative holiday tins, and personally hand-delivered it to everyone in her neighborhood. When she wasn't volunteering at some local shelter or church, she was knitting. She was an amazing knitter. She could look at a sweater and reverse engineer how it was made, then knit you a sweater that looked just like it. She'd make her own pattern after a quick Google search!

Needless to say, when I walked outside and caught a glimpse of her short, round frame coming towards me with a tote bag in one hand and a bottle of Pepsi in the other, I knew that bag was full of yarn and needles. I smiled and greeted her, "Hi, Carolyn, thanks for coming over so early in the morning. Do you need a hand with your things?"

She smiled and said, "Hi, Lexe, good morning to you too. And it's no problem, I can carry all of this just fine. I'm happy to help you and your dad out. Honey, it's the least I can do while Michael is away at drill. It seems like he just came back from deployment, and now he's off somewhere else. At least he's only an hour away at Fort Indiantown Gap. Once we get inside and I put these things down, we can hug. I know you have to leave soon to catch your train, so I won't take up too much of your time. Call me later tonight to let me know how things go and how your dad is, okay?"

I agreed and held the door for her. She stepped in, placed her things on top of my washer and dryer counter, and gave me a huge, bear hug as soon as I walked in the door. Did I mention she gives the best bear hugs in the world? Then she went into the kitchen, said "hi" to my dad, and gave him a big, bear hug too. As she turned to take off her coat and hand it to me, I could see the concern in her eyes as she and I made eye contact. I could tell she noticed how thin and frail he looked.

The kids were dressed and ready for breakfast. Thankfully, Carolyn was familiar with the kids' morning routine and bus schedule. I didn't need to review anything with her. She had her knitting and her Pepsi, and that's all she needed. As I put Carolyn's coat in the closet, I took out Dad's button-down, barn coat and intended to just hand it to him. But then, I noticed how dazed and confused he suddenly looked and decided against it and chose to help him put his coat on instead. It was lined with a heavy, red-and-blue-quilted flannel, and I swear the coat felt like it weighed more than him.

He staggered back under the weight of the coat and slumped against a wall in the mudroom for support. I helped him regain his balance and then reached back into the closet for his hat and gloves. As he donned them, I grabbed my tan, double-breasted, knee-length, cashmere coat, quickly put it on, and cinched the belt around my waist. I grabbed my hat and gloves and was ready to go. Carolyn was standing by to give out more of her huge, bear hugs and kisses on the cheek. She handed me my purse and Dad his briefcase, and off we went. She waved goodbye to us as we left through the side door to the garage.

By the time I was in the car and buckled in, Dad was still opening the passenger door. It felt like it took him hours to open the car door, sit down, swing his legs inside, close the door, and put on his seatbelt. I just stared at him with raised eyebrows and never said a word. I don't know what happened to him between breakfast time and now, but he was moving slower than molasses and seemed more dazed and confused by the minute. At least we were on time and left the house at 8:15, as planned, to catch the 9:10 train down to Suburban Station.

As we drove to Exton and talked, I couldn't shake the feeling that something was off about him. It was like he had aged a hundred years in the last hour. We made small talk as we made our way down Route 100 to the train station. We lucked out and found a spot close to the platform, which was a blessing because it took Dad ten minutes to walk the couple of steps to the platform. Other commuters saw how he struggled and made room for him to sit on one of the benches. We had about ten minutes to kill before the train came.

Once the train arrived, we were the last to board, and the conductor helped Dad up the stairs and onto the train. He seemed so disoriented. I talked to him and told him to follow me, and we'd get a two-seater facing forward. He took the window seat, and I took the aisle seat. Thank God it was the express train, because he literally asked me the same five questions over and over again. It was as if he had developed an acute case of Alzheimer's the instant he sat in the seat. I don't know what happened, but he just went downhill from there as the day went on. He couldn't remember where we were going and kept asking me.

Then, he needed help getting off the train, and I had to hold his arm and support him as we walked through Suburban Station to JFK Boulevard.

Once we made it outside to the Boulevard and caught a sharp breath of the fresh, cold, winter air, I felt revived. He still looked out of sorts as we walked down the sidewalk. We missed two traffic lights to walk across the street to City Hall because he was disoriented and needed to get his balance. At the rate we were going, we'd miss his 10 o'clock appointment. I kept asking him if he was okay, and he replied, "Yes," every time.

While we walked across the expanse of sidewalk, he was leaning on me for dear life. He noticed the snowflake decorations hanging from the lampposts and asked me if it was Christmas. I turned to him and said, "No, Dad, it's not Christmas, but we are in December, and Christmas will be here in about three weeks. Do you need to stop and take a break? Or can you keep walking?"

He had this spaced-out look in his eyes and replied, "Yes, let's keep walking; this is nice." As we slowly made our way towards our destination, he looked up at City Hall, turned to me, and said, "Lecky, are we going to that church?" At that point, I was just done in; he hadn't called me "Lecky" since I was a child. I could almost feel my life come crashing down around me like a building being dynamited. It was like the dust and rubble of my ruined life were flying everywhere with every word he spoke and every labored step he took. I was getting more alarmed by the minute. *What is going on with him?*

It should not have taken us over fifteen minutes to walk from the train station to City Hall. *Will he remember what office he needs to go to and what forms he needs to sign? Is he losing his mind? Am I going to have to take care of him for the rest of his life? Does he have money to go into a nursing home? How could this be happening? Is he having a panic attack? Is this sudden onset dementia? Is that even a medical condition?* I felt so alone and helpless.

We found the correct office and sat for about 45 minutes before being called to an agent window. He seemed to come to his senses while we sat there. I had brought a bottle of water with me and several granola bars. He ate two bars, drank half a bottle of water, and seemed to feel better. *Maybe he had just been dazed and weak with hunger?*

Luckily, he seemed competent enough to conduct his business and sign his paperwork. When it was all said and done after all debts were calculated and settled, Dad was only going to receive a whopping $7,000 for the sale of Mom's house on Conlyn Street. I was shocked. *How could this be?*

I had gone online earlier in the week to see what houses were selling for on that block of Conlyn Street, and duplexes were easily fetching $90,000–$115,000 in fair to good "as-is" condition with no modern updates to the façade, interior finishes, or floor plan. His mother, my dear grandmom, who I fondly referred to as "Mom" and was known to all as "the Miller," would have been rolling over in her *grave*.

She had lived in that house for over fifty years. She was the last living elder on the block, the block's Matriarch, and everyone's adopted grandmother. She was *the Miller*. If there was anything you wanted to know, she was the go-to person on the block and in town. Before it was a thing to be an influencer, she was an influencer. She had a mouth on her that could cut like a knife, she didn't take any BS, and she was adored and feared by many. I knew she would have been furious about this transaction and how Dad had let the house fall into disrepair and rented it out to the worst person possible. From all the stories passed down, she and the Old Man, my grandfather, had purchased that house as an income property and an investment to leave to their children.

My father had inherited their duplex. He could have lived on the first floor and rented the second floor as an income source. *Talk about botching things up badly.* To see what my father did to her home infuriated me. Instead of growing the legacy of wealth, he drained it dry and burned it to the ground. I sat there stewing as my father finished up the transaction. I wished to God she had left the home to me. I could have done so much with that property as an interior designer. I could have flipped that house or fixed it up, let Dad live on the first floor, and rented out the second floor. Sadly, the only real profit Dad received from the sale was peace of mind, which to him was priceless, so I guess, in that respect, it was a profitable venture for my dad. He'd finally be rid of that headache and all the memories it held. He was finally free to pick up the pieces of his life and make a fresh start in his new home.

We had thirty minutes until the next train to Exton arrived; that would give us enough time to use the restrooms and take our time getting back to Suburban Station. My Dad did walk a little faster on the way back, but he still leaned on me for dear life and had a death grip on my arm as we crossed the street. We made it to the train with no event, and the conductor helped him board. Luckily, he fell asleep on the way home and woke up more like his old self.

The rest of the ride home was uneventful. We stopped at Wholefoods for lunch, and he complained about how expensive the food was and poo-pooed my attempts to explain the benefits of eating non-GMO, organic, and locally sourced food. He said the dollar menu at McDonald's tasted better. The banter made me feel good; it was like the dad I knew and loved was back! Finalizing the paperwork and getting a decent meal in his belly seemed to infuse new life into his frail frame, and he appeared more aware and oriented.

On the ride back to my house, we made small talk, and I felt like a million pounds had just come off both our shoulders. Dad left before the kids came home from school; he wanted to avoid rush hour and didn't want to drive home in the dark. As he pulled out of the driveway, I waved goodbye from the side door and thanked God that Dad's dizzy, disoriented spell was brief and not anything serious.

I headed into the kitchen to prepare dinner and called Michael to give him a recap of the day's events. I was grateful to have this behind me. This was a bad chapter, and it was finally closed. No more stress, no more issues. No more "Dad drama." We could finally get back to life as usual. *Thank God!* I exhaled greatly and felt my shoulders drop; it was like the weight of the world had just come off. I lost myself in the moment and watched the water swirling in the pot as I prepared dinner.

CHAPTER 10

"Merry Christmas!" It was the most wonderful time of the year again. What a difference a year made. Michael was home, Gil was resting in peace, and I was free to redefine my career. At the moment, I was busy in the kitchen preparing the turkey, mac and cheese, and candied sweet potatoes. The kids were playing with the new toys that Santa had given them, and Michael was frying up bacon for his green bean casserole.

There was a knock on the door, and on cue, my mom and mother-in-law arrived promptly at 1:30 p.m. with food in tow. We were having an early dinner at 2:30, so the grandparents could get home before it got too dark for them to drive home safely. My mom was in charge of bringing her yummy coleslaw and her mouth-watering dinner rolls handmade with love and lard. My mother-in-law, Carolyn, was bringing her sausage stuffing, gravy, and mouth-watering pecan pie. Her pecan pie was to die for. Every year in October, she received a couple of pounds of pecans in the mail from her dear mom, who lived in Texas. Carolyn swore the fresh pecans made all the difference and was the secret to her mouth-watering dessert. It was odd not having my father-in-law, Gil, with us. She made her pecan pie in honor of him. It was Gil's favorite. My dad was coming too; he was bringing toys and, most likely, a cheese ball from Hickory Farms for the appetizer.

Around 2:30, we could hear the familiar, loud hum of my dad's van pulling into the development. We'd have to open presents quickly or wait until after dinner if we were going to have dinner any time soon. We were supposed to be sitting down to eat at 2:30, not greeting guests. As he neared the house, the faint, engine hum grew to the sound of a roar, and when I opened the side door to greet him, the van idled with a deafening roar that rattled the entire house.

As he slowly climbed down from the van, he shouted in his booming voice, "Hi, Lexis! Get Michael to come out and give me a hand with all these presents." He slowly made his way around to the passenger side to slide open the side door. He looked skeletal in his black slacks and shearling coat. The garments hung off him like he was a skeletal wire hanger. As he walked toward me, I didn't want to be rude and stare at him, but I couldn't help myself. He looked like a bag of bones; if he hunched forward any further, he'd look like Victor Hugo's Quasimodo.

It broke my heart to see him like this. He looked horrible. He looked like he had lost even more weight since I saw him last. As he reached his hand forward for help walking up the side stairs, I caught a glimpse of his skin. His hand looked so boney and frail, and the skin was tissue thin and crepe-like. I blurted out, "My God, Dad, are you eating? Are you okay?"

He looked quickly at me and said, "Yes, money is tight, so I'm mostly eating frozen TV dinners."

My eyes bulged; he couldn't live off that processed food. He needed real food. I quickly said, "Well, we'll make sure you load up on leftovers, Dad. Seriously, take home as much as you want."

I hung up his coat, and he walked into the kitchen to greet every-one. Meanwhile, Michael made several trips to the van to bring in the presents from the back of my dad's van. No one else commented on his appearance. We had been snacking on some nuts and keeping the food warm in the oven while we waited for my dad to arrive. As soon as the kids laid eyes on him, they were squealing with delight to open their presents.

We ate dinner first; and we all over-ate and thoroughly enjoyed each other's company and the warm glow of the twinkling, Christmas-tree lights. As soon as dinner was over, the kids opened presents from Pop-Pop Miller first. My dad basically ate and ran. It truly was a shame he didn't come earlier, so he could have spent more time with us. But I knew he had an hour-plus drive back home, and it would be dark by 5:00.

He was warming up the van and leaving our driveway at 3:45. As I waved goodbye to him from the driveway, I praised God that he was sober, ate a good meal, and left with tons of leftovers. Lord, he was thin. Shortly after, Carolyn left the festivities to go home and care for her fur baby. This Christmas was bittersweet for her; this was her first year celebrating the holiday without her husband, Gil. We hugged longer than usual before we said our goodbyes. My mom stayed behind to talk with Michael and me, play with the kids, and help clean the kitchen. She and I talked and laughed as we washed the tableware and silverware by hand, dried them, and packed them up in boxes. She left around 6 p.m.

After my mom left, we clowned around and let off steam. The kids got ready for bed, and we all sat down in the family room to watch a Disney movie and munch on some Christmas cookies and milk. Around 7:30, the phone rang. When we paused the movie, I assumed it was some distant family members calling to wish us a

"Merry Christmas!" I didn't recognize the caller ID and was going to ignore it, until I realized it was the police calling. I picked up the phone, and it was an officer from the Bensalem Police Department who asked to speak to me about Alec Benjamin Miller III. "I'm sorry, ma'am, to have to tell you this on Christmas."

Before he could continue, I gasped, clutched my chest over my heart, and pleaded, *"No!"*

He took a deep breath and said, "He is safe. We found your father asleep in his parked vehicle. He was parked in the Wells Fargo bank parking lot on New Falls Road and Route 413 in Levittown. We found him during our nightly patrol of the area. The van was turned off, and he was at the wheel with a coat on but no hat or gloves. The weather has dropped into the teens tonight, ma'am. If we had found him any later, he might have frozen to death out here. He awoke as soon as we knocked on the van door and called out. He said he couldn't see well at night and pulled into the parking lot to get his bearings. He gave me your number as next of kin. After seeing his license and registration, we knew he didn't live far. Maybe six minutes, tops. We drove to his house in the patrol car, and he followed us in his vehicle. We escorted him to his side door, and he just went inside."

There was a long pause. I didn't know what to say or how to process this. Michael was looking at me while the kids dunked their cookies in hot cocoa, oblivious to it all. Time stood still. I could feel my eyes welling up and my face scrunching up to cry. I heard the officer speaking, but nothing was registered with me. I was in shock.

After several long blinks, I heard, "Ma'am, are you there? Hello, are you okay? Hello?"

I quickly pulled myself together, wiped the tears away, and spoke, "Um, yes, I'm here. I heard every word. I'm just trying to take this all in. Thank God he's okay. Thank you for calling. I don't understand. He seemed fine when he left our house. He wasn't drinking. He left before dark. I don't know what happened. He should have had plenty of time to get home; he left my house around four. His house is an hour and fifteen minutes away. It would have been dark by the time he reached his neighborhood. I didn't know he was that bad off. I'm so glad he's safe, and no one was hurt. Thank you, Officer James."

I really don't recall what else he said or what I said; it was all a blur and too much for my soul to take in. I told Michael what happened as I speed-dialed Dad. After what felt like hours had passed, he finally picked up the phone.

"Dad, are you okay? I just got off the phone with a police officer who said they found you asleep in your van in a bank parking lot tonight." As I anxiously spoke those words into the phone receiver, I could not believe they had come from my mouth. This was not happening. This was not what I had planned for my life—taking care of an aging parent? *I had kids to raise!* I could not possibly take care of this man, too!

Dad started speaking, "Well, yes, I guess that's what happened. I drive slower now these days, and I should have left your house earlier. I was on the turnpike when it got dark, and I missed my exit and ended up in Willow Grove. I got back on the turnpike and headed towards home, and took the correct exit for Bristol. But it was pitch dark by then, and I couldn't find my way. Things looked different to me. I saw my bank and pulled in there. I meant to call you, but I guess I fell asleep, and I don't know what happened to the van. The next thing I knew, someone was knocking on the window, and I was freezing cold." My dad stated this all matter-of-factly and sounded coherent and in his right mind.

I, however, was losing my mind. I was pacing the floor in the kitchen at this point as I listened to him recount the events he could recall. Thank God Michael was keeping the kids occupied in the other room.

I had one hand on the phone receiver and the other over my heart as I talked with Dad. I felt so helpless and trapped. He was my *dad*, I looked up to him, and he could do anything in my mind's eye, and it pained me to see him like this. It petrified me to know that I was the only family he could depend on. I wondered, "Am I up for this responsibility of possibly caring for an aging parent?"

I breathed deeply and asked Dad some more questions about how he was doing. I prayed he was being honest when he said, "Yes, Alexis, I'm fine. I just don't see well in the dark. The police officers helped me find my way back home and made sure I was safe and warm in the house. I drove behind one car and the second police car drove behind me. I felt like President Barack Obama getting an official police escort through town! I can't find my wallet, though. I might have left it in the van. I lose it a lot lately. I lose my VA benefit ID a lot too. I have to get a new one."

He sounded convincing enough, but I wasn't buying it. I knew that I'd have to keep a closer eye on him going forward without making him feel like I was eavesdropping or emasculating him and treating him like a child. I silently vowed to help him and call him twice a week. Hopefully, it wouldn't be too smothering, and hopefully, he'd open up more about what he was going through and ask me for help instead of trying to tough it out on his own with a stiff, upper lip and treat me like I'm a child who doesn't know anything. This would be a delicate balance, as our roles evolved right before our eyes. He came off hard as nails, but he really was soft as a gentle, summer breeze. I just needed to get past that hard demeanor. I decided to consult Professor Google for help.

I stalled the call longer as I tried to muster the courage to ask him if he'd consider having a social worker help him manage his affairs. I had been putting off asking him if he wanted that kind of help, but after this latest event, I had to muster the courage sooner than later. It was so disconcerting to witness my formerly capable father, my superhero, who could do anything, deteriorate right before my eyes. I did not want this to happen. I resisted and wrestled the idea of becoming his caretaker to the ground and squashed the life out of the notion every time it dared to pop into my mind. But now was the hour to step up and be bold.

I mustered the courage to blurt out, "Dad, would you get a social worker? I'll set everything up for you. They can keep tabs on your doctor appointments and make sure you get to them."

He said, "No."

I asked him if he would accept Meals-On-Wheels, and he said, "No."

I asked him if he'd consider moving into a VA nursing home. He refused and followed by saying, "I will be fine. I'm going to marry a fast woman, and she'll take care of me; we'll live in a motor home and travel cross-country to all the cities with VA hospitals. I'll get care there when I need it and live all over the country. Don't worry about me, Alexis."

I was speechless and just dropped my jaw. I don't remember what we talked about after that. I was sure my father had lost his mind. And boy, did I worry. I didn't sleep a wink and had nightmares every time I drifted off to sleep. *What is happening to my life? What will become of my dad? I'm his only family. Do I want this responsibility?*

He had so much baggage. It might have been easier to swallow if he wasn't a drunk. I did not want that drama under my roof.

CHAPTER 11

I was seeing Jeanette for another hair appointment, just in time to look fabulous for the New Year's Eve party Michael and I were attending. My hair was growing and getting stronger every day. Michael and I had been so excited for a night out without the kids, but honestly, after Christmas night with my dad, I wasn't much in the mood for celebrating and kicking off the New Year.

What do I have to look forward to in 2017? I didn't like this rotten attitude that was beginning to take root and needed to nip it quickly. I mentally searched for *anything* to give appreciation and thanks for. It was a stretch, but I blurted out loud nonetheless, "Well, it *is* a blessing to be able to afford to go to the salon, and I *am* blessed with a safe and reliable car to take me there, and I *am* blessed with eyes to see the beautiful holiday decorations strung along the buildings on Germantown Avenue."

I gave a swift sigh of relief and felt my mood lightening and my attitude improving. The rest of the drive to the salon felt more pleasant as I took in the change of scenery from Chester County farm country to the quaint cobbled streets of Chestnut Hill. I loved seeing Germantown Avenue decorated for the holidays. The swags of greenery and Yuletide cheer displayed in the shop windows lifted my spirits.

I planned on talking to her about my dad and what happened on Christmas night. Perhaps she'd have some personal experience or could share advice from what other clients of hers did in similar situations. I needed help fast. I entered the salon in a better frame of mind and happily greeted Jeanette. I always received more from these visits than just a new hairstyle. I was so grateful for having her in my life. She was an angel in disguise.

As we greeted each other at the reception desk, she ran her fingers through my hair and sized it up. "Hmm, your hair is growing out nicely, Alexis! And it doesn't have that rough, resistant drag when I run my fingers through it. It feels fuller, too; I don't see down to your scalp anymore. In fact, your hair looks like it's on its way to being shiny, luscious, long, healthy, and full again! Well done, keeping up with the at-home treatments and regular cuts every six weeks. I know it's been a lot for you to drive down here and pay for extra sessions with me. But I really see a change in your hair for the better. It's not so dull and damaged."

I was beaming as I took a seat in her salon chair.

We talked about the holidays as she worked on relaxing my hair. I was glad that the texture was improving and there was less shedding. I was using the frequency at which I switched out my Swiffer dry sweeping cloths as my hair recovery gauge. I used to have to change the Swiffer cloth at least five times a week because it looked more like a furry black cat being pushed around on a mop than a floor sweeper. By now, I was only switching out the Swiffer cloths twice a week, and there was less and less hair on them each time. I was glad to see the improvement. I took it as a sign that I was keeping my stress levels at a healthy state *despite* all the "Dad drama."

Instead of filling the time talking about my hair rehabilitation, we talked about my dad's situation. She had some great pearls of wisdom to share with me from her own life experience, what some of her clients had done in similar situations, and how they dealt with aging parents. I left armed with a new hairdo and a greater sense of confidence, knowing I wasn't alone in this experience. I loved Jeanette and gave her the biggest hug when I left the salon. She is so much more to me than just my hairdresser. I breathed a sigh of relief as I stepped back out into the crisp winter air and prepared to make the trek back home, filled with a renewed sense of gratitude and hope for the new year.

I may have looked fabulous for the NYE party, but inside I felt like crap. My mom came over for the night to watch the kids. She didn't know what was going on with my dad. Michael and I hadn't told anyone. But I could tell she sensed I was feeling off. Thankfully, she let it drop and didn't press me on anything.

Truthfully, I just wanted to be home and make sure Dad was okay; I was worried about him. I had deep-dived on Google after talking with Jeanette and was shocked by how expensive adult home health aides were. Michael and I couldn't afford that kind of care for Dad, and we sure as hell didn't want to take care of him. We worked and had a family to provide for. Nevertheless, I shoved this all down, put on a happy face, and went to the party.

We made small talk and gave each other "the look" when it was time to go. Michael and I had agreed ahead of time that we'd leave by 1 a.m. This year, my mind was elsewhere. Normally my resolutions revolved around me making goals towards improving my health, mindset, and sleep hygiene. This year, my main goal was to call Dad at least once a week to keep tabs on him and help him stay healthy. "Grace" was my anchor word for 2017. It was like my true north, to help me navigate through life's chaos and stay the course with my goal. Despite our shortcomings, I desperately wanted grace to be given to me, my dad, and my family.

When we arrived home around 1:30 a.m., my mom and the kids were already asleep. We trudged upstairs to bed, and I walked over to the home phone on my nightstand to check the messages. The phone base was blinking; someone had left a message. I played the recording back. It was a message from my dad; he was shouting with his booming voice that carried, *"Happy New Year, Michael, Alexis, Chad, Arianna! It's me, Pop-Pop Miller. Love y'all. All right, now; take care. Bye-bye."* He paused between our names, like he was trying to recall them. I chuckled when I heard him announce who it was; there was no mistaking who owned that loud booming voice. It was so sweet. I started to delete the message from the machine, but as my finger reached out to press the erase button, I felt a quickening inside me, and I got the sense that I should save his message. I decided to heed the advice, withdrew my hand, and saved the message. I asked Michael to save the message, too. It just felt like the right thing to do.

As the winter cold gave way to warm air and longer days, I kept my promise. I consistently checked in on Dad weekly throughout January, February, and March. The last thing I wanted was for him to be lost on the side of the road again, frozen like a popsicle. He was sober more times than not, and I felt like our relationship was stronger because of our weekly talks. I was hoping that he'd trust me more and finally open up about what was going on with his weight and his memory. If all went well, maybe he'd even be open to receiving my help.

After three months of consistently calling him weekly, I found out he was subsisting on frozen pot pies, whiskey, beer, and coffee because he needed three root canals. He kept forgetting when his dentist appointments were and would then forget to reschedule the appointments and arrange for a Veterans Transportation Service van to drive him to and from the appointments at the Philly VA. I was shocked. I guess that explained why he had lost so much weight and maybe why he balked at the idea of receiving food from Meals-On-Wheels.

When I asked if he needed any help, he just replied, "No thanks. I can manage on my own." I vowed to continue asking him every week if he wanted me to arrange for him to receive Meals-On-Wheels food deliveries. He was a hard nut to crack.

As the weather warmed up and the first flowers of spring burst their purple heads through the last of the snow, Dad started to open up more and trust me. I was glad that I had invested the time in deepening our relationship. Prior to that, we were lucky if we talked once every three months. His drunk calls didn't count in my book, and I doubt he even truly remembered how many times he drunk-dialed me over the past six months.

Around late March, he asked if I could take him to his bank the following week. I wasn't working, so I had the time to help him. Doing this for my dad was a big deal. He wanted to add me to his personal and business checking accounts. Despite my mom warning me not to do it, I agreed. He had ruined her credit when they were married, and thirty-five years later, she is still nursing her wounds and holding a grudge. I was the only family he had, and I decided to take a chance on him and help him. He was my father, and I felt a duty to be there for him, regardless of his past transgressions.

As I drove down the turnpike towards Levittown, I thought about what we'd say to each other. I wondered how much money he had in his accounts and why he wanted to add me to them now, of all times. Maybe there was something more going on with his health than he was letting on. He looked so ghastly thin when we saw him over the Christmas holidays. I couldn't get the image of his frail frame out of my mind.

As I pulled up to his small, Cape Cod house and parked in the driveway, I said a little prayer for us and our dealings at the bank. Before I could pick up the phone to call him, I saw his side door open, and he slowly made his way out, slowly closed the door behind him, and slowly stepped down the two steps while holding onto the side of the house. He carried a ragged brown leather briefcase in the other hand. I guessed that his bank documents were in the briefcase.

He had on his shearling jacket, corduroy pants, and nubuck work boots, even though it was almost 50 degrees outside. I guessed that his thin frame made him cold; he didn't have an ounce of body fat left to keep him warm. I got out of the car to hug him and help him into the passenger seat. It took what felt like eons for him to bend down while holding the sides of the car, sit in the seat, use one hand to swing each leg into the car, buckle in and then hold his briefcase. It was a good thing I arrived at 9:30 for our 10 a.m. appointment.

We arrived at TD Bank ten minutes before our appointment, and it took all ten minutes for him to get out of the car and walk into the bank; he clutched my arm for dear life as we slowly walked into the bank. The pace we walked was unbearably slow, and, in my head, I was screaming. My soul was crying out in agony. When he spoke to the teller at the customer service desk, he was so loud that I'm positive the customers at the drive-thru heard him in their cars. After what felt like hours, we signed all the paperwork to add me to his accounts. We officially had joint checking and savings accounts together. Our new checkbooks would arrive in the mail in a week or two.

I had planned to take Dad out to lunch after the bank appointment and then to the grocery store to restock his pantry with anything he needed. He refused and said he was too tired to do anything else for the day. We didn't talk much on the ride back to his house; though he did divulge that he wanted me added to his accounts in case anything happened to him. That was the extent of the explanation.

I walked him to his door, and we said our goodbyes. I watched his frail frame disappear inside the house, and I fought back tears as I backed out of his driveway. My dad wasn't as forgetful as he had been when we went to City Hall together, but I still wasn't convinced that he didn't have early signs of dementia. On the ride home, I decided to call my mother-in-law and pick her brain about dementia. She'd lost her husband to it last year, so she was a fount of information on the topic.

As soon as I was on the turnpike, I speed-dialed Carolyn and asked her about dementia. I told her about my dad's erratic behavior, forgetfulness, the police call on Christmas night, today's bank appointment, all of it.

She was shocked; she just kept saying, "Oh, my gosh; I had no idea it was this bad. I'm so sorry, honey. I wish you had come to me sooner. Next time, promise me you won't wait. I'm here for you." She went on to tell me about what she learned while caring for her late husband during their eight-year battle with his dementia. She wanted me to know key things, like how to recognize the classic warning signs of dementia. She rattled off things my dad was exhibiting, like asking the same question over and over again, becoming lost in familiar places, not following through on medication changes, getting appointment dates and times mixed up, not being able to follow directions, and unexplained weight loss. I was cringing as she said these things.

She said, "If he seems confused or disoriented with his surroundings, do these things to help him feel calm and get oriented: make direct eye contact with him, reassure him of what he's to do next, give simple instructions if he's lost or can't remember how to do something, walk next to him—not in front—be calm and conversational with him, ask him if he understands you, *wait* for him to actually respond, address any concerns he has, be direct and personal, reassure him, speak slowly and use simple terms without being condescending."

She paused, then said, "I know I just said a lot, and you're driving; I'll send this to you in an email. These tactics really helped to lessen the confusion and frustration when Gil was in the early stages. Also, if you go to more appointments with him, make sure the person is addressing you both in the conversation. It used to burn me up when the doctors ignored Gil and talked only to me, like he wasn't even in the room. We finally found a really great doctor who established a great rapport with Gil. She talked *with* him, not *at* him. When she said to him things like, 'It seems to me that you are becoming more forgetful. Are you noticing this? May I make some suggestions? If it's alright with you, I'd like to…and does this sound like something you'd be interested in or willing to do?' I knew I had found a keeper!"

I was in tears by then, and Carolyn said softly, "Oh, Lexe, honey, I didn't mean to upset you. I love you so. I'm sorry. Please know I only meant to help. Are you okay?"

I was really shaken up by all that she said; it confirmed my suspicions that something was wrong with my dad. As I drove down the turnpike, I was fighting back tears. The longer I talked, the better I felt; I had been keeping so much bottled up. I told her, "I thought it was just the alcohol. I was praying it was just the alcohol. Why is this happening? My concentration is shot; every time the phone rings, I'm worried that it's either him calling to tell me he's gotten lost, or it's the police telling me that he's driven off the road into a ditch, and they just found his body. I can't concentrate on anything anymore. I feel like I'm going crazy. I'm trying to act normal for Michael and the kids, but inside, I'm a nervous wreck. How did you do it with Gil for so many years?"

Carolyn sighed and said, "Lexe, honey, I'm glad you're feeling better; please pull over to a safe area if you need to cry. I want you to stay safe! Promise me, okay?"

I said, "Okay," and she continued on.

"Well, for starters, of course, you can't concentrate. Who can concentrate, let alone think clearly, in survival and fear mode? I couldn't concentrate, and my creativity was shot. Once I got home healthcare set up through the social worker, I could breathe more, rest, and collect myself. Having home health aides made all the difference in the world. I was able to get away to myself and have the time and peace to collect my thoughts, pray, journal, and hear my own inner wisdom. In time, I began to feel a sense of safety and deep-knowing that the next, right steps would always be revealed to me, no matter how precarious things became with Gil, as his condition worsened. An abundance of resources also began to present themselves, as I reached out and asked for help and sought answers. God provided for Gil and me in ways I can't even begin to describe."

I mumbled a barely audible, "Okay," and she continued on.

"Don't try to avoid this and think it will go away; at some point, you must surrender and accept the fact that your dad is changing; he may or may not ever have a formal diagnosis. But for your sake, it will do you wonders to make peace with his current condition, surrender to what is and seek clarity and action from that perspective. The longer you put off facing the inevitable, the worse things usually get, and it could end up hurting you or your dad in the long run. You've got to face this head-on. But you don't have to do it alone.

Getting connected with a support group and a good doctor made all the difference in the world in my situation. As did having family close by. All the support that you, Michael, and your mom provided me was a lifesaver. I am here to support you; please lean on me. You are not alone and don't have to try to be some superwoman and do this alone."

Oh, but I did feel so alone. I hated to bug people and ask for help, but at this point, I was about to snap mentally, and I knew I'd have to reach out for help sooner than later from my family and friends. As if on cue, Carolyn said, "Don't wait until you're overwhelmed. Allow me to check on you; it is okay to need help. You cannot manage all of this and your family life on your own. You do not have to do it all on your own. Please remember that. You are going through a lot, and that doesn't make you weak if you ask for help or allow someone to help you. It takes a lot of courage to ask for help and accept it. I'm here for you."

We talked some more on my long drive home. Carolyn shared many pearls of wisdom that would carry me through the darkest days that were yet to come.

As the weeks passed, I faithfully called Dad at least once a week. I regularly talked with Carolyn and my mom and arranged for the kids to sleep over at one of their houses every other weekend. It was mid-April, and I had just dropped the kids off at school and was making the drive to Dad's. I was meeting with his lawyer to draw up my father's will, financial power of attorney, and medical power of attorney. He was entrusting me to execute his wishes, yet he still denied that anything was wrong with him.

I remember saying, "Dad, is there something you want to tell me? Is there something going on I should know about? Why are you doing this out of the blue? You just added me to your bank accounts, and now this? What's going on? Is there something you're not telling me? Please tell me what's going on."

He just sighed and plainly stated, "Alexis, I'm fine; don't worry about a thing. I just want to get my affairs in order. I've been wanting to do this since last year when Gil passed away. His death made me realize I better get my act together. He was younger than me, so if he could go, who's to say when my number's up? I wanted to do it sooner, but you were working, and I didn't want you to have to take off work. Now that you've got more time on your hands and Mom's house is finally off my plate, the time is right. That's all. Nothing more."

That was it, end of story. He just said he wanted to get his affairs in order. I didn't believe a word he said, but agreed to take him and sign the paperwork.

CHAPTER 12

I was dreading the upcoming legal appointment with my dad. It was about a 90-minute drive to his house, and from there, it was almost a two-hour drive to his lawyer's office on Township Line Road, off Route 3. I wish he could have chosen someone closer! At least, this was just a onetime appointment.

As I drove along the turnpike toward Bristol, I listened to podcasts in the car to pass the time. My dad's neighborhood was close to the turnpike, and I called him as I pulled into the driveway. Thank God, he answered and remembered why I was calling. I went to his side door to meet him. As he opened it and stepped outside, I heard a faint buzz; several flies darted out at me, and a waft of some terrible stench assaulted my airway and nearly took my breath away. I started coughing as I batted away the flies. Finally, I managed to sputter out, "Hi, Dad, do you need a hand walking down the stairs?"

He replied, "Hi, Alexis, good morning. Can you take my briefcase while I lock the door?" He handed me his battered, old, dark-brown, leather-bound, hard-side briefcase. It had seen better days. The once shiny, gold closures had been worn down to a scratched, dull, yellow, and brown patina. Once I regained my composure and stopped coughing, I couldn't help but notice how frail, shriveled, and small he looked. His once thick, dark-brown afro was now thinned and turning grey. I always wondered if he colored his hair, but I never saw hair color in his medicine cabinet in all the years I snooped inside it throughout my teens and young adulthood. I would have loved to have known if he colored his hair to impress the ladies.

It was a warm day, yet he wore corduroy pants, a long-sleeve cotton plaid shirt, suspenders, and Naugahyde work boots. He moved slower than a 300-year-old tortoise as he locked his door, double-checked that he locked it, turned on his little landing, and slowly walked down the two steps, using a step-to-step pattern for stability, making sure each foot was on each step at the same time, before stepping down to the next one.

I was glad he was safe, and I stood close by with a wide base of support, and my core braced, in case I needed to drop the briefcase and assist him. My years of training as a physical therapist were on autopilot, and I was ready to assist. Thankfully, he was able to walk independently down the two steps without a rail. He leaned on the storm door for support and hugged me when he reached the driveway. He smelled nice, so I wasn't sure what that stench was that had wafted out of the house when he opened the door, and I wasn't sure I wanted to know. I didn't bother asking him. I guessed it was nothing, and we proceeded to walk slowly to my car and make small talk.

My dad recounted his favorite tales from his youth, growing up in Germany, post-WWII, as an Army brat. I always loved those stories, and as a military wife myself, it meant so much to me to be able to visit the same city centers that my father visited as a child when I traveled to Europe with my husband and children. The lively conversation was a positive distraction during the long drive to Upper Darby.

Before I knew it, we were turning off Route 3 onto Township Line Road and pulling into the parking lot next to the Dutch Colonial housing the legal office of Jeff Lubick. When we walked inside, the interior had been converted into office spaces, and we waited in the lobby for our appointment. The room was cozy and quiet despite facing a noisy street, and the deep sofa was comfortable. While we waited, I checked my phone, and Dad dozed off to sleep. Within minutes, Jeff saw us, and the fun began.

Initially, Dad couldn't remember why we were there, and Jeff had to remind him. Jeff looked at me, and I looked at him. Our eyes locked in a mutual moment of awkward understanding. Aside from that one moment of forgetfulness, my dad seemed fairly coherent for the rest of the appointment. His hand shook as he signed the documents, and he needed reminders as to where to sign and why he was signing so many papers. As we wrapped up, he said he understood everything. Yet, when Jeff left the office to prepare the documents, Dad turned to me and said, "Alexis, remind me again why we're here."

I gulped and calmly explained that he had made this appointment to assign me as the person in charge of his medical care, finances, and property. I finished by saying, "Dad, we just signed your will, financial power of attorney, and medical power of attorney; those papers say that you want me to take care of you if you can't take care of yourself and your money anymore. And when you pass away, I will oversee your property and money."

He looked over his glasses at me with big, watery eyes and blinked all this information in. Finally, he nodded in agreement and said, "Yes, that's right, just checking to make sure *you* understand; that's my girl."

I laughed nervously and said, "Okay, good; I'm glad *you* understand too; you had me worried for a minute there."

We both laughed and waited for Jeff to return.

Once all the formalities were finished, Jeff gave each of us his business card, heartily shook our hands, and asked us to call if we needed anything. I had every intention of calling Jeff; I needed to arm myself with as much legal information as possible in case I needed to have Dad placed in a home and take over his affairs. I also found out during the appointment that Dad's house was not in his name; it was in the name of his company. Apparently, it was more advantageous for him to do this for tax purposes. However, his business had been non-operational for years; I planned to ask Jeff if this was something I needed to be concerned about. Now that my name was on everything, I needed to cover myself.

God, I could hear my mom now: "Didn't I warn you, Alexis, not to put your name on any of his papers? He will drag you down into his mess. I warned you."

I prayed her words didn't ring true.

After a long appointment, we left with documents in hand and headed back down the highway for Bristol. On the drive home, we chatted about his good old days in Germany, and he recounted most of the same stories he told me on the drive to the lawyer's office. I just smiled and enjoyed the conversation with Dad. We hit traffic on the way home and arrived back at his place around 4:30. I was pleasantly surprised when Dad invited me inside to help put his documents away for safekeeping.

He was stiff getting out of my car, and it took a while for him to walk to the side door; then, he dropped the keys twice while trying to open the door. Luckily, I was there to pick them up. As he swung open the door, that same stench from this morning came tumbling out, assaulting my airway, and it nearly burned my eyes.

As he stepped into the house and I stood outside, I made a full body shake, the hairs on my arms stood on end, and I thought, "My God, what *is* that smell?"

As he stepped through the doorway into the kitchen and plodded across the black carpeted floor, I hesitantly walked up the two side steps towards the doorway. As my face approached the house's threshold, it was as if the entire front side of my body met the resistance of a warm, gaseous, invisible force field of stench. I paused briefly at this invisible, nonetheless perceptible warning and, against my better judgment, decided to cross the threshold into his house then closed the door behind me. I was not prepared for what I saw.

It was still light outside, and as I quickly looked around the small kitchen, I saw dirty dishes piled in the sink, on the counters, and on the stove. There wasn't a square inch of clean space on the counters. Dozens of flies loudly buzzed throughout the kitchen. They briefly landed on surfaces and quickly took off again. There was trash piled on the floor in every corner, like rotted food, used napkins, empty food boxes, cartons, frozen food boxes, and plastic cutlery. It was piled so high that it crested the top of the counters. The tiny kitchen was overrun with trash. Everywhere my gaze rested, there was trash.

I stood at the door in shock. There was a clear path from this side door, to the sink, to the fridge, to the dining room, and to the hall bath and Dad's bedroom. Aside from that, every bit of floor space was overrun with garbage, piled as high as it would go before toppling and making another mini-mountain of trash. I looked straight ahead into the narrow hall that led to Dad's bedroom. He was walking down the hall and turned back to say, "Come on back to my bedroom, Alexis. Have a seat on the sofa, so we can talk and sort these papers."

I turned to the left to peer into the small dining room; the card table and folding chairs that had been set up in the center were gone. Instead, the room was now a receptacle for empty Miller Light boxes. The blue boxes were piled high in every corner up to the ceiling and encroached on the center of the dining room. There was a path through the room to the tiny, center-hall entry and front door. My mouth dropped as I took in the scene, and I quickly covered my hand with my mouth to block any flies from zooming inside it.

I blinked my eyes several times because they burned from the acrid odors. Tears streamed down the sides of my eyes from the rancid stench, and I covered my nose and mouth with my shirt as I followed Dad down the short, narrow hall to his small bedroom. The room was no more than 8' x 8', and if my memory was correct, he had installed a nice, tan-colored, frieze-style, looped carpet in the room to complement Mom's heirloom, wood-carved bedroom set. That set was a childhood favorite of mine. It had a beautiful, inlaid-wood floral pattern on each drawer and along the top of the head-board. I looked forward to seeing the beautifully carved bed frame, nightstands, and chest of drawers!

As I approached the room, I uncovered my nose. The full-size bed was directly in front of me as I walked into the room, but something looked different about it as Dad plopped on the bed and looked at me. *Why does he look so short?* I could remember leaping into that bed as a child during sleepovers at my grandmom's. I instantly recognized the burled walnut nightstand beside the bed, and facing the bed was a small, tattered, faded, green, velvet loveseat, which I played on as a child at my grandmother's house. To the left of the loveseat was a plastic zippered wardrobe, and to the right was a small closet door.

There was a small window behind the sofa, and it had an A/C window unit perched in the lower part of it. But it wasn't turned on.

The room was sweltering and smelled like hundred-year-old urine preserved from the lion exhibit at the zoo. As I stood in the doorway, Dad was facing me as he sat on his bed with his briefcase resting on the bed next to him. He beckoned me in and said, "Come on in; I don't bite. Take a seat over there on the sofa."

I stood in the doorway, and my eyes bulged. The acrid odor was even worse. Mail littered the floor. It was piled high in every corner and tumbled out into the walkway. A narrow, clear path on the tan carpet enabled Dad to get out of his bed and shuffle past the loveseat and over to his wardrobe. Hopefully, there was nothing important in the closet because it was basically barricaded by knee-high piles of mail. I debated going any further; my senses were on high alert, and my first mind said to bolt it the hell out of there. But I wanted to help Dad, and I had to know why his place looked like it did.

Has he lost his mind? Then it hit me; the bedframe was gone!

As I faced him in the doorway, where I stood frozen like a statue, he smiled and gestured again to his left for me to sit down. I really didn't want to go in, but against my better judgment, I did anyway. As I walked past him, what I saw staggered me. The beautiful, full-size, ornately carved, burled walnut bedframe, that had been in the family for two generations, was gone. My dad was sitting on a folding cot with a thin mattress plopped on it; the mattress was covered with some yellowed, rotten, old, sheets and a wretched, brown blanket. My stomach lurched, and I had to swallow back a gag. I had to collect my nerves and steady myself, and get the hell out of there as soon as possible. I was starting to break out into a cold sweat.

There were unopened piles of mail littering the floor. It was piled everywhere, and the new tan carpet, that *was* so plush you could sink your feet into it, was matted and brown. It was only visible in a small pathway around the bed.

I nodded, willed my legs to move me into the room, and deliberately made my way along the narrow matted brown path with much mental effort to stay on the path and avoid brushing up against any piled trash. The last thing I wanted to do was walk too fast, brush against the piled papers, and trigger an avalanche of crap falling down around my bare legs and ankles. I walked over to that small loveseat, mechanically lowered my body down, and perched on the seat edge. Flies buzzed incessantly around me, and I thought I'd lose my mind from the high-pitched, buzzing sound and the putrid stench.

Why does it smell like hundred-year-old, fetid, wild, lion piss in that room?? My eyes were blurred from the acrid stench, and I didn't dare touch my face with my hand. Lord knows what grime and foulness were on the surfaces in his place. I hated to think this way about my father's circumstances, but I was completely grossed out and shocked. I sat facing him as he sat up on his bed with his legs crossed. Finally, I looked past his stockinged feet at him directly and said, "Dad, what's happened to your house? Why is there trash everywhere? What is going on? Where is Mom's bed? Why are you on a cot?"

He looked at me, completely unphased. As if this was normal and completely fine. He casually gestured his hand around the room and said, "Oh, this, I didn't want it to look like I was living in the house, just in case the township came by when I was having the house remodeled. I guess I got used to leaving trash around. Then I got so busy with trying to evict Dooley Pine, and selling Mom's house, that I guess I just never got around to cleaning the house. It was easier on my nerves just to leave it like this. I'm used to it now. Like I said, I never got around to cleaning it. Now, I don't even notice it."

I blinked back the shock and said, "Uh, no offense Dad, but how can you *not* notice that smell, the piles of trash, and the flies? And what are you sitting on? Where is Mom's pretty, wooden, bed frame that's been in the family for ages?"

He nonchalantly replied, "Oh, the flies, yeah, I have some flypaper hanging up. I keep forgetting to buy more. And I gave Mom's bed to that nice African couple who used to be my upstairs tenants in the house on Conlyn Street. They needed it more than I did. They were on hard times, and I never asked for it back."

I was not buying this. There was no way Dad was okay living in this filth. I said, "I am happy to help you clean this up. I'm not working, so I have the time to come over. If that doesn't work for you, I can even hire someone to come in and clean your place. Think of it as a clean slate; from there, you can just maintain keeping it clean on your own. What do you say, Dad?"

He sat on his bed, which seemed more like a folding cot with a 5-inch-thick mattress on it; I could hear the springs creak when he changed positions. "Thanks for offering to help. I can clean it myself. Now that all these legal matters are out of the way, I'll have the time to tend to the house. I can go to the store and get a bucket and some rubber gloves and give this house a good scrubbing. Thanks for offering, though, Alexis."

With that subject officially closed, he proceeded to slowly unlock his brown, leather briefcase as he sat on his bed. He took the paperwork out and systematically fanned it out across his bed like he was getting ready to set up a game of cards. It was all surreal to me. *How is this happening to me? How is it possible that I've found myself sitting on a raggedy, faded, green, velvet loveseat in a vile, stench-filled room overflowing with piles of trash heaped up in every corner?*

I thought a million times about getting up and running out of that room screaming, and never looking back. Yet there I sat, as if my buttocks had been glued to that faded, green, velvet loveseat. I was sweating profusely and trying to hold back my gag reflex. *I have to get out of here. I can't do this. This is sheer insanity! If I stay here another minute, I will keel over from the stench.* Yet, I remained rooted in my spot and watched him painstakingly carry out his task.

Slowly but surely, he placed my copies of the will, financial power of attorney, and medical power of attorney into a manilla envelope and gradually folded it closed, pushed the gold clasps through the rings, and pressed each one down. He repeated this slow, systematic process for his copies and secured them in his raggedy, brown briefcase. As he closed the metal clips on the briefcase, he looked up at me and said, "There! Now that we're finished with that, you will take your copies home and keep them in your firebox. As for my briefcase, I need you to put it in that wardrobe next to you, on your right. Once you unzip the opening, look down in the bottom. There's a spot down there."

As if on command, my buttocks became unglued from the loveseat; I rose, stepped over papers scattered on the floor, and gingerly walked along the path of carpet around the bed to where Dad sat. He pushed the briefcase over to me and lifted it up for me to grab the handle. Once I had the briefcase, I turned around to walk on the carpet path toward the white, quilted, plastic, clothing wardrobe. It had a clear, plastic window in the top quarter of it, showing the shoulders of the contents hanging on the metal, clothing rod. I set the briefcase on the loveseat to unzip the wardrobe.

My dad watched and said calmly and precisely, "Okay, now I want you to look down on the right side of the wardrobe; you'll see two shoeboxes. Take them out and put them on the loveseat. Then put the briefcase in that spot and put the two shoeboxes on top of the briefcase. It will be safe there. I keep all my good clothes in there and my important papers. I have mothballs and cedar chips in there to

keep everything smelling fresh and to keep the moths and flies away."
He said this so nonchalantly, like it was no big deal that we were
sitting in a crap hole of trash piled up in every corner of this room,
with flies swarming around our heads and the smell of rotting hell.

My whole body shook when he said this, chills ran up my spine,
and the hairs on my arms stood on end. I could not take this insanity.
I looked around and just wanted to dart down the carpeted pathway and run for the door. But I guess out of some twisted sense of
daughterly loyalty, I stayed and carried out his commands as if frozen
in time, fighting back my gag reflex. It was so hot and wretched in
there; the air had a palpable texture from the odorous funk. It was
like stench had built up and was almost transforming from a gaseous
to a solid state that weighted on my body and made it hard to inhale.

He carried on with the conversation about the briefcase and sorting the contents. I had no idea what he was saying; I couldn't take it
anymore. There was a piece of hair stuck on my face, but I didn't dare
touch my face or hair with my hands until I'd washed them. I had to
go to the bathroom so bad, I thought my bladder would burst, but
I didn't dare use his bathroom. *If this is what his bedroom looks like,
what in the hell does the bathroom look like?*

When I unzipped the wardrobe, it smelled like mothballs and
cedar. I happily plunged my head inside to breathe a sliver of *fresher*
air. It was a refreshing change from the foul, pungent air that filled
the rest of the room. One look inside the wardrobe, and I instantly
recognized the clothes I pushed aside to reach the shoeboxes. I was
shocked to see how neat, clean, and orderly the wardrobe was when
I looked inside. All the clothes were pressed, and the smell of cedar
chips and mothballs wafted out. He had about five, tweed jackets
on wooden hangers, three, black, wool slacks folded over on hangers, and several dress shirts. All the slacks, jackets, sweaters, and

button-downs that Dad wore to our house were inside this wardrobe. That explained why his clothes didn't smell of stench when we hung out. It was like a shrine inside there. It was like the contents had been transported from someone else's home and placed amongst this crap pit. Everything was neat, clean, and organized. The stark juxtaposition of realities befuddled me.

Is this a joke? How can the man who identifies with the squalor he is sitting in be the same man who identifies as the clean, neat, and orderly chap who owns the contents of this wardrobe? My mind was racing for an answer. *Is he trying to con the government out of something to get extra public assistance? Is he scheming money from some crisis intervention agency by pretending to be a crazy hoarder? Why are his going-out clothes so clean, neat, and organized, yet the rest of the house is a crap pit??* I was stumped.

I recognized the clothes; he wore them to our house for family dinners and annual birthday parties. Why would he live every day in such a hovel and reserve the best just for special occasions? It saddened me to my soul to think that he prized and protected these inanimate objects better than himself. It seemed like he paid no regard to his everyday clothes, or himself, for that matter. Thinking of him sitting behind me on that poor excuse for a bed, surrounded by piles of trash, broke my heart and gave me the impression that he felt like he was equal to nothing more than the trash he was surrounded by.

My heart ached for this man. How did his life come to this? I blinked back the tears and took a deep breath as I bent down and pulled out the heavy shoeboxes; my guess was they contained the dress shoes he wore to our house. I placed the boxes on the loveseat, picked up the briefcase, and carefully placed it inside the wardrobe. Once everything was placed back inside, I breathed in the last drop of cedar-mothball-scented air, zipped and secured the wardrobe, and steeled myself as I turned to face him.

I forced a smile and wondered how I was going to get myself out of this. My copy of the papers was still sitting next to him on the bed. I was spent. Somehow, I had to grab them and go. I had finished my task. I had to go. I couldn't take it anymore. Seeing him sitting in that squalid heap of crap was more than I could take in and comprehend.

He was satisfied that his briefcase was secured, held out the manilla envelope and said, "Here you go, Alexis; you did good. Thanks for putting the briefcase away. Make sure you keep your copy of the documents in a safe place. You have a fireproof lockbox, right?"

I nodded yes as I leaned forward to take the papers from him.

"Good," he said and gestured for me to sit back down on that faded, green, velvet loveseat.

My heart was breaking. I had to get out of there. His living conditions were like an outward manifestation of his stormy, internal, mental dysfunction. And I was sitting smack-dab in the epicenter. As odd as the scene looked, there was something very ceremonial and "right-of-passage-like" about the experience. As if he was transferring something *of* himself to me. He hadn't alluded to any reason in particular for why he was doing this. He just said he was getting his affairs in order to make things easy for me. I looked him square in the face and said, "Dad, are you sure everything is okay with you?"

He smiled and nodded, "Yes, Alexis, I'm fine. I'm sorry if this is morbid. I'm just getting my ducks in a row while I'm able to. I'm fine. I'm just being proactive. All is well; there's nothing to worry or be morose about. Okay?"

I nodded. My father looked so frail and pale and hollowed out. It broke my heart to see him sitting on that makeshift cot surrounded by piles of trash. I needed a mental distraction to be an anchor for the frayed cords of my sanity. I searched for something nice for my eyes to land on and give them a rest from the sensory overload. I noticed the patterns on the burled walnut nightstand next to his bed; it had been my grandmother's, and she used to have a matching set on either side of her bed when she lived at the Conlyn Street house. I looked to both sides of Dad's bed, but the mate was missing. I guessed he had given that to his former African tenants, too.

I looked back over to the left and rested my eyes on the remaining nightstand. His ancient-looking push-button telephone and answering machine sat on it, along with some papers. I looked at my watch and blurted out, "Oh, would you look at the time! Dad, I've got to get going. It's a long way back to my house, and Michael and the kids are waiting on me. Can I get you a glass of water or something to eat before I leave?" I was kicking myself for mentioning something to eat. *I have no intention of cooking him anything; I need to leave!*

He looked at his watch, noted the time, and exclaimed, "Oh boy, yes, look at the time; I didn't realize it had gotten so late. Nah, don't worry about me. I'm sure you've got to be getting home; it's almost 7 p.m. I'm all set. I'll fix myself something to eat. I've got steak in the fridge that I took out of the freezer. Thanks anyway, though, Lexis." He swung his legs over the bed and rested one hand on the nightstand to support him as he stood. I followed out behind him.

We made our way back down the black, carpeted path, past the trash. It was getting to be dusk, and when he turned on the kitchen light, critters scattered, and I noticed dead roaches stuck in the congealed grease in the frying pans on the stove. I walked over to the sink, dodged a couple of low-hanging, flypaper strips on the ceiling along the way, took in the rancid sights rotting in the sink, angled the faucet to the lowest pile of dishes in the sink, squirted a drop from the liquid soap next to the sink, turned on the water and wedged my hand under the faucet so as to not disturb the piles of dishes and decay. Then I turned the handle off with the back of my hand and shook my hands dry. My dad had produced a clean paper towel from somewhere; I took it gladly, dried my hands, and kept the rolled paper towel wadded in my left hand. I was tempted to use it to swat away the flies. Their cacophony of high-pitched, frenzied, fly-buzzing past my head nearly made me lose my mind.

We said our goodbyes and hugged. He assured me that everything was just fine. We hugged goodbye again, and he thanked me for my help. He pulled a set of keys off the wall hook next to his side door and said, "Oh, before I forget, here is a set of keys to my house, the van, and the Dodge Stealth."

I took them and put them in my jacket pocket; something was up. He might not have admitted to it tonight, but this move confirmed my suspicion that something was going on. I stepped out into the fresh air and breathed deeply. I turned and waved to him and said, "It was nice spending time with you today, Dad. Have a good night. I'll call you in a couple of days."

I got in my car and sat there for a few minutes before turning it on. I was in shock. I needed to get away from this mess. I replayed the night's events in my head as I drove down the familiar streets in a dazed, semi-aware state of consciousness.

I was on the turnpike in a couple of minutes when the waterworks started. I couldn't hold the tears in anymore. Crying hysterically on the drive home was not how I envisioned my day ending. I was hoping to make it all the way home, but as I approached mile marker 228, near the King of Prussia mall exit, I had to pull into the highway rest stop and park my car. It wasn't safe for me to be on the road anymore. I hastily pulled into the nearest parking spot, slammed the car into park, and turned off the ignition. I didn't care who saw me sitting in the car crying with snot running down my face. I could not process what had just happened.

What the hell happened to him? As far as I knew, no one on his side of the family had been a hoarder. I had so many unanswered questions, and it ripped my heart into pieces to see my father living like this. This was my father! *What happened to the sharp-dressed man in all those black and white photos taken in his younger days?*

I was vainly searching through my purse and my glove compartment for tissues. I finally found a small, travel pack of Kleenex under my seat. I dabbed at my face as I replayed the events over and over in my head. Clumps of tissue stuck to my face as more tears streamed. *Have I just sat in the eye of the storm of this man's madness?*

I clutched my hair and wanted to pull it out of my head. I had worked so hard to grow my hair and nurse it back to health, and now this. *What the hell?* At this rate, I feared I'd be bald by summer. I had to clear my head and needed to decide what I was going to do.

Has he lost his mind? Is this a part of his dementia? Has he just forgotten how to clean and take care of himself? Or is this hoarding? Whatever it was, he seemed to be in a dark and troubled place, and I wanted no part of it. I rubbed my eyes and tried to stop the stream of tears that kept flooding them. I talked out loud to myself and didn't give a flying fig who saw me. I shouted out, "How could this happen? What happened to him? How long has he been living like this? Why did he let his place get like that? How can he live in that wretched, filthy place? Where did he go to use the bathroom and shower? Has he lost his mind? Why didn't he ask for help? Why? Why? *Why?*"

My whole body heaved as I sobbed, hands clinging to the steering wheel; I sobbed for a long time. I had no idea what time it was. I had rubbed my left contact out of my eye, and snot was running down my face and dripping on my thigh. I didn't have any tissues left in my car and used the satin inside of my jacket to wipe my face off. I folded the jacket up and placed it on the passenger seat. Then, I sat back in my seat and just breathed deeply. The windows had started fogging up. I turned on the ignition to lower the windows a crack, and I looked out into the darkness at the cars and tractor trailers speeding past on the highway.

I started replaying the day's events in my head, and tears started streaming down my face again. I willed myself to stop crying and began using my hands to fan my face and cool down and dry off my tears. I began talking out loud to myself again, "Well, my dear, *consider today the day you said 'goodbye' to your father*. All that's left is a shell of a man, a fractured, wounded soul who's making his way back home and is checked-out of this world. Your dad, as you knew him, is long gone." I wrapped my arms around myself and hugged myself hard, and tears started streaming again.

I eventually gave myself over to my grief and just laid my forehead on the steering wheel and wept. I wept for the man I knew as my father. I wept for the boy this man once was. I wept for the past that shaped him. I wept for the man I had just hugged in that tiny, messy, little house in Bristol.

I flung my head back onto the headrest and began yelling at the top of my lungs at God, "Why, why, why, why did you do this to him? How could you let this happen? Why him? Why *me*? What did we ever do to deserve *this*? I'm a good person; I've volunteered every damn year of my life since I was 12! I dedicated a decade of my life to caring for special needs children. I go to church. I turn the other cheek. I tithe. I pray for world peace. What the hell else can I do? Isn't that enough? Why is this crap happening to me, God? Why my dad? Why did I have to be born into this crap? Aren't I good enough for a good life? Why? Why? *Why?*"

I was spent and reclined the seat back and closed my eyes. I would rest and wait on God for an answer. A sliver of cool, night air crept in through my partly lowered window, and I welcomed the breeze across my face. I focused on my breathing and just let the night descend upon me. Gradually, the rage and sorrow flooded out of me. I felt a gentle calm descend upon me, and I felt like I had cried all my tears out. I cried to the point of laughing. I just sat there shaking my head back and forth, laughing. Laughing at what just happened with my dad and laughing at myself for sitting in the car wailing. I laughed at the memories we had made over the years, the infinite paths I could take, and how this could unfold and transform our lives.

Clarity came upon me. I realized I had a choice of how I could see this. I could let it wreck me and end up bitter like my mother. Or I could choose to see this differently. Happiness is a gift that I could choose to give myself, despite the circumstances. I could choose to see this in the best possible light, no matter how crazy it looked. I got to choose how I wanted to feel about this, how I wanted to look at this, and what meaning I wanted to assign to it. I chose to look for the good and decided to choose happiness, even in the storm. I wanted my children to look up to me and see me handle this with grace and strength. I wanted them to know that even when life gives you something tough, you always get to pause and decide how you will respond: with fear and negativity, or with hope, faith, optimism, and love. I decided that I would choose to make the best of it. No matter what.

I felt a deep sense of peace, let out a sigh of relief, and decided to pray. "Thank you, God, for getting me here safely tonight. Please forgive me for wallowing and despairing. I trust that this is happening for a reason. I trust that You have plans to prosper me. I trust that

You will see me through this. What would You have me do? Please be with me. Please be with Dad. Please help me to help him. Please give me discernment, courage, help, and protection. Bless my dad and keep him safe. Thank you. Amen"

That moment, I decided that tonight's farewell embrace with my dad marked the moment I said "goodbye" to my father as I had known him. Going forward, I chose to see this new version of my dad as a man doing the best he could, a man I would make new memories with. The idea of parenting my parent didn't sit well with me. I believed that seeing him from this new perspective would ease my angst and make things easier for all concerned. I'd love, respect, and care for him, but for my sanity, I had to detach and put space between us. Whatever he was going through, I decided that I would help him as best I could while protecting my heart and mind and my family.

The matter was settled; I breathed deeply, turned on the car, and texted Michael to let him know I was alive and on my way home. What a tale I'd have to tell one day. This might not be easy, but I knew in my heart that it mattered and hoped that in the end, it would be worth it,

CHAPTER 13

I practically staggered in the door around 9:30, tired and drained from the day's events. I walked into the kitchen, and Michael looked up from his laptop to greet me. "Wow, you look like crap! Why are your eyes so puffy?" Not the warm greeting I was expecting when I came home, but he was not one for sugar-coating anything. He was a blurt-it-out, tell-it-like-it-is, kind of guy. He did not mince words. At least you knew where you stood with him because he was brutally honest.

I sighed and gave him a quick recap of the day: my dad's hoarding, and the deplorable living conditions at his house. Michael was shocked. Luckily, the kids had already gone to bed, so we could sit and talk things through. He was a good shoulder to lean on, and I was grateful for his company. We didn't come up with any solutions that night, and I decided to sleep on it.

I called my mom in the morning and told her about Dad and his living conditions. I hated to pull her into his mess, but I had to tell her. I *needed* my mother's support and insights. She *was* married to him, and to the best of my knowledge, she was the *only* other living soul who knew anything about him. Maybe she could shed light on what was going on.

I spilled the beans to the effect of, "Ma, I need to talk to you about Dad. You might want to sit down. Not to alarm you, just to forewarn you. Um, as you know, I've been helping him draw up his will and power of attorney, which he legally added me to yesterday, and I accepted. Well, after we went to the lawyers, I went back to his house. I hadn't been inside it for a while, and what I saw shocked me. Do you know if he was ever a hoarder? Or did he have anyone in his close family who was?"

I could hear her suck in her breath before exhaling and sharply answering, "So, you went through with it *despite* my warnings. Well, do what you want. To answer your question, *no, Alexis*, your father was never a hoarder." Her tone softened as she recollected, "I mean, well, he always stocked up on things like a case of toilet paper or a case of soup when the grocery store was having a sale. He learned that from his mother, who grew up during the Depression, and from his childhood experiences oversees when food was rationed in WWII. But no, he was never a hoarder, and I don't recall anyone else in his family being that way. Why do you ask?"

"Well, I ask because his house is basically a hot mess full of trash. I don't mean a bag of trash here or there. I mean piles of papers, piles of empty beer cases, and piles of mail everywhere the eye can see throughout the first-floor kitchen, bathroom, dining room, and even in his bedroom. It smelled wretched. There must have been a hundred flies buzzing around in there. The house smelled like a combo of rotten, hard-boiled eggs, diarrhea, and hundred-year-old urine. I didn't want to hurt his feelings, so I was literally fighting back my gag reflex, and it took all my willpower not to run out of there screaming. I couldn't even use the bathroom if I wanted to; the floor was literally littered with empty beer cans and whiskey bottles. He tried to do something about the flies by hanging flypaper, but the strips were completely covered in flies. It was surreal. It was like a scene straight out of one of those hoarder reality TV shows."

"And did you ask him why his house looked like that, Alexis?" she said.

I replied, "Yes, Ma, I did. All he had to say for himself was that, basically, he staged the mess to throw off the township in case they did a random inspection when his house was being remodeled. Apparently, the contractor didn't get any building permits from the township, and Dad seemed to think it was illegal for him to live in his own house while it was being remodeled. I know plenty of people who have lived in their homes *while* they're being remodeled, but that was the story he told me. He claims he left trash around to make it look like he couldn't possibly be living there. But that remodeling work finished ages ago because the lousy contractor skipped town with Dad's money and never completely finished the remodel. Why Dad never cleaned up the garbage is beyond me; that's why I called you. I was hoping you could shed some light on the subject."

She snapped back, "Getting taken advantage of, being gullible, lying, and trying to get around the rules has always been classic Alec traits. That's part of the reason why I left him. I'm sorry to hear about his sad state of affairs, and I don't have any answers for you, my dear. Did he say why he needed to get a will and all the other paperwork drawn up?"

"No, Ma. He hadn't alluded to any reason in particular for why he was doing this. He simply said he was getting his affairs in order to make things easy for me in the future. Who knows, maybe Gil's death shook him up, and he decided to get his own affairs in order?"

There was a moment of silence, and my mom dropped one of her classic cold, Carla comments. She said, "Alexis, do you *really want* to do this? Do you *really want* to be caught up in this mess? I've been there, done that, and added that to my list of regrets. I'm telling you, and heed my words; unless you *must*, don't. Do not let that man drag you down like he did me. It took me years to recover and get my credit right. I don't want that to happen to you. Preserve what fond memories you have of him as your father; do not go down this road. Who knows what you might find out about him?"

I breathed a sigh of disappointment and frustration. Why did I bother calling her? She seemed so bitter and resentful, even after being separated from my father for decades. I didn't think talking to her would be that easy, but I wasn't prepared for *that* cold, Carla comment. I scrambled to respond. "Well, thanks for sharing your opinion. I will have to decide for myself what I'm going to do. He *is* my father, and if I can find a way to help him without entangling myself in his mess, I intend to do so."

"Well, my dear, I hate to break it to you, but you're too late for that. You became entangled the *second* you signed your name to those legal papers. All the best to you with *that*. Now, if you have nothing else of value to talk about, I'm going to bid you goodnight."

We said "goodbye," and that was that. *She just had to insert another cold, Carla comment.* I cleaned up the dishes from breakfast and went into the family room to play with the kids to take my mind off things and dull the sting from my conversation with my mom.

The weather was unseasonably warm for the beginning of May, and I decided to sit outside on the back patio after lunch and give my mother-in-law, Carolyn, a call. Maybe she could offer better advice. The flagstone pavers were hot under my feet as I walked across the patio to sit in a cozy, overstuffed, lounge chair under the patio umbrella.

Thankfully, she picked up right away when I called. She sounded worried, "Hi Lexe, is everything okay, honey? What's wrong, honey? It's odd for you to call this time of day."

I paused and tried to muster the courage to tell her everything that had happened the night before. I told her about the lawyer's appointment and how Dad forgot why we were there. I recounted the state of the house and Dad's nonchalance about the stench and piles of trash that practically engulfed his emaciated, little, boney body. I told her about the wardrobe and how he asked me to place his documents there. I told her that he swore to me that he was fine and had just hit a rough patch. She took this all in and sighed.

In a soft, tender voice, she slowly said, "Oh Lexe, I am so sorry to hear this turn of events with your dad. Alec is such a good man, and I've enjoyed his company over the years. We've had a lot of good laughs together and have enjoyed watching our grandbabies grow up. It sounds to me like he needs help and, above all, grace. I noticed how thin he looked the last time we were at your house. I had no idea he was that bad off. Did anything traumatic ever happen to him in his past that you're aware of?"

I paused to think and finally responded, "No, honestly, nothing that he ever shared with me. I believe his father was a strict man. He talked fondly of his dad and always recounted fond family stories. But now that I think of it, he never, ever referred to his father by any name other than 'the Old Man.' I always wondered why but never plucked up the nerve to actually ask. Mom called him 'the Old Man,' too, and she also called him 'Dad.' I wonder if he had a tough childhood living abroad as a military child?"

We talked some more; ultimately, she recommended I continue to persuade him to reconsider getting a social worker and emphasize that they could provide resources to clean his house and obtain healthy meals. That way, he wouldn't feel like he was burdening me. He'd have his dignity and pride intact by choosing to set up his own services.

She continued on, "Especially if this is truly a hoarding situation. He may need to eventually address whatever the underlying emotional or mental issues are that surfaced as hoarding. Whatever you do, do *not* hop online and search for 'hoarding.' That will lead you down a rabbit hole and probably upset you unnecessarily."

After a deep sigh, I said, "Thank you for sharing that with me, Carolyn; that means a lot. I have always looked up to you and saw you as a strong, successful, intelligent woman."

She took a deep breath and said, "Well, thank you, sweetheart. Coming from you, that means a lot. I love you like a daughter. You know, I never shared this with you, and I don't know if Michael has either. I hit a very rough patch financially after Michael's dad and I split up. I was really down on my luck and was quickly running out of options. I showed up at my sister's doorstep with nothing but a suitcase. She took Michael and me in. She had a family of her own yet made room and shared her resources with me while I got back on my feet. As a big sister, she had seen red flags early in my relationship with my ex, but I ignored her advice and warnings. I thought I knew better and would finally outshine her in one area of my life for once. Boy, did I blow that."

She laughed bitterly and continued, "I tell this to you, not to encourage you to invite him to live with you, but to highlight the fact that when I was down and out, my sister chose to support me in the way she knew how and most of all, most of all, she showed me *grace*. Never once did she rub it in my face and say, 'Serves you right; I told you so.' Never once did she judge me or shame me or lecture me. She simply held space for me to heal, process, and get back on my feet. I love her more than words can say. We had a strained relationship before that, and it took all my courage and self-respect to humble myself and show up at her door. She graciously welcomed me in when other family members slammed the door in my face, literally and figuratively. Please consider keeping the proverbial door open with your father. Show him grace. This is one moment in his life. Think about all the good times."

I appreciated hearing about her past and said, "Michael did share with me that you and he lived with his aunt for a stretch, but he never went into the details. Thank you for the advice. I also wanted to talk to you about the possibility of it being Alzheimer's."

Carolyn spoke, "Lexe, honey, based on my experience with Gil and his Alzheimer's, this can either go well or it can go bad. Either way, it is going to go. Do your best to stay one step ahead versus getting walloped by crap hitting the fan. Take time for yourself. Ask for help when you need it. Trust your intuition; don't wait for things to come to fruition. Otherwise, you're digging yourself out of a hole and compounding the problems. Get help from professionals, like a social worker or an aide to take your dad to appointments. See if the VA has services for him since he's a Vet. Keep calling him regularly; that consistency builds trust. He may never open up and admit to needing help. He may not want to be evaluated and diagnosed with anything. If he does agree to help, move fast on this and get support set up. Your situation is different because he's your dad and not your spouse; I will help you in any way I can. Whatever you need, if I don't know the answer, I will find it for you. If he doesn't agree to help, be patient, keep offering, and know that ultimately, he may refuse until the bitter end. At least you know you tried."

Her feedback helped, but it didn't make me feel warm and fuzzy inside. I asked, "How long do you think it might take for him to accept that kind of help?"

"Well, honey, one can never tell. In my experience, problems don't fix themselves, especially if he's been used to avoiding them and silencing the feelings associated with the issues. He's been numbing out on alcohol and drugs for decades for a reason. Just keep showing up and show him grace as best you can, while setting boundaries about what you will and won't do for him. You have a family to think about and your sanity. Do not neglect your mental well-being. You can only do so much. You cannot pour from an empty cup. That just breeds resentment, in my experience. You don't want to be helping him from a place of guilt or resentment. People can feel that from a mile away, and it might push him away."

I knew she was right. We talked some more, and she was most helpful. I decided to call Dad regularly and, if all went well, set him up with a social worker and Meals-On-Wheels.

It was no easy task. As May rolled on, I hadn't made any progress. He refused to consider getting a social worker. He refused to consider moving into a VA nursing home. He refused to have Meals-On-Wheels delivered because he didn't want to open his door to strangers with food. Handouts weren't his thing, especially from strangers. Meanwhile, he was living in squalor and eating a liquid diet of beer and whiskey, peppered with sodium-laden, frozen food-like substances picked up from the dollar store.

He'd always let me down gently and followed it up with his brilliant solution. He'd simply say, "No, Alexis, I don't need any help. I am all set. I am going to marry a fast woman, and she'll take care of me. We'll live in a motor home and travel cross-country to all the cities with VA hospitals; I'll get care there when I need it and live all over the country in the motor home."

I'd just nod and say, "Okay, Dad, that sounds excellent." There was no point in arguing with him or pointing out that no woman in her right mind would want his shriveled-up, old, broke ass. *Who would want to cart him around cross-country in a motor home, going from VA hospital to VA hospital? Was he for real!?*

I was due to go to the hairdresser right before Mother's Day. My hair was getting fuller and longer, so my stress couldn't be that bad, right? I actually dreaded seeing her. What would I say when she asked about Dad? When I went to see Jeanette, I carefully chose my words. Normally, I gushed about my life with her, but this situation with my dad just hit differently. We talked about our kids and our plans for their summer camps. I glossed over Dad's situation. I didn't mention the hoarding, just the weight loss and Meals-On-Wheels.

She commiserated for a bit and noted how long and thick my hair was getting. As she processed my hair, we talked about summer plans and upcoming holidays. I mentioned Father's Day, "I'm trying to make reservations at Pharov's Middle-Eastern restaurant. But Dad's notoriously late; I will kill him if he doesn't show up on time, and we lose the reservation."

We laughed and made more small talk. Before I knew it, I was finished and back in my car, heading home. I felt relieved to be out of there. What was normally a relaxing and enjoyable experience felt like walking on eggshells or stepping around landmines. I decided to call Dad on the way home and let him know about the Father's Day plans for dinner at Pharov's and tell him my Aunt Dot was in hospice. I got no answer.

Mother's Day came and went, and he never called me. I knew his memory was fading, and I tried not to take it personally. I called

Monday morning and still got no answer. I called and called around the clock on Monday and still got no answer on his home or cell phone. I waited a couple of days and called him, and there was still no answer. I decided to keep a log of my calls and increase the frequency.

Sunday, May 14th, 2017 – 8 a.m., called Dad, no answer.

Monday, May 15th, 2017 – 9 a.m., called Dad, no answer.

Monday, May 15th, 2017 – 10 a.m., called Dad, no answer.

Monday, May 15th, 2017 – 11 a.m., called Dad, no answer.

Monday, May 15th, 2017 – 1 p.m., called Dad, no answer.

Monday, May 15th, 2017 – 3 p.m., called Dad, no answer.

Monday, May 15th, 2017 – 6 p.m., called Dad, no answer.

Tuesday, May 16th, 2017 – 10 a.m., called Dad, no answer.

Tuesday, May 16th, 2017 – 11 a.m., called Dad, no answer.

Tuesday, May 16th, 2017 – 12 p.m., called Dad, no answer.

Tuesday, May 16th, 2017 – 2 p.m., called Dad, no answer.

Tuesday, May 16th, 2017 – 4 p.m., called Dad, no answer.

Wednesday, May 17th, 2017 – 9 a.m., called Dad, no answer.

Wednesday, May 17th, 2017 – 10 a.m., called Dad, he answered.

"Hi, Alexis. How are you?" was all he said after being M.I.A. for days.

I tried to remain calm and respectful, "Hi, Dad, it's good to hear your voice. I've been trying to reach you for days. Where were you?" I knew better than to ask how he was doing; that would get me nowhere, and he'd just respond with a generic "fine." I cut to the chase and asked direct questions—no time for BS. I wanted answers.

He replied, "Well, funny, you should ask where I've been. I just came back from Lower Bucks Hospital. I was there for the last of my prostate cancer treatments."

I was stunned, and my hand was shaking so badly that I nearly dropped the phone as I slumped against the kitchen counter for support. "I'm sorry, what?" was all I could muster.

Casually, he said, "Yes, I was in the hospital for a couple of days; the medicine I was on made me weak, so I had an ambulance pick me up on Saturday and take me to the ER. They admitted me, and I've been there recovering. I felt better today, was discharged this morning, and walked home."

I lost it. "Why didn't you tell me you had *cancer?* All this time we've been talking, and you just simply forgot to mention it?" I was trying hard to remain calm, but my voice was rising.

He casually replied, "You have so much on your plate with work and the kids, and I know you and Michael are always so busy, and with his deployment and all, I knew that must have taken a toll on you. I didn't want to bother you; I figured you had enough on your plate. It was bad enough that you had to help me with Mom's house and Doolie Pine."

I blinked all this in and snapped back, "Well, Michael's not deployed now, and I'm not working, so why didn't you call him or me to pick you up from the hospital? Why would you *walk home?*"

He sighed and said, "Alexis, I'm fine. You and Michael are busy raising your family and living your lives. You live over an hour away. I would not ask either of you to drive all this way to take me home. I live five minutes from the hospital. It was literally a fifteen-minute walk thru a nice neighborhood, and it was a warm, sunny, spring morning. After being cooped up in that hospital, I enjoyed the fresh air, and I could sit at park benches when I needed to rest."

All I could envision was a frail little old man shuffling down the street at a snail's pace. There was no way he walked home in fifteen minutes. I calmed my nerves and exhaled deeply before speaking, "Dad, after being on bed rest for five days, for prostate cancer treatment, I can't believe the hospital would discharge you and let you walk home. What kind of hospital does that to a person in your condition? It's over now; no point in beating a dead horse. My point is, next time, please call me. For the love of God, it is not an inconvenience. Please call me, Dad. Please. I love you and want to make sure you are safe. That being said, how are you feeling?"

He sighed and said, "Well, thank you, Lexis; I am tired from the walk, I just finished a snack, and I'm going to lie down after this call. Thanks for offering to pick me up in the future. I am happy to report there will be no next time. The cancer is all gone now; I have a clean bill of health, so you don't have to worry. There won't ever be an ambulance at this house again! And I won't ever be needing a ride from the hospital again in life!"

Sadly, he couldn't have been more wrong.

We talked some more after that. I broached the subject of getting Meals-On-Wheels set up for him, and he said he'd think about it. He casually mentioned that the hospital recommended he have a social worker, and he asked me to help him get one. I was grateful for this change in his attitude and glad he'd agreed to a social worker.

After I hung up the phone, my legs gave out, and I slid down the kitchen cabinet onto the hardwood floor and just curled up into a ball on the floor and cried. *Thank God the kids are at school and won't see me like this.* I cried body-heaving sobs for a good half-hour until I was all cried out. On one hand, I was glad and relieved that he was cancer-free. On the other hand, I was ticked off that he didn't tell me sooner. *Why is this happening to me!!* I was so tired and overwhelmed with Dad's drama. Why didn't he just tell me about the cancer? It would have made life so much easier, and I could have helped him. I wasn't working and had the time.

I needed help fast. I didn't know what else to do, so I prayed. I got on my knees and prayed, "Please, God, take this burden off my shoulders. I can't do this anymore. Heal Dad's body, mind, and soul. Please open him up to accepting my help and help from social services. Thanks."

I was exhausted and needed to go for a walk with Michael to clear my head. I replayed the events to him and just couldn't fathom how Dad never told me about his cancer. *How long had he suffered and shouldered this burden alone? And why would he, when he had family who loved him?*

I couldn't make sense of my father, and trying to understand him was wearing me ragged. I just wanted this all to end. I just wanted my normal life back and my old, familiar dad back. I just wanted things to go back to the way they were. I had no clue how much longer I could sustain this relationship. It was like I had a third child. It was such a weight off my shoulders when he agreed to a social worker. Now my task would be to set that up ASAP and get home health and meal services set up for him. That house was a mess, and he deserved better.

CHAPTER 14

My mind was cracking in two, and I was losing it. I had a throbbing migraine and felt like I was losing any semblance of control that I thought I had in my life. It was noon, and I was still in bed. Keeping up appearances was no longer an option. It felt like there were no more highlight reels to post. I could no longer keep a stiff upper lip and carry on like everything was just fine. My house was a mess, I couldn't keep up a happy mommy façade for my kids, and I was snappy with Michael. I was losing it: no dinner, no sex, no play dates, no gardening. Just anxious thoughts running in my mind, going down the rabbit hole online till all hours of the night and dragging myself out of bed to face the day, exhausted and defeated. Something had to give.

Life became bleaker with every passing week. Getting Meals-On-Wheels set up turned out to be a huge fiasco. My dad said he agreed to receive food, but as his memory failed, he didn't recall the arrangement and refused to open his door to strangers. For the first three weeks of May, I received a call daily from Meals-On-Wheels, telling me that a driver was at my dad's but unable to deliver the food. I'd call Dad; he'd pick up and tell me a stranger was at his door. I'd remind him that I sent someone to drop off food for him.

He'd pause and usually say, "Okay," but still wouldn't open the door. It would take a second phone call and me staying on the line with him as he opened the door, before he'd actually accept the daily meals. By the last week of May, he finally got the hang of it and willingly opened the door when they knocked. No more calls needed to orchestrate the drop-off. *Thank God.*

Whenever we talked on the phone, he'd ask me when I was coming over to the house with the kids, and I kept avoiding the topic. Finally, I relented and said, "Dad, no offense, but your house is a mess. I cannot bring my kids into your home in the condition it's in. I won't ever step a foot in there again until it's cleaned."

There was a pause, and he responded, "I'm fine now; my doctor gave me meds. I have more energy, and I'll take care of it. Don't you worry; you and the kids can come over real soon. I'll buy a bucket, gloves, and some cleaning supplies. Then you and the kids can come over to see me at the house."

I wasn't holding my breath but said "yes" to the invitation anyway, under the stipulation that the downstairs was clean. He agreed, and the matter was settled. We made plans for me, Michael, and the kids to all visit him on Father's Day and take him out to dinner. He didn't like the idea of going into the city for Middle Eastern food, so we agreed to take him to his favorite local restaurant, Outback Steakhouse.

Just to be on the safe side, I was mentally devising a Plan B in my head in case his house was dirty. If the house wasn't clean when we got there, we simply wouldn't go in. He had a backyard, and I decided I'd bring a set of folding chairs with us. We could sit outside in his backyard and chat until it was time to take him to Outback Steakhouse for dinner. We'd also stop along the turnpike to use the rest-stop bathrooms before we went to his house. Too easy, problem solved.

He sounded so happy. It broke my heart to think of that frail, old man cleaning that dirty house, piled high with trash. I asked him about his social worker, and he gave me her name and contact information. Apparently, she had been to the house already, and according to him, she saw no concern with his living arrangements or the state of his house. I didn't believe it for a second but dismissed it and continued with our conversation. I'd call her later and find out firsthand what her impressions were and what could be done to help my father.

During our call, he seemed in good spirits and in his right mind, so I asked him about the idea of moving into a nursing home. He had balked at the idea several months ago, but it was worth a shot. "Dad, what do you think about checking out some local nursing homes? There's a Veterans' nursing home close to where Michael works in Spring City; maybe that would be a nice place to consider. What do you think? Would you want me to get you some information about the place? Just to read over?"

Before I could get another word out, he shot back, "Nah, I don't need that. I'm going to marry a fast woman, and she'll take care of me; we'll live in a motor home and travel cross-country to all the cities with VA hospitals. I'll get care at one of their centers when I need it, and we'll live all over this great country."

I was flabbergasted. *Who would want to marry him in his current condition?* Damn, he was delusional. I just chuckled and said, "Okay, we'll talk about it later. I'll be over next Friday, June 2nd, to take you to the bank. I'll call you before then. Aunt Dot's in the hospital, by the way. I'm going to see her tomorrow to celebrate Memorial Day with her. It was always her favorite holiday. Remember how she'd make that cherry-red Kool-Aid with the lemons floating in it for her annual Memorial Day BBQ?"

We talked some more and reminisced about family times and Aunt Dot. I was glad Dad still had his core memories from the past to hold onto.

I thought the call went well, and we were making progress, but the news of Aunt Dot's condition must have pushed Dad over the edge. His drunk calls came back with a vengeance. When I did pick up, it would be the same sad stories. He'd reminisce about his days as a ranch hand in Colorado, or he'd tell me about the time his truck caught on fire, and he walked into Sears covered in soot, and the nice, sales lady gave him a free outfit, underwear, and all. That would segway into the time he owned a liquor store in California with an arcade in it; that was right around the time Chuck E. Cheese started, and he was giving them a run for their money.

Then he'd top it off with the love story about his lady with a tattoo on her ass and how he loved her and wanted to bring her home to meet his mother, but the lady was too wild to take home. Then he'd start blubbering and talk about getting a motor home and driving cross-country with his lady friend. She'd take him to all the VAs and care for him.

I'd nod and go along with it for a bit when I felt like it. Other times, I'd use the kids' dinner time or homework as an excuse to cut the call short.

He kept inviting the kids and me over, saying he'd set up tray tables and lawn chairs in the living room and we could watch TV. I'd stress that I'd love to, once the house is cleaned up and the flies are gone. I'd tell him that I'd come over to help him. He'd reply that he was going to get a bucket and rubber gloves to clean the house. We'd play this game all the livelong day; we had this same dialog damn near every day. I didn't dare *not* to pick up just in case he was in distress and actually needed my help.

In June, he started refusing Meals-On-Wheels again.

I talked to the social worker; she said hoarding was not grounds to strip him of his rights and put him in a home. He was not off his rocker enough to be declared insane or incompetent. He could have his house any way he wanted. She said she'd circle back at the end of June to administer some standardized tests to ascertain his cognitive function and ability to function independently. That would have to do. My hands were tied, and I was frustrated beyond words. I was running on fumes and at my wit's end, trying to help him and keep him safe, fed, and alive.

Friday rolled around, and I was making the all-too-familiar trek down the Turnpike to the Bristol exit to pick up Dad, take him to the bank, and go out to lunch. I decided not to mention his behavior over the past few days. I was too weary to pick a fight. I just wanted to spend a normal day with my sober father, like old times, and then go back home to my life.

When I pulled up to his driveway, I called him to let him know I was outside. Thankfully, he answered the phone, remembered the date and time of his appointment, and was ready to go. I had called him three times this week, leading up to this event, to remind him. It was mentally draining, but at least it guaranteed a better chance of success. When he appeared in his doorway, he was wearing a nice, plaid, long-sleeve shirt, a brown, leather vest, khaki pants, and loafers. But the belt was cinched tight, and the clothes were hanging off him. *I remember when those clothes were snug on him.*

I didn't go inside; I met him at his side door, greeted him, slowly walked him to the passenger side of my car and helped him inside, then closed the car door. He looked feebler than before. I wondered if he was eating the meals provided to him through Meals-On-Wheels.

When I got in the car and turned to face him, Dad said, "I'm fine now; the doctor gave me meds. The kids can come over to see me at the house. I can clean; I have more energy. I bought a bucket and cleaning supplies. I'm cleaning the house for you all."

I smiled, thanked Dad, and told him I was looking forward to coming over on Father's Day with the kids. We planned out the day; he asked me to bring the kids' favorite DVDs and toys along to keep them entertained. I told him I'd make the reservations at Outback for 5:30 p.m. We talked about my visit with Aunt Dot. Her condition had worsened since then, and I was glad to have spent the day with her.

The bank appointment was uneventful. I signed some more papers, and the bank gave us hard copies of our joint account information for safekeeping. Despite my mom's warnings, I signed them anyway. I decided not to let her bitterness and resentment cloud my own vision. She still hadn't forgiven him for ruining her credit before they separated.

My Aunt Dot passed away peacefully in her sleep on June 6th, and the funeral was scheduled for June 14th. I dreaded calling Dad with the news. *Would it send him into an even deeper spiral of despair? Would this push him over the edge? He was already hitting the bottle again. What would this do to his resolve and will to live?* I was hoping his clean bill of health and being declared cancer-free would give him a new lease on life. He seemed excited to be getting the house cleaned for our visit. How he'd pull that off in less than a week, in time for Father's Day, was beyond me. But hey, maybe that was just the challenge he needed to feel like he had a sense of purpose and a reason to live.

Ironically, when I visited Dot in the hospital and told her about my dad and his plans to drive cross-country in a motor home with his girlfriend, she was the only person who thought my dad's plans sounded wonderful. She said she was happy that he was living out his dreams. In fact, she was grinning from ear to ear as I told her of his plans to trek cross-country with his sweetheart. She was sitting up in her hospital bed, listening intently to every word, and her 14k bangles shook gently on her arms as she clapped her frail, bony hands together in delight over my dad's plans.

Meanwhile, I was thinking, *she's clearly lost her mind, too, and was now operating under the wisdom of innocence, no longer encumbered by the weight of adult logic and sensibility. She's free to embrace all possibilities.*

And as if she could read my mind, she stopped laughing on cue, looked me dead in the eyes, and said, "Darling, you have no idea what's possible; just be happy for your father."

When Dad heard the news of her passing, he was stunned and saddened. He declined to come to the services. After his mother's funeral, he vowed that he'd never attend another funeral except his own. I told him I'd call him afterward and confirm our visit for Father's Day dinner at Outback.

I decided to float the idea of living in a nursing home past him one more time while I had him on the line. "Dad, um, have you given any more thought to moving to the Veterans Home and letting them take care of all the household stuff and provide you with three square meals a day?"

There was an ungodly long pause, and then he spoke, "Yes, Lexis, I think that it's time. I'd like that. Can you bring me information when you come this Sunday for Father's Day?"

I was shocked when he said yes. I told him we'd discuss it when I came over for Father's Day. I called Coatesville VAMC to get resources for Dad about their drug and alcohol recovery day programs and contacted the Veteran's Home to find out how Dad qualified to become a resident of their nursing home.

Dot's funeral was held on Wednesday, June 14th. It was a sunny day, and all the family came together to mourn and celebrate her life. People asked where my dad was, and I just said he wasn't feeling well and sent his condolences. I called Dad when I came home and got no answer. Life after that became more excruciating by the moment. As the days passed, I ramped up the intensity of my efforts to reach him and ensure his safety. As if I could control any outcomes. But I called in vain, anyway, to feel like I was at least doing something productive to reach him and show that I cared.

Thursday, June 15th, 2017 – 11 a.m., called Dad, no answer.

Thursday, June 15th, 2017 – 7 p.m., called Dad, no answer.

Friday, June 16th, 2017 – 8 a.m., called Dad, no answer.

Friday, June 16th, 2017 – 10 a.m., called Dad, no answer.

Friday, June 16th, 2017 – 12 p.m., called Dad, no answer.

Friday, June 16th, 2017 – 2 p.m., called Dad, no answer.

Friday, June 16th, 2017 – 4 p.m., called Dad, no answer.

Friday, June 16th, 2017 – 6 p.m., called Dad, no answer.

Friday, June 16th, 2017 – 8 p.m., called Dad, no answer.

Friday, June 16th, 2017 – 10 p.m., called Dad, no answer.

Saturday, June 17th, 2017 – 8 a.m., called Dad, no answer.

Saturday, June 17th, 2017 – 10 a.m., called Dad, no answer.

Saturday, June 17th, 2017 – 12 p.m., called Dad, no answer.

Saturday, June 17th, 2017 – 1 p.m., called Dad, no answer.

Saturday, June 17th, 2017 – 2 p.m., called Dad, no answer.

Saturday, June 17th, 2017 – 3 p.m., called Dad, no answer.

Saturday, June 17th, 2017 – 4 p.m., called Dad, no answer.

Saturday, June 17th, 2017 – 5 p.m., called Dad, no answer.

Saturday, June 17th, 2017 – 7 p.m., called Dad, no answer.

Saturday, June 17th, 2017 – 8 p.m., called Dad, no answer

Saturday, June 17th, 2017 – 9 p.m., called Dad, no answer.

Sunday, June 18th, 2017, was Father's Day.

I was beside myself by Sunday. I didn't want to make the hour-plus drive with my family to Dad's house. What if he was passed out drunk or indecent when we showed up? I didn't want my kids to see that. Worse yet, what if something had happened to him? I didn't want to walk into that with my kids in tow. I was getting scared. Was he back in the hospital? Dinner was at 5:30, and I needed to reach him ASAP, to make sure he was okay. I had to make a decision by noon. I wrestled with myself all morning and prayed he'd pick up every time I called.

Sunday, June 18th – 8 a.m., called Dad, no answer.

Sunday, June 18th – 10 a.m., called Dad, no answer.

Sunday, June 18th – 12 p.m., called Dad, no answer.

Sunday, June 18th – 12:15 p.m., decided to call Lower Bucks Hospital. He wasn't admitted.

Sunday, June 18th – 12:30 p.m., called the police. They sent an officer to the house.

CHAPTER 15

At 1:30 p.m., Officer Hopkins called my cell. The moment he began talking, I knew what he was going to say. "Ma'am, I'm so sorry to have to tell you this, especially on Father's Day. There was no answer when I knocked on the front door or the side door. After getting no response and based on the description you gave of your father, I kicked in the side door to gain entry. I'm so sorry to have to tell you this; I found your father deceased in his bed. His body was badly decomposed. When did you talk to him last?"

As I formulated my response, tears rolled down my face, and I quietly said, "Thank you for going inside. I last talked to him June 13th to check in on him. He sounded fine. I've been trying to reach him ever since, but it just went to voicemail. I can't believe he's gone. I just talked to him."

Officer Hopkins replied, "Thank you, ma'am. And again, I'm so sorry. There was no foul play on the property, and he appeared to have died of natural causes. I've called an ambulance, and in cases like this, the coroner does not perform a full autopsy. There'd be a fee if you wanted one."

I was sniffling, holding my head in my hand. I quickly replied, "No, an autopsy won't be necessary."

He replied, "Understood, ma'am. I will stay here until the ambulance arrives, and when they leave, I will leave. I recommend securing the side door before nightfall. Again, I'm truly sorry."

I quietly thanked Officer Hopkins and told him we'd be over to secure the house before nightfall. He was arranging for an ambulance to take my father's remains to the morgue.

I was sobbing when I hung up the phone. I didn't care if the kids saw me or not. I was pacing back and forth in front of the fridge, crying. Michael came into the kitchen and held me in his arms; I sobbed into his chest. I was so grateful his weekend plans changed; he was supposed to be working the entire weekend at Fort Indiantown Gap. Luckily, he and the other soldiers received a 48-hour pass to be home for Father's Day weekend. I was so grateful he was home.

There was no way I could have gone over to that house by myself. I had no idea how to secure the door. He normally missed important family events because of his military duties. Thank God he was here now. We stood there for a couple of minutes until I was able to stop crying and get words out. I told him what had happened, and the kids were in the kitchen asking me why I was crying. I told them Pop-Pop Miller had passed away and gone to heaven. They really couldn't process it and just said they were sad and wandered off to play in the family room.

I sat down at the island, and Michael brought over some Kleenex and a glass of cold water. He sat next to me and said, "I'm so sorry, Lex. Your dad was a good man, and he loved you. You did all you could to help him."

I started crying again, and as I dabbed my face, I turned to Michael and said, "Did I really do all I could do? Maybe if I had been more present in his life and went out of my way to spend more time with him, he would've told me about his cancer and let me help him. Maybe he'd still be alive right now, instead of giving up on life and laying down to die in that wretched hovel all alone in a vile bed of trash."

Michael rubbed my arm and said, "Maybe so, and maybe not; who knows? He's gone now and can't tell us. Don't get hung up on what-ifs; that's a losing game."

Damn, I hated his bluntness, but I knew he was right, and I also knew that I had no time to wallow and lament. I needed to find a funeral home fast. I needed to cancel the dinner reservation and call my mother-in-law to come over and watch the kids so that I could hightail it to the house to secure it and get out any valuables, drugs, prescriptions, and weapons. I said a quick prayer and said out loud, "I love you, Dad. You'll always be my dad. You'll always be my angel. I'll make sure my kids remember you."

As soon as I uttered those words, it felt like a little peace washed over me. I knew I had to let him go. He was not meant to be here anymore, and I knew it. Let's face it; he had been wasting away for the past year. I knew he was preparing me for his demise that night at his house when I put that briefcase in his wardrobe. It felt way too ceremonial, like a ceremonial farewell or passing of a torch that bestowed wisdom and reasonability upon me. I knew it! I tried to save him in vain.

I wished I had more time with him. I wished I knew more about him. I hoped he died peacefully. I was sad he died alone in that wretched house. I hoped he made peace with his demons and set things right with God. Most of all, I hoped he knew he was loved and respected. I missed my dad. I wished I had spent more time with him.

I Googled the closest funeral home in the Greater Northeast and left a voicemail. I'd need them to receive the body, cremate it and handle setting up a funeral service followed by a repast for family.

They called me back within the hour, and I started making the arrangements. Michael posted the news on Facebook.

I called Outback and canceled the dinner. As Michael drove us to Bristol, I secured a date at the funeral home and arranged the cremation and funeral service. Lastly, I called my mom and told her the news of his passing. She, like Michael, has a way with words. "I'm sorry to hear the news of your father's passing. Alexis, I suggest you walk away from that house and his mess. Don't get wrapped up in his messy affairs. It sounds nice on paper to choose to be transformed by one's bad experiences, but that's a crock. A part of you will always be destroyed by the experience. There's no getting around that. I know you tend to be optimistic, but in my opinion, you are *too* optimistic. You don't know what kind of mess he's leaving behind, and it could very well destroy you. Maybe not the *exact* way your dad was destroyed by the weight of his problems and lies, but the secrets he kept drove him mad. Who knows what uncovering those secrets will do to you? Don't play with fire. Don't let his mistakes ruin your life like they ruined mine. Alexis, don't be a fool. Some secrets are best left hidden; heed my words and walk away."

Great. Exactly what I *didn't* need to hear at a time like this — another cold, Carla comment. *Why did I bother calling her?* I regretted doing it.

She had but a drop of remorse mixed in with her salty bitterness. "Look, Ma, I don't know what happened between the two of you. I am his only living relative, I don't know where Aunt Vicks is, and I doubt any of his distant cousins from California are going to pop out of the woodwork and take care of this. I agreed to be his executrix earlier this past year, and I am going to honor that. I'm going to work with a realtor and a lawyer and wrap this up as quickly as possible to sell the house. I was going to try to renovate the house myself and flip it but given the condition it's in and the fact that he died in it, I just want to have the trash all hauled out and sell the place as is. Then get on with my life and never look back on this chapter."

My mom sighed and said, "Well, suit yourself. Best of luck; I'll be talking to you at the funeral. Bye."

I said goodbye and wrote her off as a source of help. It looked like I was going to be on my own with this.

It was almost 3 p.m. by the time we arrived at the house. My Dad's van was still in the driveway; I half-expected him to come out and greet us from the side door. But I knew that wasn't going to happen. Before getting out of the car, I dabbed a Kleenex with a blend of lavender oil and water and stuffed the wadded Kleenex into each nostril. I had to breathe, and since I didn't have a respirator, this was the best I could do to keep from smelling the stench.

I didn't know what my eyes would see and prepared myself for the worst. I steeled my nerves for what was about to come next as we walked up the tiny driveway and approached the side door. It was on its hinges, but the frame was damaged, and the door couldn't be locked. Michael was carrying several 2x4s and a drill case. I was carrying a box of trash bags and two pairs of rubber gloves. We paused at the door and looked at each other; chills ran down my spine. It was now or never. We stepped inside, and the "fun" began.

The house smelled worse than death; even with lavender-soaked Kleenex stuffed in my nostrils, I could still smell the wretched stench. My eyes watered, and I felt sick to my stomach. The number of flies had tripled since I was there last, and I thought my eardrums would burst from their frenzied, high-pitched buzzes. There was no point in swatting them away; there were just too many of them to fend off.

It was sweltering in the house. It was about 90 degrees outside, but the inside of the house felt like a convection oven set at 450 degrees. Before going into Dad's bedroom, we did a quick sweep of all the other rooms on the first and second floor, making sure all windows and doors were secured, and rooms were undisturbed. Then we worked on securing the side door. We barricaded the door pretty quickly. I held a 2 x 4 across the door, and he drilled it into place in the door frame. We wedged a second 2 x 4 under the doorknob for extra measure. Thanks to the carpeted flooring, that wood wasn't budging. The only thing left to do was go into the bedroom.

Sweat was running down our faces at this point. I exclaimed, "My God, why is it so hot in here? Did you hear that? It sounded like heat just came on in that floor vent next to us." I bent down and put my hand next to the register, and sure enough, heat was coming out. In the middle of June, the heat was on. "Why is the heat on? Do you think my dad was so frail that he was actually cold? Or had he lost his mind and put the heat on by accident? Or did he do it on purpose to kill himself?"

Michael looked up from closing his toolbox and said, "Lex, I don't know why the heat is on. Who knows? Don't worry about that; just go find the control and turn it off."

He was right. It was a waste of my mental energy to ponder on pointless things. I looked around and saw the control in the adjoining dining room against the far wall. I trudged through the piles of empty beer cases to the thermostat dial. I looked over my shoulder at him in the kitchen and said, "Michael, the heat was set at 80 degrees! What in the blazes! It's all good. I turned it off. When we go into Dad's bedroom, we can turn on his window unit A/C."

He nodded and headed back towards the bedroom. I shuddered and followed suit. When I entered that room, what I saw sent shivers down my spine and haunts me to this day.

CHAPTER 16

Dad's room was exactly as I had last seen it when I put the suit-case in his plastic, portable, zippered wardrobe. Only this time, there was a blood-stained body indentation on that thin mattress with the dirty, yellow, fitted sheet. I don't know how long his body laid in that position, but the imprint was molded into the mattress, and putrid, dark fluids had gathered in the deepest middle part. The top sheet was gone; I guess the paramedics gathered him up in it. I couldn't take my eyes off the bed. But I had to look away, or I'd faint. My eyes wandered to the top of the bed, and my gaze rested on the pillow; *Damn, if there wasn't an indentation in that too!* There was a hollowed-out cavity where his head would have been, and parts of it were filled with his curly, brown hair, like some morbid toupee that had come unglued.

Michael was staring at the scene, too. I broke the silence and said, "My God, help me. Give me the strength to do this, sweet Jesus! Michael, please take those blankets at the foot of the bed and cover the entire bed and pillow. I can't be in this room and look at that gory stuff. In fact, why don't I walk over to the other side of the room and put on the A/C? Because I swear, this tan carpet is undulating every time I look down at it. I swear it's wriggling."

Michael replied, "Yeah, no prob, I'll take care of it. You know, as badly dehydrated and malnourished as he was and with the heat cranked on 80 during this past week's unseasonal heatwave, he *had* to have practically been a *skeleton* when that police officer found him! I've heard that if left undisturbed in a room, the body does the majority of its decomposing the first four to five days post-mortem. The rest of the year in the coffin is minimal decomposition. Depending on whether the coffin is wood or metal and whether or not water penetrates it."

I stared at him, dumbfounded. Before he could say another word, I interjected, "You know what, babe? I *don't* need to know *that*. My head is spinning from all this, and I swear that carpet is wriggling every time I look down at it; flies are buzzing all around us, and I have to dig through the piles of crap in this room to find his wallet and any other valuables or contraband. Your scientific commentary is *not* helping the situation. Please stop."

I didn't know where to start. I set the box of trash bags down on the faded, green, velvet loveseat to put on my rubber gloves. My hands were sweaty, and I had to work hard to shove them inside the gloves. I kicked some trash aside to get to the wardrobe but decided to walk past it to get to the window on the far side of Dad's bed. I wanted to make sure it was locked. When I approached the other side of the bed, I almost hurled.

I shouted, "Michael, there's a big metal bucket next to the bed, and it's nearly filled to the top with urine! He must have been using it for a really long time because there's mineral deposit-like, crusty bits lining the entire inside of the bucket. Gross!"

He replied, "Well, dump it; the last thing we want to do is kick that over. While you're doing that, I'm going to look under the bed for your dad's shotgun and samurai sword."

The bucket was directly under the window, so I'm guessing he used it like a chamber pot and dumped the contents out the window. That explains where he was relieving himself. I had to dump that stuff. I lifted the roller shades, unlatched the window, and raised it. His neighbor's side yard was literally a stone's throw away from this window, but thankfully the neighbors had a tall wooden privacy fence along the entire property line that completely blocked their view of Dad's property. When I poked my head out the window and looked down, the grass was dead under the window, which confirmed my suspicions. I ducked my head back in, gingerly raised the bucket, and held it out the window to dump its contents carefully. That partially explained why the house smelled so bad on my last visit.

I turned to Michael as he squatted down and looked under the bed. He poked his head back up and looked serious, "Um, Lex, I don't mean to alarm you, but I have some good news and some not-so-good news. Good news is, I found two shotguns and the sword. The bad news is, they're covered in blood that's dripping out of the underside of the mattress, and the carpet isn't moving; it's actually wriggling maggots all over. That's what you saw moving. All these flies in here were attracted to the body. The flies laid eggs, maggots hatched and began feeding on the bod—"

"I get it! Okay!" I interrupted. "You don't have to mansplain the fly's lifecycle to me and what they feed on. This is my dad you're talking about, not some science fair project. And I'm standing on maggots!! I don't care how they're born. I have maggots on my shoes! We are standing on maggots, and I'm holding a crusty piss bucket! The flies buzzing around us were on my dad, and now they're landing on us!! His piles of trash are lying on a maggot-encrusted floor, and I have to wade through all of these trash piles to look for his wallet and stuff. It's a thousand degrees in here, and it smells like death and diarrhea."

"*Please* don't make this any worse than it already is. I'm about to lose my mind. I am holding it together by a string right now. No more science talk or gory stuff. Please, just take care of the guns and the sword, and use the inside of one of the blankets to wipe them off. And then turn the blanket back over so I don't see the blood. I have to get out of here; I'm going down to the basement; maybe it's cooler down there. I have to get out of here for a moment."

He just looked at me. Honestly, sometimes he had the emotional intelligence of a troll.

I tiptoed around the bed and walked on the undulating carpet path to leave the room. In a few steps, I was at the basement door. I was petrified to go down there alone. I'd never been down there before and didn't know what I'd find. I opened the door cautiously and flipped on the light. Thankfully, the basement lit up, and the stairs looked sturdy and new. It sounded quiet when I opened the door, and the air felt cooler as I descended the stairs. There was a finished wall on the left side of the staircase with a hand railing; the right side was unfinished and completely open. I couldn't help but notice that this would most certainly *not* pass code.

As I approached the last step, I could hear a steady drip hitting on a hard surface. To the left of the stairs was a finished entryway to the finished rec room. That side was carpeted. To the right of the stairs and at the landing, I was greeted by a concrete floor and an unfinished basement with nothing more than a washer, dryer, and utility sink. The sound was coming from the unfinished side, and I decided to have a look. I hoped it wasn't a leaking pipe. That was not what I wanted to deal with.

I didn't have to search long for the source of the sound, what I saw on the floor stunned me and nearly knocked the wind out of me. I staggered back and fell up against the cinder-block wall. I wanted to bolt up those stairs and never come back. But I had to take a closer look. The floor was covered in rusty, wet-looking fluid, and as it splattered, it looked like an eight-foot diameter splash art project for an art installation. I walked as close as I could without getting splattered. I looked up and knew the spot was directly below Dad's bed. The underside of several wood floorboards was drenched with bloody, body fluids, and the fluid dripped through the floor joints.

The power and data wires running along the floorboards were bathed in the fluid. The drips took turns slowly falling in succession or sometimes simultaneously. Why was there so much blood? At that moment, I was too grossed out to care. I had to leave. I had to leave *now!* I backed up and turned and ran towards the stairs. I suddenly halted and decided to walk into the finished basement to quickly see the handiwork. The walls were white; the floor had a nice wall-to-wall, tan Berber, the drop ceiling and fluorescent lights were installed nicely, and there was a bathroom with a stall shower!

So, his buddy, the shady contractor, did do a decent job after all! The sink still had the manufacturer's tags on the faucet, and the toilet still had the manufacturer's seal across the seat. Why hadn't Dad gone downstairs to use this toilet, instead of using a glorified bed pan and clogging the upstairs toilet with crap? I had seen enough and gave up pondering.

I ran upstairs, flipped off the light, slammed the door shut, and stopped at the entry into the bedroom. I breathlessly blurted out to Michael, "Babe, you'll never guess what I found downstairs! The blood soaked through the carpet, dripped through the floor joints, and splattered all over the basement floor. It's dripping as we speak.

Why is there still so much blood? His body isn't even here anymore. How much blood did that man have? He was skin and bones! Oh, and there's a finished side on the other side of the basement, which looks nice and has a brand-new bathroom that's never been used. Never! Why didn't he use the downstairs bathroom!?"

Michael was covering a shotgun in a towel as he spoke, "Well, Lex, there's so much fluid because it's not just blood. All the organs basically liquified, and the ever-increasing internal pressure caused all that liquified goo to ooze out of every imaginable orifice. Eyeballs can even—"

I cut him off fast, "Stop it! Stop telling me this! It's not helping; I don't care to know the gory details. I need you to help me and comfort me. And spewing gross facts isn't helping. That was a rhetorical question; I don't want you to *literally* tell me what anything is anymore. I don't give a crap about organs and what happens to them when we die. I don't care!" My nerves were shot. I tried not to get upset with Michael, but we squabbled over stupid things a couple more times before the night was over.

I wanted to retch in a corner, but every corner was piled high with mail. I walked around and looked at the shotguns he had lying on the bed. It sickened me to see them resting on that deathbed splattered with blood and wriggling maggots. I looked at Michael and said, "Thank you for cleaning the weapons and making sure they're not loaded. Once you're finished, can you help me find Dad's wallet? I'm going to try to look through the piles of mail, but I feel sick to my stomach. I don't know how much longer I can be in here. Between the flies and the maggots and the stench, I can't take it. How could he live this way? It breaks my heart to think of Dad living and dying here."

I could feel my eyes welling up, and I averted my gaze to stem the tears. My gaze landed on a pile of trash near his wardrobe. I don't know how I missed it before, but right before my eyes, I saw my grandmother's old, Jackie O-style, black, alligator top-handled purse perfectly perched on top of a pile of magazines. My grandmother was one of those old ladies who carried her handbag wherever she went. She either clutched that bag in her hand, or had it draped on her forearm, everywhere she went. It's the only purse I can remember her carrying throughout my entire childhood and adulthood. She wore it with everything, from sweatpants and jeans to her finest, vintage, polyester pantsuits.

As I held up Mom's old purse, I exclaimed, "What in the hell? Why would he put that there? Why does he still have Mom's old purse? Of all the things Mom had, why did he keep *this*?"

In an irritated tone, Michael said, "Lex, I don't know. You're asking me questions I can't answer. Who knows why he kept it? Maybe it reminded him of her. Who cares?"

At that moment, I really wanted to hit Michael across the head with that handbag. Instead, I grabbed it and took it home with me. It was a memento of my grandmom. Maybe he had kept it as a keep-sake? Maybe it was the last thing his eyes saw from across the room when he took his last breath. I don't know. I just knew I felt compelled and had to take it with me. I put it in its own trash bag, sealed it, walked it into the kitchen, and set it on the makeshift tarp I had made with some of the trash bags.

When I walked back into the bedroom and looked around, my eyes landed on that faded, green, velvet loveseat. Sitting there, on one of the seat cushions, was a black book. When I moved closer, it was a black, leather-bound, zippered bookcase, and on the front, engraved in gold, were the words, "Holy Bible." I blurted out, "Michael, look at this; it's a Bible! What is happening here!? Where did this come from? Neither my dad nor grandmom *ever* talked about God or religion. I didn't even know they believed in God, let alone had a Bible!"

I reached down and picked up the Bible. It was about seven inches by eight inches in size and looked well-kept and unused. I opened the leather-bound cover and flipped through it. I instantly recognized my grandmother's handwriting as I skimmed the contents of the Miller family tree written in her penmanship. I knew for a fact that Bible was NOT in this room the last time I was here with Dad. I mused out loud to myself mostly, "Wow, who knew she had a Bible? I wonder…did he use this to pray during his last living moments on earth? Did he leave this here for me to find? Or is it here for some other reason? Or no reason at all? I don't know, but I'm keeping it."

Michael didn't even acknowledge me. He was engrossed in cleaning the shotguns. I felt the urge to keep it. It was our family's Bible. I wrapped and sealed it in a trash bag, walked it into the kitchen, and set the bag on the tarp with the other bag.

It was almost 4 p.m., and the bedroom had started cooling down thanks to the A/C window unit. As I made my way around Michael, I ignored the undulating carpet and looked past him, vigorously rubbing blood off the sword sheath. Thankfully, there were no maggots on the piles of mail. I decided to tackle them and look for Dad's wallet and keys. I looked around and felt like the piles on the right closest to me were a good place as ever to start. My hands were sweating in the rubber gloves, and I prayed I found the things quickly.

I went through those two piles and found my dad's wallet, keys, and cell phone. Thank God. I noted bills with overdue marked on them in big, red-stamped letters. I couldn't deal with that now. That would have to be for another day. I placed his belongings in a trash bag, sealed it, and placed the clunky bag on the tarp in the kitchen. I didn't care how empty those bags were; I was sealing them and starting fresh with a new bag.

The next thing to tackle for the day was the wardrobe. I wanted to be out of there by five, and that wardrobe was packed full, last time I looked inside it. But I knew the first things to look for and exactly where to find them. In hindsight, I was grateful for that peculiar evening when I first set foot in this gruesome den of dismay and disorder. I was grateful for the time with my dad, glad that he had asked me to put his things away, and even more glad that I had agreed to help him. I knew exactly where to look for the will and other documents. Just as he had instructed me that fateful night, I faced the wardrobe, unzipped it, and looked inside. Thank God the contents looked exactly the way I last saw them.

The muscle memory was still in my body. As Dad had instructed, I looked down on the right side of the wardrobe and saw the two shoeboxes. I bent down, took them out, and put them on that faded, green, velvet loveseat. Then I went back for the briefcase. It was right where I left it. I pulled out the tattered briefcase and placed it on top of the shoeboxes. I opened it, confirmed the contents, closed the briefcase, and placed it in a trash bag on the loveseat. I went back to the wardrobe and started going through all the pockets in the trousers, jackets, and vests. I found nothing.

Then I started methodically taking out two shoeboxes at a time that were also stacked in the bottom of the wardrobe. There were about eight boxes, and they all had dress shoes in them. I looked inside each shoe; nothing was inside them. I placed them all back inside the wardrobe in the exact order I took them out.

Four, larger, boot-sized shoeboxes were stacked on the bottom-left side of the wardrobe, and I started going through them next. I grabbed the top two, and they were heavy. When I placed them on the loveseat to inspect the contents, they were both filled with old VCR porn tapes. *Gross.* The covers were lewd—naked black men with white women. BBC was the predominant theme. I rifled through them and didn't find anything else. I really didn't want to know my dad's sexual fetishes, but here we were, and this was happening. I tried to make the best of it.

Michael just chuckled.

When I took out the next box and peered inside, it was more of the same. Damn, Dad! Yet, as far as I knew, he never actually dated any white women. The only women he ever introduced me to were black or Hispanic.

The last two boxes went from bad to worse. The third box had drug paraphernalia in it. Based on the little mirrors, razors, pipes, and filters, it looked like he was into snorting stuff and smoking weed. I didn't find any drugs, just paraphernalia. The last box was old, love letters and nude photos. I cringed. They were all old, yellowed photos from the early 80s based on the envelope postmarks, the décor in the photos, Dad's thin frame and full head of dark hair, and the ladies' feathered hairdos.

Some photos had the date on the back, too. Every sultry, half-naked woman in the photos was white, and I didn't recognize any of them. Based on the time frame, that's when he was living in San Jose, California. He had dropped completely out of my life during that time, and I was lucky if I even received a call from him at Christmas. I could feel decades of old hatred, loss, and feelings of abandonment cascading down upon me as I shoved the contents back into the box and put the lid on it. I put that box in with the briefcase and sealed the trash bag. Maybe the old letters would shed some clues on his past and the facets of this man I never knew.

By then, it was nearing 5 p.m., and I was spent. I could not process another ounce of this man's life or death. I placed the remaining shoeboxes back in the bottom of the wardrobe and zipped it shut. We turned off the A/C, gathered the guns and sword, and placed them in a couple of trash bags to conceal them, gathered our things, the bags on the tarp in the kitchen, and made our way for the front door. It took two trips, and as I locked the front door, I noticed two brightly colored pieces of postage from the township stuck on the door. They were notices stating that this house was going up for sheriff's sale at the end of the month if taxes weren't paid.

Great, I have less than a month to decide what I'm doing with this property. Do I keep it and try to sell it or let the state take it and get on with my life? Maybe the weight of his life's circumstances had a role in his death? Had the stress of it all taken a physical toll on him? Who knows what other demons he was battling or secrets he was hiding. Oh, Dad, I wish you had talked to me about your financial situation!

We didn't talk much on the drive home. I left the sealed trash bags in my trunk for days. I hoped the sweltering heat in my garage would bake the life out of any creepy crawlies that had hitched a ride on the objects. I completely shed all my clothes at the garage doorstep, walked into the house naked, and went straight to the shower. The stench was on my skin, and I wanted to scrub it off and let the day's memories wash down the drain with the soapsuds. Happy Father's Day.

CHAPTER 17

I tossed and turned all night. I dreaded facing that place by myself tomorrow. Unfortunately, Michael had to go to work. My mind raced. I enjoyed a moment of relief, knowing that Michael had a military background. He agreed to handle all the Veteran's benefits and military burial arrangements. I did not have the capacity to handle any of that, and the thought of government red tape made me cringe.

But as the minutes ticked by, images flashed into my head again: the maggots, flies, stench, the deathbed, and the blood puddle in the basement. These images filled my dreams and tormented my mind. I dreaded going back to that house. When I'm under stress, I bake desserts, clean every nook and cranny of my home, down-size and organize my closets, and make to-do lists. So, in the morning, after I dropped the kids off at camp, I organized the pantry, threw out expired spices and flours, and labeled the kids' toy bins. Then, I made a list of the people I needed to contact about my dad when I got home and a list of the things I needed to buy before going back to his house: two packs of surgical gloves, menthol VapoRub for lining my nostrils, and bug foggers to kill the flies and maggots. As I walked past the pile of clothes on my garage floor, I could still smell the stench from last night.

As I made the familiar drive to Bristol, the dread set in deeper and deeper. I sat in my car in his driveway with the A/C on blast. It was a sweltering day, and I was in jeans, a tee shirt, a button-down, long-sleeve, chambray shirt, socks, and cruddy sneakers. I rubbed a little of the menthol VapoRub on a tissue and plugged my nostrils with wadded up tissue bits. I hoped it would lessen the smell of stench. I had a garbage bag to gather essentials. I was mainly looking for money, prescriptions, weapons, and jewelry. My plan was to stay at the house for an hour, set off the foggers, and run like hell out of there.

I opened the front door, locked it behind me, and started crying as I looked at the trash around me. I furiously swatted at the flies swarming me. I was so overwhelmed by the sea of trash. Everywhere I looked, trash was all I saw. Where was I even going to begin? I had no one to help me.

"Look at this mess! How am I going to find anything in it?" I said out loud to myself. "He could have hidden things anywhere in this house. What am I going to do with my one, dinky, thirty-gallon garbage bag against this house *full* of garbage?" There was trash piled everywhere. I couldn't go into that bedroom; I couldn't bring myself to see that bed. But I had to go in there. That was the main room he essentially lived and died in. Anything of major importance was bound to be in that room and *that* room only. I looked upstairs first, and although the two bedrooms were clean and bug-free, the heat was staggering, and I was about to pass out. I couldn't be up there. I'd have to bring a fan with me on the next visit tomorrow.

"Lord, God, help me; what am I going to do? How am I going to do all this?" I pleaded out loud. I looked around at the piles of food cartons and beer cases in the dining room and kitchen, felt the flies buzzing around me, and broke into a sweat. I tried to breathe through gritted teeth to prevent flies from going into my mouth. Having my nostrils blocked made me sound like Donald Duck and made it hard to breathe. Those flies made me irate and sick. I imagined that those were the same flies that were flying on his corpse yesterday, and I wanted to gag.

I started frantically swatting them away from me and ran toward the front door. I was about to unlock it, yank it open, and run out screaming. Then I paused to look into the tiny living room, long enough to check the two windows and make sure they were securely closed and locked, and noted that there was no trash in there—just a mid-century, modern credenza with a huge, flatscreen TV sitting on it. I remember when my father bought that TV. It was the first-generation digital TV, and it cost him a couple grand, but he had to be the first on the block to have it. It looked like it was mine now.

The pause bolstered my courage, and I decided to stay. The number of flies increased as I got closer to the kitchen. It appeared just to be empty beer cases piled in the dining room as I walked along the narrow, one-foot-wide passage of floor space in a sea of empty beer cases. There was no furniture, and the gold, four-candle chandelier looked oddly out of place hanging down over a sea of boxes. I made my way into the kitchen, and my head fell. I had to start somewhere. I looked around in the kitchen, and the only trash piled up appeared to be half-eaten food in Styrofoam food containers and empty, frozen-food dinner containers.

I scrunched up my face and frantically swatted away flies that were buzzing by me in frenzied, erratic circles and zigzags. They'd fly past my eyes, land on a counter or the ceiling, buzz past each other, buzz past my nose or ears, or land on my clothes. I frantically swatted them away and fought off the urge to scratch myself silly until my skin was raw. I looked toward the bedroom and steeled myself. I knew I had to go in there. That bedroom was where he spent the majority of his time. I knew that any important things had to be in that bedroom. It was the epicenter of the storm, and I had to go in there.

I pulled my rubber gloves out of my shirt pocket, wiped the sweat off my brow with my shirtsleeve, and steeled my nerves to walk down that narrow hall towards the bedroom. I walked three feet and froze; I got as far as the hall bathroom; I couldn't do it. I could not face that room. I could not go in there just yet. He had died in there. *He died alone in there, surrounded by piles of trash, a bucket of his own urine, and God knows what else. Maggots wriggled all over that bed and carpet at that very moment, and flies that touched his rotting corpse were now flying all around me.* I had to get out of there.

It was hot as hell in there and smelled like death. I frantically swatted flies away from my right ear and slapped at one that landed on the side of my neck. I wanted to scratch my face so badly, but I didn't dare touch my face. I had to leave. I nearly gagged, and chills ran down my spine. My hair was on end all over my arms. *I have to get out of here.* The sound of swarming flies was more than I could stand.

I was there almost twenty minutes at that point and was only going to give myself an hour to get in and get out. It was too hot; the stench was horrible, and the flies were disgusting. Not to mention the fact that Dad had just died in the room next to me, the bloody outline of his body was hidden under that blanket, and the hairy, concave indentation was in that pillow from the weight of his head. I knew all too well what was under that blanket, under that bed, what had seeped down through the floorboards and over the wires running in the basement directly below, and what had splattered all over the concrete basement floor like splatter art. I couldn't face that bedroom.

I knew both windows were locked in it. I knew the windows were locked in the bathroom and the kitchen. I couldn't go into the epicenter of it all and see those maggots, hear those flies, or face that bed. Eventually, I had to go in there, but today was not that day. God only knew what important documents were stashed in all those piles of trash. But I peeled the gloves off my sweaty hands and put them back in my shirt pocket. *Baby steps. Baby steps.* I remembered what Carolyn had told me when I had a problem as big as an elephant; the best way to tackle it was one small bite at a time. Today was a nibble. I was mustering as much courage as I possibly could to show up and face this mess. Something was better than nothing. Tomorrow would be another day to chip away at this.

Before I left, I set up the bug foggers. Based on the 1,200-square-foot size of the home, I put one fogger on each floor. I started upstairs on the second floor after double-checking that the windows were all shut and locked. I placed the canister in the center hallway between the two rooms and activated the trigger. I had a couple of minutes to get out. I ran downstairs to the basement, set one in the center at the bottom of the basement stairs, left the door open, and set the last one on the first floor in the center of the kitchen. I pulled the plug, bolted to the front door, and slammed it behind me. I heaved a sigh of relief so hard that I blew the tissue plugs out of my nostrils. That was enough for one day. I was emotionally spent. I could not fathom how I was going to do this.

I got in the car and drove off crying. My grief came in waves. I had to show up and still be a mom and wife. It wasn't fair to act sullen around my family. I kept up a good spirit as much as possible around them and only cried in the shower or the car, seldom in front of them. I tried to focus on the positive. This was a crappy situation. I wanted to have the best mindset possible to deal with it while holding space to process the pain, grief, anger, loss, and whatever else cropped up.

Most days, there was more love than grief. I hoped and prayed there would come a day when there were just bittersweet, loving memories. Today was not that day. I did my best to allow the wave of grief to flow through me, while holding space to focus on the goodness around me. I wanted to remember to appreciate life's little pleasures, like sunshine and butterflies and puppy videos on Instagram. That was the best I could muster.

I have to go back there tomorrow. I was dreading it already as I made the trek back home. As soon as I got home, I stripped in the garage, gathered all the smelly, vile clothes, and washed them. I headed to the shower to clean up and have a good cry. I decided to leave the sealed trash bags in the trunk to bake off any remaining flies and maggots. I couldn't deal with that stuff today. I stuck to my original game plan and called my realtor, the funeral home, and the lawyer who drew up Dad's will and power of attorney. I had no playbook on how to remain calm and bury one's parent and clean out the contents of their hoarded house. So, I decided to make it up as I went and figure it out along the way. I chose to keep the faith, accept that I'd fail along the way and trusted that the help and answers would come to me as I needed them.

My realtor, Rob, became my lifeline over the next six months. Rob sold Michael and me our first house well over seventeen years ago, and we'd kept in touch all these years. He was a great source of help during my time of need, and thankfully, he had a lot of experience handling situations like mine. In speaking with him briefly, it was a relief to know that I wasn't the oddball client with weird circumstances rarely seen before. There was a comfort in knowing I wasn't the only one who had dealt with situations like this. He was quite familiar with helping grieving families sell their deceased loved one's homes and all the baggage that can come along with it. He also referred me to a great lawyer who worked in-house at his real estate office, and it was a much-needed source of help.

During this time, I just felt very overwhelmed by all of this. I had no idea how I'd manage to single-handedly pull all this off. Rob and I agreed to speak in more detail and set up a time to meet in his office to determine what the next steps would be. I felt a glimmer of hope after speaking with him. I hadn't felt hope in so long. For the past year, it honestly had felt like a never-ending stream of crap showering down on me. To have this glimmer of hope pop up was like a much-needed lifeline. It meant more to me than I think he will ever know.

I went through the rest of my day feeling a sense of relief and, dare I say, joy! The support and acknowledgment of my circumstances and the assurance that I wasn't alone, and this was actually common, meant the world to me. By the time Michael came home with the kids, I felt like a new me. I was able to show up for my family from a much better frame of mind, and I slept soundly for the first time in a very long time. I could honestly say that I was looking forward to waking up to a new day.

CHAPTER 18

Yesterday's unexpected highlight gradually wore off as I made the solo trek to Bristol. By the time I pulled into Dad's driveway for day two, there was barely an ounce of joy or hope left. I shouted out, "God, help me!"

After about fifteen minutes of deliberating in my car as to whether or not I was going to step inside the house, I decided to do the dang thing. It was now or never. I didn't drive all the way over here to sit in this driveway and talk to myself. I could feel my energy welling up, and stamina summoned forth from somewhere deep inside me as I shoved that Kleenex up my nostrils and flung the car door open. As I bounded to the passenger side, I swung my sweat jacket over my shoulders, forcefully shoved my arms in, and zippered it up. As it zipped, I could feel my courage rising. *Keep going,* a voice said inside me.

I plucked up the courage to walk up to the front door and step inside. Although the place still smelled, it was eerily silent. Dead silent. For once, there was no frantic buzzing from the multitude of flies. But now I was facing the hot, thick, silent air. I was alone with my thoughts, and there was no distraction. I wasn't sure how long I could stand to stay in the house. *Keep going,* a voice said inside me. I was staggered by the scene before me, and that voice was silenced.

The momentum of courage was blocked and came to a dead halt. I stood in the doorway, just staring at the piles of trash for a good ten minutes, breaking a sweat in my jeans and hoodie. What happened to all that courage I had just summoned?

The idea popped into my head to call Carolyn and ask her for advice. She picked up, and I just blurted out, "Hi, Carolyn, can you talk for a minute? I'm at my dad's house, surrounded by piles of trash, and I don't know where to start. I was hoping you could point me in the right direction. Thanks."

She could tell I was nervous and out of sorts. I never just call her out of the blue to ask for advice. "Well, Lexe, honey, I bet your dad has bills that need to be paid; that might be a good place to start. Look for anything that looks like a bill. And start sorting them and then open them and write on the front of the envelope when they're due. As you go through the piles, you'll start recognizing a pattern of what bills come monthly and which ones only sporadically. Does that help, Lexe?" Boy, was she brilliant.

I exclaimed, "Oh my gosh, yes, that's a big help. I'm so overwhelmed, I can't think straight. Yes, I will gather a bunch of his letters and start looking for bills. Thanks, Carolyn; I think I can do this now. I have a starting point to focus on. Thank you. I'm going to go now; thanks for picking up. I'll call or text when I get home. I'm only going to stay here for an hour. It's still too much for me to be here."

We said our goodbyes, and I felt like a wind was in my sails. I instantly tapped into that energy and swiftly walked to the back of the house and headed for the bedroom. I was determined to keep my stride because if I faltered, I would likely turn back and run out the front door. I summoned every ounce of courage I could muster to will my legs to move and barreled through the piles of empty beer cases, rounded the corner, and briskly walked past the bathroom with laser-focus on the bedroom doorway and that blanket-covered bed that faced me. I was nearing it, I was in the doorway, I was breathing faster, and my hands clenched the box of trash bags.

I stepped over the threshold into the bedroom and turned right towards that faded, green, velvet loveseat. I did it! *Baby steps,* I made it into the bedroom—a major victory in this tender, quiet, solitary moment. Tears streamed down my face. I turned away from the bed and faced the wardrobe and piles of mail all around it. I kept my back to the bed and just worked on donning my gloves and grabbing handfuls of letters from the nearest waist-high pile. I shoved them in the trash bag as fast as my slender arms could go. *Just a little while longer. You can do this!*

I didn't know how long my courage would last. I had to move as fast as I could. I blindly threw letters into that trash bag as tears streamed down my face and dropped from my cheeks onto the papers. Thank God the carpet was no longer gyrating and moving. Dead flies were everywhere. They littered the papers; they littered the bed. They littered the floor. I didn't care if I smashed them as I walked. I'd scrape them off of my shoes when I left the house. I was on a mission to gather these papers. And I prayed to God that I could do it without throwing up; the house smelled like death.

I stayed for about an hour, and that was all I could tolerate. Tomorrow would have to be another day, and I'd try to stay for two hours, but an hour was all I could muster for now. I had to get out of there. I practically ran out. After I locked the door behind me, I checked the mailbox mounted on the brick exterior. There was a pile of envelopes inside. I skimmed over the labels and gathered these were for his cell phone, credit card, life insurance, electric, and medic transport services. *What the hell?* As I flipped through all of these bills, they all had a big, red "OVERDUE" stamped on them.

What am I getting myself into? Should I do this, or should I just walk away from this? Maybe my mom was right. I had to call my realtor, Rob, and talk to him ASAP before I did anything. I had until the end of the month to decide what I was going to do before the house went up for sheriff's sale, and I was down to two weeks. I dropped the letters into the trash bag and headed to my car to add this bag to the growing collection in my trunk. I pulled a trusty Kleenex out of my pocket and dislodged the wadded-up tissues in each nostril with one hearty blow.

This ritual would be repeated daily for many days to come. Old me would have been mortified to be seen in public like this. At this point, I didn't care who saw me do this. I flopped into the hot car, cranked up the A/C, and patted myself on the back for the mission accomplished. *I did it! I went into that house and went into the bedroom.*

I sighed, exhaled with deep satisfaction, and checked my voicemail as the car's A/C cooled down the interior. My goal was to gather one pile of mail from the bedroom and pile it into a trash bag. *And I did it!!* My heart swelled, and I sat there and wept. One bite down; how many more to go? I decided to leave that trash bag in the trunk along with the others to kill off any living things that might be amongst the papers. From there, I planned to sort the contents outside in a shady spot. Now to actually go through with that plan.

I wiped my tears, exhaled, and picked up my phone. I had a voice message from my realtor, Rob. *Thank God! Perfect timing!* I pulled myself together and spoke to him as I made the drive home. At first, I was embarrassed to go over the sordid details of my family situation. But Rob remained calm and collected and didn't appear to be passing any judgment on me, so I let my defenses down and spilled my guts about the gory details and the financials. If we were going to work together, he needed to know the whole truth and nothing but the truth. I decided to trust him implicitly.

I told him the details of my dad's house and that I was the executrix. I told him about the house's condition: the bloody mess, the maggots, the flies, the stench, the garbage and papers piled downstairs—the condition of the basement and upstairs…the papers piled everywhere, overdue bills in the mailbox with "Final Notice" stamped on them in red…the property tax notice on the door and pending sheriff's sale at the end of the month, if not paid. As I sped down the Turnpike, talking to Rob, the events just spilled out of my mouth.

I remember telling him, "Rob, I've never seen anything like this before in my life. Have you? I just can't wrap my mind around how my father could have lived like this! Part of me wants to go in and fix this house up on my own. I am an interior designer. I can flip this house and maybe make a profit. But then there's a part of me that doesn't want to have anything to do with this. Especially now that I know it's slated for sheriff's sale in less than two weeks. Who knows what I'm getting myself into? I don't want to pull my family into this. It's not fair to Michael and the kids. I have no idea what I could possibly be getting myself into, and I don't want to get into financial ruin. I have no idea what additional monies my father might have in other accounts. I'd have to sort through every paper piled in that house to solve that mystery. As far as I know, his existing bank accounts barely have $3,000 in them, combined. And I'm in no position to be bailing out someone else. I'd really appreciate your advice."

Rob replied in his typical calm voice, "Alexis, I've seen this a thousand times before. Please know that you're not alone in feeling this way and having these questions. Other people do grapple with these same issues. You are not alone, and I am here to expertly guide you and help you arrive at the best decision for you and your family. I am going to send you an email today with a link to a video. Please watch the video. I think you will find it very helpful. Then, I recommend just sleeping on it. We can talk again tomorrow afternoon. Okay?"

I agreed to look at the video and just sleep on it. Honestly, at this point in time, I was so overwhelmed with everything else, I appreciated this simple request. Watch a video, go to bed. Done. It sounded simple enough—no added stress or work. Just sleep on it and talk to him tomorrow. At this point, I needed simple. I needed sleep. I could handle this. It didn't feel like another impossible burden to overcome. I felt like my plea for help had been heard and was being answered. I called Carolyn and Michael to share the good news.

I waited until the kids were in bed and the house was quiet before opening Rob's e-mail and watching the video. I got comfortable on the sofa, and what I saw flabbergasted me. It was actually a story of a couple named Tony and Tina, who went through a situation very similar to mine. The scene opened with the husband and wife debating what they were going to do about her dad's house. She wanted to fix it up and sell it. The husband thought it was a great idea too.

Tony and Tina had the great idea that while the market was hot, they would flip the house and make a huge profit that would set them up for life. But when Tony and Tina stepped inside her childhood home and saw all the possessions and garbage her father had accumulated, she became overwhelmed and too worked up to face the task at hand. She could not imagine going through her father's possessions, let alone demolishing the rooms that held so many of her childhood memories. Long story short, they decided to hire a company to clean out the contents of the house, hired a contractor to fix up some minor issues, and sold the house as is.

After watching the video, I set the phone down, closed my eyes, and just rested for a bit. I must have fallen asleep because it was about two o'clock in the morning when I woke up. I dragged myself upstairs, climbed into bed, and completed the rest of my assignment for the day, which was to sleep on it. I woke up the next morning with no real sense of clarity or purpose. So, I went through the motions, got the kids up, fed them, took them to camp, came home, and mentally prepared myself to drive over to Bristol and face the house. I took the full trash bags out of my trunk and dropped them in the garage. I made the trek to Bristol, more confused than ever, only armed with an ounce of courage, a drop of faith, Kleenex, and a box of trash bags.

Tears streamed down my face as I drove along the all-too-familiar roads to his house. I pulled into the driveway and sat in silence, summoning the courage and strength to go inside and face that giant mess. The clock was ticking, and I needed to give Rob an answer today about what I was going to do. *Should I try to flip the house, sell it as is, or just walk away from it and let it go to sheriff's sale?*

I felt a responsibility to honor my father. Surely, he didn't go through all that trouble to set me up as the executrix if he just wanted the house to go to sheriff's sale. If that were the case, he would have never gone through all of those measures to add me to his bank accounts and appoint me as his power of attorney to handle his affairs. Obviously, this was his way of telling me he wanted me to handle his affairs properly and see this through. In my opinion, he didn't want this property to go to sheriff's sale. I wish he'd had the courage in his living days to tell me the full story instead of leaving it for me to find out myself, like some iceberg underneath the water, having no idea what's truly beneath the surface. But what's done is done. He's gone now, and I can't change the past; I just need to figure out how I'm going to move forward.

When I felt strong enough, I willed myself to get out of my car and march up to that front door. I propelled myself into that living room and was determined not to look at anything around me this time that would distract me. I couldn't stop at the front door for another ten minutes like I had done yesterday. I willed my legs to keep moving. I kicked aside the piles of empty beer cases. I just ignored the mess in the kitchen and ignored the mess in the bathroom. I also ignored what was on that bed. I just focused on the piles of trash. I randomly decided to look to my right and started with a random pile of letters. I just willed myself to shove the letters in the bag as fast as my arms would go. I must have looked robotic and comical, and I didn't care.

I filled one entire thirty-gallon, multi-purpose bag full. It was so heavy I could barely pick it up. I could see the black plastic giving way to the weight of the mail as I tried to lift the bag. I set it back down and started frantically pulling out half the contents. I could feel my anxiety rising, and I could feel myself getting frantic and panicked. I was losing my cool and about to snap into a full-blown panic attack. I had to remember to breathe and calm my nerves before I lost my mind. Otherwise, I'd start flinging paper everywhere and run out of there screaming. I took a moment just to breathe. I couldn't look around at anything because it would freak me out. I didn't want to close my eyes because I was petrified to be in that house by myself, so I just looked down at my feet.

Then that started freaking me out because I thought about the maggots on the floor. I cried out, "God help me; I can't do this!!!" I was getting lightheaded, and my peripheral vision was fading to black. I shook my head, and my vision cleared. I took a deep, belly breath in through my nose and out through my mouth. I rolled my shoulders and counted down from ten to zero. I stared at the window shade; it was solid white with a barely perceptible, grass-cloth pattern embossed on the plastic material.

I focused on counting those fine little vertical and horizontal lines. Their repetition helped to calm my nerves. That was always one of my go-to tricks when I felt overwhelmed in any situation. I would look for repeating architectural or design elements that I could just count over and over, boring, predictable, neutral, safe—like the joint lines between hardwood floor planks, the mortar between bricks, the pleats in drapery, and the mullions in a window. Something about counting those repeating elements calmed my nerves and stemmed my panic attacks.

So, I just stood there and suspended all sense of space and time and just counted the little lines until I felt calm. Then I proceeded to fill a second trash bag and a third trash bag. And that was enough for the day. Mission accomplished. I was there for about an hour and a half. I couldn't stay there any longer. I had to get out. The stench was unbearable. I tied the bags up, gripped them tightly, and just kicked my way through the piles of trash, ignoring everything to my left and right. I couldn't look at anything. I couldn't take in any of the scenery in my peripheral vision; I had to get out of there. I slammed the door behind me, locked it, and ran to my car.

I sat there in my car and wondered what I had gotten myself into. Feelings of fear and overwhelm washed over me. There was still so much more of this metaphorical elephant to chew and swallow, and I felt like I was getting full. *How much more can I eat? Can I pace something this gigantic? Can I expand to take all this in? God help me.* The contents of this house felt insurmountable, and I felt alone, outnumbered, and out of ideas. I sat in the car and wept as the A/C blasted and cooled the air.

I cried out, "God, help me! What am I doing? I can't keep coming into this house. I hate it. I hate it. I never want to see this place again. What was I thinking? I can't flip this house. That was a horrible idea. Yes, I'll sell it, but I'm going to have to call a junk removal company to clean this place out. Do I settle his debts? What if he owes a fortune? What am I going to do? Please help me. I can't do this on my own! I need help. Please, God, help me. Help me! God, help me!! *Help me*!!!" I was practically begging and pleading; I was blinded by the tears running down my face. I didn't care if all the neighbors saw me sitting there crying in my car. I rubbed my eyes on my shirt sleeve and sniffled. I breathed and swallowed hard. I guzzled some water, cleared my throat, and began to bargain with God.

In a deep and steady voice, I said out loud, "Are you going to face this? Are you going to walk with this pain and fear or run away from it? Are you going to avoid it or take it on? Are you willing to step up and be uncomfortable and do the work of processing this? Or are you going to numb out and go back to your habit of avoidance and fake, superficial perfection? Will you take this on? Will you open your heart to this?? Will you *face this challenge and rise up to meet it or slink away* and go zone out on the internet and be comfortable?"

Tears streamed down my face, and I sat in silence.

The *internal* bargaining and bickering continued, "You are going to have good days and not-so-good days, anyway. Why not take a chance on this all working out in the end? You have faced frustration, anger, pain, guilt, stress, suffering, and the unknown before. You will have to humble yourself and ask for help to get through this. And it will always be provided. Always has and always will. Are you willing to walk this walk? Are you willing to do hard things? You know you can. You have in the past. You can do it again."

I cried and wrestled with my thoughts and fears. I shouted out, "But I don't want to! I don't want to do this anymore! I know I agreed to help him and signed all those legal papers. But I don't want to do this by myself. It's too hard! I have to muster up my courage every day and face this, and it's not getting any easier. How am I going to last and do this?"

When times get hard like this, I think of Oprah. I could hear her talking about her childhood and breaking into her TV career. I could hear her saying to me, "Alexis, you are stronger than you know, child. Stop running. You've been running and avoiding pain your entire life, yet you've still had pain anyway and faced it and thrived. Stand still and stand up for something. Do the right thing, even if it's hard, even if it's scary, even if you don't know what you're doing. You are never alone. God will provide. He will step in when you can't take another step. But you have to step up to the challenge first."

I blurted out, "*But what if it doesn't work?* What if he owes *millions in back taxes and loans*?? *And now it's my problem?*"

I was emotionally spent. I was tired and needed to clear my head. I checked my phone and saw a message from my mom. I hadn't spoken to her since Dad's passing. I braced myself to hear another cold, Carla comment. Her message was a turning point for me and sealed the deal, "Hi, Alexis, Help your father. Show up every day the best you can. You aren't working; Michael is home. You have the time to do it. I will help you. Ups and downs happen. Painful things can give rise to beautiful blessings. I've had a change of heart. I will help you. Call me. Love you, my sweet girl."

I sat in the car and wept. The chains of pride and illusion of aloneness were broken. The tears of their remnants poured out of my eyes and traveled down my cheeks. I felt a welling sense of power and hope filling me. I wiped my eyes on my sleeves and stared at the phone in disbelief. *That actually just happened? My mother just agreed to help me with Dad's affairs.* That was nothing short of a miracle for that woman to put aside her anger and resentment to come to my father's aid. I sat there, momentarily stunned.

My blank gaze was broken by the image of an older couple walking across their front lawn toward me. They were Dad's next-door neighbors. I hadn't met them yet, and it looked like they were coming over to my car. As they walked across the driveway and approached my car window, I wiped my tears away and lowered the window to speak with them. They introduced themselves as Willie and Erma, Alec's next-door neighbors. For the next few months, I would know them as my guardian angels.

Willie was a stocky man with a well-groomed grey beard and mustache that exactly matched his grey hair. He kept his hair trimmed close to his scalp, smelled of Aqua Velva, and his summer uniform was khakis and a golf shirt. He drove a Cadillac and washed and waxed it every Saturday in the driveway. The rest of the time, when it was not in use, he kept it safely tucked under the carport.

Erma was a thin-framed woman with a light-brown complexion and a silky, blonde bob. She always wore a sundress or Bermuda shorts, a polo shirt with matching espadrilles, and a braided, cotton belt. They made a cute couple. I stepped out of the car to extend a handshake and get to know them.

Willie said, "We've seen your car in the driveway and wanted to give our condolences. Alec was a good neighbor and a nice guy. We enjoyed talking with him on Sundays when he was running errands. We hadn't seen him in a while and knew something must have been wrong when we saw the ambulance. We are sorry for your loss and wanted to let you know that we will keep an eye on the property.

We wrote our number and address down on this paper for you to contact us."

I was stunned. Hadn't I just prayed for help? *First, my mom, and now this! Look at God! That was fast!* I thanked them and gave them my cell phone number.

We chatted a bit more, and they invited me to come over for lemonade the next day.

I backed the car out of the driveway, feeling full and surprisingly happy. As I drove down the street, I told myself, "You have a choice to make, right here and now. You either sell this house or walk away from it and let it go to sheriff's sale. If you sell it, there's no telling what you're going to dig up about your dad's finances and his past. Know this; you *will* face whatever surfaces. If you are selling it, turn right and drive directly to Rob's office. If you are walking away from it, turn left, drive home, and never come back here."

I was nearing the T-stop intersection, and a car was driving up behind me. I knew there'd be no going back; I had to decide quickly. *What am I going to do?* I had a glimmer of hope thanks to the unexpected help from my mom and the next-door neighbors. *But what if that was just beginner's luck?* If I chose to help my father and settle his affairs, there was no telling what I'd unearth and have to face. But if I walked away, I'd never know what could have been! Worst of all, how would I ever face myself in the mirror if I didn't at least *try* to help my dad? I essentially gave him my word when I signed those papers.

The moment had come. I was at the stop sign and had to decide.

I prayed, "God, help *me*. What am I supposed to do with this house? God, if this is NOT for me, please close this door in a way that I can never open. If this is for me, *please* show me the way and open the door in a way that no one can ever close."

The car behind me was quickly approaching. It was now or never; I had to decide. It felt gut-wrenching. It was time to make a move. No more thinking. Time to either leap in faith or rot in fear. My inner voice shouted, *"Do it!"*

I obeyed, put my blinker on, and turned right. My armpits were tingling with sweat, and my palms were sweaty and shaking. But I did it. The decision was made in that swift, holy instant, and I never looked back. My courage was growing and my glimmer of hope was giving rise to faith.

CHAPTER 19

I decided to clean up the house and sell it as is. I could feel my excitement mounting as I drove to Rob's Chalfont office. I hadn't worked with him since he sold Michael and me our first house in Glenside seventeen years ago. I called him on the drive to his office, and he was available to see me immediately.

His secretary greeted me at the door, and I sipped on a lemon water while I waited for him. The real estate office was open-concept, with a couple of moveable dividers separating the space. There were three, glass-walled offices and a conference room behind the reception station. The spaciousness reminded me of a car dealership showroom. Rob came out of his office to greet me. He hadn't changed after all these years. He was tall, dark, and handsome with a dazzling smile, a prominent chin, and a deep dimple in his left cheek. His black hair had a few more greys than I remembered, but it was still thick as ever. He wore tan khakis and a navy, polo shirt with his REMAX™ logo embroidered on the chest.

Before leading me to his office, he greeted me with the standard issue sympathies, "Alexis, it's so good to see you; I wish it was under more pleasant circumstances. My condolences to you and Michael. Thank you for choosing to work with me. What have you decided? Did you watch the video?"

I replied, "Thanks, Rob; I appreciate your help at a time like this. I did watch the video. Thank you, it was a real eye-opener. After giving it thought and consideration, I've decided not to flip the house. I'd like to sell it as is, once I clear out the clutter and furnishings."

In the privacy of his office, I showed him photos of the house's interior and exterior. I gave him the home address and a set of keys. He gave me a list of things to consider and tasks to take care of. My memory is fuzzy, but I think I signed some papers. I told him my goal was to quickly sell the house in the fall to a person who would transform that hovel into a lovely home. I envisioned the fully renovated house getting a fresh start with a new family who would put down roots and create beautiful memories that blotted out the wretched, gruesome past.

After we talked, Rob introduced me to Harry Cohen, who rep-resented the legal leg of the REMAX™ team. Harry was a short, thin man with pale skin, kind, brown eyes, and dark, wavy hair. He walked briskly and talked fast. He was quick with a smile and looked very intellectual in his tortoise-shell glasses and business suit. I had never retained a lawyer and trusted Harry implicitly to help and guide me. I had no idea how to handle Dad's affairs. At this point, the cost didn't even matter. I needed the help.

They say ignorance is bliss, and this is a prime example of just that. I was blissfully ignorant of what I was signing up for. Little did I know it at the time, but Harry would be in constant communication with me for the next several years as I navigated Dad's estate, taxes, and business. I met with Harry in the large conference room and explained what I knew to date about my father's property being on the sheriff's-sale list and the house's condition. I also explained that the house's title was under the business name, not my father's, which didn't faze him in the least.

We set up a time to meet later in the week so he could review the legal documents I had co-signed with my father. Harry talked me through the process of contacting the county to settle the lien on the property and prevent the sheriff's sale. When I left the meeting with him, I had a laundry list of things to do: sort mail, find the life insurance policy, get copies of the death certificate, track down any and all bank accounts and investments, and look for files on Dad's computer. The list went on and on and felt daunting. As if that wasn't enough, he also wanted me to keep a log of all miles driven and expenses incurred while conducting matters related to the estate or Dad's company. I took in all this information and felt the overwhelm mounting. Dad had only been declared dead three days ago, and this is what I was doing!

There was no time to lay in bed and mourn. No time to sit and process what had happened. The show had to go on, and I was the one leading it. I had to process my grief in segments. I still usually cried in the car or the shower. I didn't know what else to do. I still needed to finish planning the memorial service and had less than a week to get that together, notify friends and family, and find a venue for lunch. What a mess!

I had no idea who to contact to arrange a military burial in the military cemetery where my grandfather and grandmother were buried. Luckily, I could rely on Michael to handle that. I was depending on him to know what government agency to contact to request this kind of burial. I was grateful to have this task taken off my plate because I still needed to track down Dad's primary healthcare provider, cancel Meals-On-Wheels and find someone to mow the lawn. I was on a mission to accomplish these tasks and wrap everything up as quickly as possible.

I posted the memorial service on Facebook, and my mom graciously volunteered to call family members. The following week, I hosted a small memorial service and luncheon. It was a lovely tribute to my dad; only my childhood friends and my mom's side of the family were in attendance. I had no contact information for Dad's cousins in California, and I wasn't able to track down his older sister, my Aunt Vicks. I wish I could have found her, at least; maybe she could have shed light on what happened to my father.

Michael took care of the military burial. It took several weeks to get Dad's military service records from the National Archives. Michael worked with the funeral home director to take care of everything and see to it that Dad would be buried with military honors.

Throughout the remainder of June and most of July, I made trips to the house on Mondays, Wednesdays, and Fridays. It didn't seem that overwhelming with this newfound sense of purpose. Every day, I'd don my work clothes and gloves and lock myself in the house for a couple of hours in the early morning before it got too hot and smelly in the house. I'd bring home two to three 30-gallon trash bags full of mail. I'd let the sealed bags sit in the garage overnight, to help kill off any crawling critters that might have hitched a ride on the bags. Then I'd start the process of sorting, discarding, and actioning on Tuesdays and Thursdays.

As I gathered and sorted, pile by pile, paper by paper, my heart was being challenged and changed. Over time, my grief was beginning to transform into a bittersweet heartache. I missed my dad, and I wanted to be free of this burden. My nights and weekends were for recuperating, recharging with family, and following up on emails from Harry or Rob.

Due to the large volume of mail that I was bringing home, I set up a makeshift sorting station in my three-car garage. Michael was a good sport about parking outside. One table was for sorting through the contents of incoming boxes and trash bags; there was a keep pile and trash pile on that table. Once I confirmed an item was trash, I tossed it directly into a large trash can placed next to the table. The keep pile was later sorted further and placed into actionable piles on the second table.

So far, the piles on the second table consisted of bills to pay ASAP, bills to pay later, documents to investigate further, accounts to close, subscriptions to cancel, and keepsakes. Mom's purse and the family Bible were some of the keepsakes. I placed her purse on the doorknob of my office. I saw it every time I walked up the stairs, and it made me smile and think of fond, family memories. I placed the Bible in the office closet along with a box of family photos I found on one of my day trips to the Bristol house. I kept a notepad handy to write down the names and numbers of utility companies, cell phone plans, credit card companies, etc.

Thankfully, the life insurance bill was in one of the first piles I tackled, and Dad had paid the balance back in May. Thank God! That gave me $15,000 to work with to apply to any of his outstanding debts and his funeral service. This was a major victory and put wind in my sails. I was able to use this money to pay off the $1,500 owed to the township and save the house from going to sheriff's sale.

I used the remaining money to pay the funeral expenses and chip away at his smaller debts. The cell phone, cable, credit card, and ambulance bills were easy to pay off and close. However, the deeper I dug into my dad's paper trail of debt, the more alarmed I became. I recalled that at every family gathering, he would brag about his investments, his bars of gold, and the day trading he was doing. Yet, when I contacted Fidelity, he only had $0.01 in a Fidelity money market account. When they cross-referenced their accounts with his social security number and business EIN, no other accounts were found.

I called every major investment house I could think of, but none had accounts in his name or business name. That led me to conclude that must have lied the entire time about his lucrative investments and day trading. Or maybe he lost it all? Aside from his house, he had about $3,000 to his name when he passed; I wished he was still alive and able to deal with this.

I had never called so many customer service helplines in my life. My heart went out to people on the other end of the line. I could only imagine the number of irate customers they dealt with regularly. I vowed that I would only call when I was in a pleasant mood with an optimistic and grateful attitude. My goal was to be grateful for their help and to convey kindness. The majority of the customer service representatives I spoke with were an absolute pleasure to work with. Nearly all of them became instantly sympathetic when I explained that I was the executrix calling on behalf of my father, who had passed on Father's Day.

All I had to do was send a copy of the death certificate, and most companies would simply erase the debt and close out the account, no questions asked. The electric company was not so accommodating. Perhaps it was because he owed *a whopping $17,000?* My hopes were dashed when I opened that bill and saw the balance owed. I wondered how I was going to get them to close the account and forgive the debt because I didn't have that kind of money! I wasn't eating or sleeping right; my mind just raced, and my heart ached. I tried to carry on, but when grief stopped me in my tracks, I'd stop and grieve and then keep going when I felt better.

While trying to navigate my new role of executrix, I was still grieving my father and receiving condolences from friends and families. Truthfully, I was exhausted from it all: the calls, DMs, text messages, casseroles, fruit baskets, and floral arrangements coming to the house. It was overwhelming. I was trying to process my grief, deal with the funeral, clean out the Bristol house, and close out his debts. It was like salt being poured into my wounds every time someone asked me what had happened or how I was managing.

Even if I gave them a canned response with vague details of his death, in my mind's eye, I was still reliving the gory events. I appreciated their concern, but I was going to crack if I had to tell one more person about Dad or elaborate on how I was feeling and how I was handling things. I wish I could have just given a onetime press release that was recorded and disseminated to everyone. Then I'd be done with explaining and reliving hell.

As the days passed, I shortened the story and left out a lot of the nitty-gritty details. I simply said that he had been privately battling cancer for quite some time and passed away peacefully in his sleep. Done. End of story. Protecting my peace of mind was paramount.

CHAPTER 20

July brought more uncertainty and closure. I was becoming an expert at walking the line between these two dualities. As I sorted and read through Dad's mail, I was learning more about him than I ever knew when he was alive. I had gone through half the piles of mail and personal items in his bedroom and planned to be finished collecting, sorting, and actioning the remaining piles by the end of July. I'd then move on to the rest of the house and hire a junk hauling service to clear out the remaining contents by the end of August.

After talking with Rob, early September would be a great time to list the house. That was the goal that would sustain me through this chaotic, bittersweet period.

Today was a hazy, hot, and humid Tuesday, and I'd been placed on hold with the electric company for over fifteen minutes. The customer service representative was threatening to send the account to collections if I didn't pay the $17,000 balance today.

I didn't qualify for a payment arrangement because the account balance was greater than $3,000. I also didn't qualify for a twenty-one-day due date extension because Dad had apparently defaulted on a prior due date extension in the past twelve months. As a last resort, I mustered an ounce of courage and a drop of faith and asked to speak to a supervisor. I was doing my best to remain positive and hopeful as the elevator music wafted from the telephone receiver. I silently prayed to God and asked that this debt be erased, and the account be closed free and clear.

I was about to lose faith and hang up when the music stopped, and a woman named Rosanne came on the line. She spoke curtly and gave me one option, "In order for us to close out your father's account, you will need to open a new account in your name. We can do this over the phone right now if you're in agreement. This will involve us turning off the power to the 6965 Winder Drive, Bristol, PA residence. It will take approximately three days to turn the power back on in your name. Mail the following four documents to my attention: an original copy of your father's death certificate with the raised seal, a copy of his most recent electric bill, a copy of the Certificate of Grant of Letters, and a copy of your valid PA driver's license. It will take several weeks to review your father's account and come to a decision. Are you interested in this option?"

I was trying to feverishly jot all this down as she spoke and stopped writing to quickly reply, "Yes, thank you for your help, Rosanne. I definitely want to use this option."

She replied, "Good; as I said, it will take several weeks to review the claim. Please take down this number, claim number 566Z-PTM. Please reference this when calling me. My direct extension is 5369. My full name is Rosanne Mendez. Please mail the paperwork to my attention at Customer Solution Center, 9308 Market Street, Philadelphia, PA 19103. Once I receive it, I will need several weeks to review the case. I recommend calling me back the second week in August. Reference the claim number. Are there any further questions?"

I replied, "No, you've been very helpful. I will get an original copy of his death certificate, his most recent electric bill, the Certificate of Grant of Letters, and a copy of my driver's license to you ASAP. Again, thank you for your help. I will call you the second week in August."

We said our goodbyes, and I literally leaped out of my chair with joy! I knew it was no guarantee, but this was a most promising turn of events. I was hopeful the $17,000 debt would be pardoned. I gathered the required documents and said a little prayer as I sealed them in a manila envelope. This was the last debt to settle, aside from any state or federal taxes owed. I was meeting with Harry soon to discuss Dad's personal and corporate taxes. I'd been avoiding that conversation and pushed it out of my head just as quickly as it appeared.

I decided to take the next couple of days off and head to the shore to celebrate this small victory, clear my head, and recharge. A dear friend of mine, Bev, offered me her Ocean City, NJ, shore house anytime I needed to get away for a few days. She and her family were in Europe for the summer, and she wasn't accepting any renters this year. I decided to take her up on the offer and planned to stay until Sunday if her beach house was available.

After a quick text message to her, she replied it was and texted me the address, key code, and photos of the house with a note about the outside shower. I'd have the place to myself, and it was a couple of houses away from the beach. Talk about heaven. I could walk to the beach and be there in a couple of minutes. Michael was able to work from home, and I'd have a couple of days away from this mess to recharge and regroup. This day just kept getting better and better.

As I packed my bags that night, I hesitated about what swimsuits to bring. I had been ashamed of my post-baby belly for the past six years. Arianna was a big baby, and after giving birth to her, I never bounced back the way I did with my firstborn, Chad. I considered bringing only one-pieces and then I thought of Dad. I thought, *"He's dead, Alexis, and can't go to the beach. You're alive. Who cares what your belly looks like? Who cares if your midsection hasn't seen the light of day in over six years? Do not waste this one precious life of yours."* I packed my bikinis and didn't bring a single one-piece. I was all in. I was determined to live my life to the fullest going forward.

I barely slept a wink that night. For once, I tossed and turned out of excitement instead of grief and anxiety. I had breakfast with the kids, dropped the packet in the mail for the electric company, and was on the highway headed for the shore at 10 a.m. My toes would be in the sand by noon. On the drive down, I sang along with all my favorite songs and stopped at the grocery store to stock the fridge. Bev had a gorgeous, newly renovated, two-story bungalow on North Street with off-street parking. The bungalow was clad in white siding with brick accents. The front porch and second-story balcony were shaded by navy- and white-striped awnings. As I walked up the front steps onto the porch, I welcomed the shady respite and cool breeze from the ceiling fan that was softly whirring. Deep-cushioned, wicker chairs were arranged on the porch, along with a coffee table with books and board games. I was looking forward to sitting on the porch at night, listening to the ocean waves.

When I stepped inside, I was greeted by an understated, chic, beach decor, pale, grey walls, and white, oak floors. I was in heaven. I exhaled deeply, dropped my suitcase, and walked around, taking in the sights. The front door opened directly into the living room, which flowed into the dining room, and the kitchen and mudroom were directly beyond the dining room. The interior architecture was Craftsman Style, and soft, pale-tan, jute area rugs were underfoot in the living room, dining room, and each upstairs bedroom. All the windows had a light-tan bamboo shade or a textured, light-tan blackout roller shade, flanked by billowy, white curtains, hung from silver rods.

The walls were a warm gray, and the ocean-themed artwork throughout the house was commissioned from a local artist. The living room had seating for a crowd with a large, welcoming white slip-covered sectional. The accent chairs were just as deep and inviting and were slip-covered in a pale blue and white classic gingham pattern. The coffee table, side tables, and lamps were white. The adjacent dining room had a beautiful, white, oak, farmhouse dining table and eight, white, slip-covered, parsons-style dining chairs.

The kitchen had white cabinets, silver drawer pulls, and Carrara marble counters. There was a deep farmhouse sink with a window above, overlooking the neighbor's yard. The center island was a contrasting navy blue with the matching Carrara marble counter. Three bedrooms upstairs all had white, wrought-iron beds, pale-grey coverlets, a sea of fluffy, navy and white ticking pillows, and white matelassé coverlets that were neatly folded at the foot of each. The master and hall baths were both marble-clad floors, and walls with floating, wall-mounted, navy, double vanities. *What a sight to behold.* I flung myself on the master bed and stared up at the white ceiling fan as it slowly spun and wafted soft breezes upon my skin.

I wished I could stay there forever. I imagined that my days would consist of waking at 8 am, meditating, praying, reciting positive body affirmations, calling the kids and Michael, getting dressed, having a hard-boiled egg, packing a snack, grabbing my beach gear, and heading to the beach by 10 a.m., where I would stay for hours letting the salt water wash away my cares allowing me to happily frolic in the water and people-watch. That would be followed by a salad for dinner, reading on the porch, chatting with the neighbors passing by, and retiring to bed by 9 p.m. as the salty, cool air and the sound of ocean waves lulled me to sleep each night.

What actually happened most days was that I cried myself to sleep at night, slept in until noon, and subsisted on pizza, trail mix, apples, and vegan protein shakes. Hitting the beach was harder than I thought. I wrestled with my fears every morning and struggled to overcome my self-doubts as I stared at myself in the mirror and debated whether I was setting foot outside in a bikini. Day one was the hardest. My stomach was so pale, and the skin around my navel was saggy and flabby.

I did my best to hold my stomach in, but no matter which way I turned in the full mirror, my stomach was a saggy mess. I almost caved and didn't go to the beach. I vowed to start doing core exercises that night. During the internal struggle, I was reminded of the promise I made to myself, to live my life to the fullest. I needed to get over the doubts in my head and push through the fear and self-consciousness. I mustered the courage to walk down to the beach with my coverup on. I sat on the beach chair for nearly fifteen minutes that first day, roasting in the sun, before I finally said out loud to myself, "This is ridiculous; no one else is thinking about your stomach. Just do it." I psyched myself up and said, "You're gonna go there in three, two, one; let's go!"

One arm slid out of the coverup; then, the other arm slid out. The countdown helped me to push past my resistance and do it scared, armed with nothing more than an ounce of courage and a drop of faith. I shed my coverup, rose from the beach chair, and walked towards the surf. Fear was losing its grip on me with every step I took. As I walked, I could feel my courage, determination, and self-assurance mounting. At this moment, fear was no longer running the show. I was creating my destiny through the lens of courage!

The air on my stomach was such a foreign feeling! My stomach hadn't seen the light of day or felt a breeze for over six years. I bravely walked to the water and stepped into the surf. I was practically giddy about my accomplishment! I looked around at the other beachgoers frolicking in the water, and sure enough, nobody was looking at me or my stomach. I was so glad I faced this fear and overcame it!

The cold water was a jolt to my senses as my feet sank into the sand and the water splashed around my ankles. I acclimated to the cold and cautiously walked in further, feeling my way across the sea-shell-strewn ocean floor. I went waist high and started feeling my defenses drop and my sense of ease rise. I hopped the waves and played in the water for a while. I cried in the salt water, letting my tears become one with the vast, salty sea surrounding me. I surrendered all cares, swam farther out to about shoulder level, and let the waves carry me as I floated and swam. It was cathartic.

Getting out of the water spiked my anxiety again. *Now people would see me!* I'd be facing all the people sitting on the sand looking out at the waves. I wanted to run and hide, but I couldn't. I had to get back to my towel and reapply my sunscreen. I did my best to hold my breath and suck in my stomach as tightly as possible, but it was no use. I couldn't hold my breath all the way back to my chair. I exhaled and let my stomach do whatever it liked, and I was fine with that. In that moment of surrender, it was as if my stomach said "thank you" to me and was pleased with my increasing acceptance and appreciation of my body for what it was in that season.

Day by day, I overcame more anxiety, and it became easier and easier to don my bikini and strut my stuff. It was as if I was reborn in the water. By day four, I was not the same person who had initially stepped into those waves. At this point, I truly didn't give a flying fig anymore about my appearance. I was over the self-consciousness;

there were people on the beach from all walks of life, and all shapes and sizes, living their best lives. And I was one of them!

Facing this fear head-on had sparked something in me. I had challenged one of my biggest fears and won! I vowed to wear bikinis for the rest of my life. No more covering up and hiding, no more bailing on invitations to attend pool parties and beach trips. My dad's death was a wake-up call about my own mortality and the preciousness of life! I refused to waste another minute playing small or being confined by fear. I used my time at the shore house to think deeply about how I wanted to live my life more intentionally. I no longer wanted fear to dictate my actions. I wanted to live from a place of courage, hope, and fun! I was determined to start challenging more of my fears, taking risks, and stepping into uncertainty more with growing faith that it would all work out for the best. It was time to reignite my dreams.

I hated to leave on Sunday; by then, I was actually sleeping soundly and hanging out on the front porch to read and chat with the neighbors. I planned on going to the beach one last time before leaving around 3 p.m. I was packed and ready to hit the beach at 10 a.m. when my cell phone rang. It was Dad's next-door neighbor, Willie. I was standing in the living room staring at the sectional as he spoke, "Good morning, Alexis; I wanted to let you know that a strong, foul odor is coming from your dad's garage. It started on Thursday, and it's gotten worse each day. We can smell it in our house with the windows closed and the A/C on. Is there any way you can come over and look in the garage to see what it is? Maybe a cat or a raccoon died in there or something."

I felt mildly deflated as I sank down into the sectional and replied, "Hi Willie, thanks for keeping an eye on the property and calling me.

I'm so sorry about the smell. I have no idea what it could be. I'm not at home right now, but I'll call my husband, Michael, and see if he can drive over tonight and find out what it is. I'll call you back when I have an answer."

I was not going to let this derail my optimism and my enjoyment; where there's a problem, there's a solution. Michael drove over, and I went to the beach for two hours to forget about my cares. While I was sitting on the beach, Michael called me, "So I found out what the smell was. When the power was temporarily turned off, it obviously cut off power to the fridge your dad had in his garage. I could smell the rotting stench the minute I stepped out of my car. All I had to do was follow my nose to the garage. As the food rotted, it liquefied and gave off gases, which built up pressure. The pressure burst the plastic wraps, blew lids off plastic containers, and burst the freezer and fridge doors wide open. There are rotting liquefied meats bubbling and dripping down the refrigerator shelves and all over the garage floor. The maggot-infested goo took my breath away. There are flies everywhere, and maggots are swimming in the goo."

God bless Michael and his technically detailed status reports. I didn't have the heart to tell him to spare me the gory details. It sounded like a science fair project of epic proportions gone horribly wrong. Michael sprayed down as much as he could with the garden hose. What he couldn't spray out into the yard, he gathered into trash bags and set the trash can at the curb. He left the remaining contents in the fridge and propped several large boxes against the fridge to keep the doors shut. Michael met Willie outside and explained the situation. I planned to call the electric company on Monday to find out when the power would be turned back on. My nerves were shot when I hung up the phone.

I waded out into the ocean and cried. I kept saying to myself, "It's almost over. It's almost over. You can do this. You can do this. You can do this. A little while longer. Keep the faith. The house will sell. Come on. Keep it together. You can do this. It's almost over."

Eventually, the rhythmic rocking of the waves distracted me from my despair and calmed my nerves. I returned to the bungalow in a better frame of mind, packed my things, and said goodbye to Bev's beautiful, beach bungalow. I was dreading Monday. I wept the entire way home.

CHAPTER 21

On Monday, I was back to my diet, which consisted of bite-sized portions of elephant. I started by tackling the electric company; according to customer service, the power would be on by Wednesday. I didn't relish the idea of working in a stifling-hot house for hours, but I drove to Bristol anyway, despite the heatwave. The trashmen had already come through to collect the garbage; thankfully, there was no trace of the foul odor Willie had described. In fact, the hot, summer air smelled fresh.

I planned to open the windows and gather more papers from the bedroom before the mid-day heat became too oppressive. The house felt like an oven when I stepped inside; as I made my way to the back bedroom, I decided to try out the window unit A/C, just to see if there was power. To my surprise, it turned on—*small victory!* The power was back on, and I didn't have to worry about the rotting food in the garage fridge freaking out the neighbors.

I gathered three bags of mail, a briefcase, and some family photos. I noticed the answering machine on Dad's nightstand, the message light was flickering, and I pushed play. It was my Aunt Vicks, Dad's older sister. I had no idea how old the message was, and she didn't leave a phone number. I decided to try and contact her when I got home.

Next to the answering machine, was a business card and a framed dollar bill. I read the business card; it was the name of Dad's liquor store in California. He was listed as the owner, along with his phone number. That card had to be nearly thirty-four years old. If my memory served me right, he closed that liquor store in 1983 and moved back to Philadelphia to repair mom's home, following a minor house fire. He kept that card all this time and had it next to his bed by his water pills, bifocals, and telephone. I bet he never forgot that store or his life in California. I picked up the framed dollar bill and turned the picture frame over. Scrawled on the back in Dad's handwriting was a note, "My first dollar earned at my liquor store, 1980." I hung my head and cried.

I felt so sorry for my father. He left his life in California in 1983 to help my grandmom recover from her house fire on Conlyn Street, and he never returned to the West Coast. He became Mom's care-taker until the day her eyes closed in 2009. I bet he left behind those half-naked women in the photos. It must have crushed him to leave his home in San Jose and shut down his business. He essentially gave up his life and must have numbed out on alcohol and whatever else he could get his hands on to dull the pain of his lost life. She wasn't feeble or helpless. I never understood why he stayed to help her.

I was nine at the time he returned, and I didn't know him at all. Yet my mom dropped me off at my grandmother's house, and I lived there all summer as he repaired the house. I was practically in a state of shock when she dumped my butt off and left me there. I hadn't seen him since I was five, and he occasionally called me once a year. His return was very awkward for me. I assumed he was going to leave us once the house was finished, so I refused to warm up to him and accept his attempts to spend time with me and show me affection and attention.

The night before he planned to return to California, he and Mom had a fight like I'd never heard before in my life. I was in the downstairs bedroom next to the living room where they argued, and I could hear every word, but I don't recall the entire conversation. She sounded mean, and her words sounded like daggers aimed at my dad. I didn't know my grandmother was even capable of being mean. I was her precious "Angel Baby," as she used to call me, and she only spoke to me with love. My dad sounded like he was pleading for his life.

I remember him sounding wounded and sad as he kept repeating, "Oh, Mom, please don't be like this. Please don't do this to me."

When I found Aunt Vicks, I vowed to ask her about that night. I had to know what it meant. What kind of hold did my grandmother have over a grown man, in the prime of his life, to make him leave his life in California and forsake it all to move back home with his perfectly capable mother? He cooked her meals, cleaned her house, and chauffeured her everywhere. He never went back to California. He was practically glued to her side for twenty-six years until the day she died. I had to know why.

On my way out of the house, I passed through the kitchen, and my eyes fell upon a new, small yellow bucket and packet of matching, yellow, rubber gloves. How had I not seen them sitting on the counter after all this time? Seeing them sparked a tinge of remorse. I wondered if these were the bucket and gloves Dad said he'd bought to clean the house in preparation for our Father's Day visit. It was too much for me to handle, and the flood of sad emotions came rushing back. I cried out, "Lord, have mercy on me; he was going to clean his house for us to come over with the kids."

In that moment, I felt like the cruelest, meanest daughter of the year. How many wasted years of not seeing him, being too busy wrapped up in work, school, the kids, and their damn sports. I missed my dad, and now there was no chance of ever seeing him again on this earth. I was second-guessing my decision not to visit him with the kids. Who cared if his house was smelly and cluttered? We could have stayed in the living room and used the bathroom in the basement. I hated this. I began to cry and decided to call it quits for the day.

On the long drive home, I also decided it was time to make a change. I decided to get counseling and attend an Al-Anon meeting. My family did not discuss mental health issues; instead, we shoved our distress under the rug and tried to ignore it. We'd rather limp along through life, destroying everything in our path in the process, instead of addressing issues and getting professional help. Well, this behavior was going to stop with me. If I was going to truly live my life to the fullest, I needed professional help. It petrified me to put myself out there and air my dirty laundry. Our family did not do this; we kept that dirty laundry hidden and put on a happy face. I wanted no part of that behavior anymore. Facing my fears head-on was my new way of showing up for life, and that's exactly what I was going to do.

When I came home, I decided to look through the keepsake pile on the garage sorting table. I read through Dad's old love letters, looked inside the briefcase, and read through the collection of thirty, yellow, Junior Legal Pads that had been strewn throughout his bedroom. The love letters were dated 1983–1984, which coincided with the time he left California to renovate Mom's Conlyn Street house.

The letters were all from a woman named Linda, who sounded upbeat and happy in the first several letters. She was grateful that Dad's mother was safe, and she was excited for the repairs to be finished. She missed him and looked forward to him coming back home to be with her and the family. The last handful of letters from Linda were dated in 1984, and they sounded like she was frustrated and devoid of all hope that he'd return to San Jose. She wanted to know why he hadn't returned her calls or letters. She wanted to know why he was shutting her out of his life.

In her last letter, she mentioned she was selling her San Jose house and driving along the coast in her new motor home. She bid him farewell in that last letter. Enclosed was a photo of her standing at the motor home doorway, waving. Her blond hair was parted down the middle and feathered. She was wearing a pair of blue, terry shorts and a white, tube top. I wept as I read the letters. *I wonder if this was why Dad said he was going to buy a motor home and drive cross-country with a fast woman every time he drunk-dialed my house last year?* I wept for the younger version of me, that little girl who he never took the time to get to know and love. I wept for the younger version of him, whose life and love in California seemed to have been prematurely snuffed out.

In his briefcase were two folders; one had legal papers regarding a patent he filed in the 1980s for a new design for truck cabs. My father was a long-distance truck driver, and apparently, he had an idea that he wanted to patent to add more interior head space to the cab and create a more aerodynamic exterior. The patent application did not appear complete. The paperwork was yet another expression of his unfulfilled dreams, literally tucked away in a tattered briefcase. *I wonder if he read through the papers with regret when he was on his deathbed?*

Why hadn't he ever told me about this patent? The other folder had papers from 1970 about his test scores for a Pennsylvania state trooper position he had applied for. I did remember that story all too well. Dad said he had a perfect test score and did well on his interviews. With his military background as an Air Force veteran, he just knew he was a shoo-in. When he went for the final call-back interview, the secretary prematurely congratulated him on receiving the position. He just knew it was his!

It turned out the runner-up, who had the second highest scores, was a Caucasian man, and the position was given to him—not my father. He always blew it off like it was no big deal when he recounted the story and the discrimination he experienced. However, the fact that he still had those papers in this briefcase almost forty-seven years later, said otherwise. *Sweet Jesus. How many shattered dreams did this man have?* Looking through his personal effects made me feel like I truly never knew my father at all. *Did he go to his grave feeling alone and misunderstood?*

Every one of those Junior Legal Pads was filled with his writing. Some pads contained his business ideas for restaurants; names, menu ideas, and recipes were scribbled on the pages. Other pads had peoples' names and numbers for loans and public relations. Other pads were lists of cars and engine parts. *What did this notepad collection mean to him? Did this man ever act on any of the items listed? Or were these unfulfilled dreams and broken promises to himself? Did the larger part of his reason for living die back in 1983 when he walked away from his life and love in San Jose? Did the rest of him finally catch up when he passed this summer? Was death a welcome relief and a chance to reconnect to lost callings?*

I felt so sorry for my father and all the unrealized dreams he had documented in these piles of paper. It made me shudder when I realized that *I* had my own collection of Junior Legal Pads, yellow Post-it Notes, and journals strewn throughout my office, bedroom, kitchen, family room, and purse. I was forever jotting down ideas and things to act on. Yet I probably only actioned 15 percent of what I'd taken the time to write down. *What am I doing with my life!?* I did not want to become like my father. *Is it already too late? Is my large collection of notepads, journals, and Post-It Notes a sign that I am turning into him!? Are my journal collections going to spiral out of control into full-fledged hoarding? Would I go to my grave deeply in debt, with a broken heart and unfulfilled dreams?*

Tears streamed down my face as I looked around the garage at the piles of papers and trash bags waiting to be sorted. I vowed that my children would never have to face this scenario after I passed. I vowed to live my life to the fullest. I was willing to change and release the familiarity and comfort of my current circumstances. It was time to choose to move with faith instead of standing still in fear. I vowed to act on my hopes and dreams. I vowed to keep more of the promises I made to myself. I vowed to live more by faith than sight. I vowed to be more spontaneous and hopeful. I vowed to start doing the things I'd always been wanting to do but was too scared to try—no more self-defeating thoughts and being my own worst enemy.

I vowed to do exciting things outside my comfort zone—no more playing small or safe. I vowed to love myself better. The spark that was lit in Ocean City ignited into a roaring fire. I spent the rest of the afternoon either on the phone or online looking up events and therapists and filling in my calendar for August and September. It was time to get help and set the wheels of change in motion. I was hopeful that this new attitude would yield results in my life that were better than I could have ever imagined. I wanted to process this experience as best I could instead of coping and hiding my uncomfortable emotions away to be dealt with at some later date.

I decided to truly get my life in order. It was time to start making the most of this silly, little ride we called life. There'd be no more ignoring difficult topics or emotions, putting off my dreams, discrediting my ideas, delaying my delight, or giving an eff what people thought about me. I decided that I would take life by the horns, savor it more, and show up for all of it. The good, the bad, and everything in between, they'd all be lessons for me to learn from and grow. I was going to get out of my own way and let life be easier and more enjoyable. There'd be no more making mountains out of molehills. Because what if, in the end, they were all molehills? I flat-out refused to go to my grave with a broken heart and dreams left in the dark, never to be realized and manifested in the light of day.

It was time to show up for life in a bigger way and take more daring risks. All this grief I'd been carrying was very heavy, and today, I was ready to start bringing it to the surface and shaking it off. The grief had pooled and stagnated in the depths of my soul. It was time to move this energy up and out. It was time to start dancing again. I hadn't danced in months. Yet dancing was like a balm to my soul. It had always been one of my favorite ways to shake off bad days, sadness, and mild depression. For some reason, I had been too busy or too sad to do it as of late.

Keep in mind; I'm no trained dancer. I'm talking about dancing around my kitchen, belting out my favorite tunes with a large, wooden spoon in my hand as the stand-in for a mic! The creative movement was like a breath of fresh air to my heart and soul. As I danced around the house to my favorite club songs and belted out the words, I could feel some of the stagnant, heavy emotions lifting off my heart. As I've told Michel in the past, I don't dance because I'm happy; I'm happy because I danced. And did I dance. I allowed the emotions to surface and be expressed. As I danced, I cried, I laughed, and I wriggled some of my blues away that day. The dancing took me out of my head and into the rhythm of the music. I felt alive!

It was just the reset I needed to power through the rest of the day and start being more intentional with my time on this Earth.

Later that night, I sat at the kitchen island with my planner and made a list of all the things I'd wanted to do for years and had put off because of lame excuses rooted in fear, scarcity, low self-esteem, and societal brainwashing. I started making a checklist of things I was going to accomplish, no matter how silly they sounded. I scrawled on the paper, "August Fear Challenges: monkey bars, French club, yoga class in a midriff-baring sports bra, meditation retreat, Paris, dream interior design job at Jenkins and Pearl Architecture Firm."

I stared back at the list and smiled. I had always wanted to successfully move across the monkey bars since I was a kid, but could never do it. I always dropped to the ground after the second rung! There was a park near me with a playground, and I decided to practice going across the monkey bars every morning until I mastered it. I wanted to sharpen my French-speaking skills, and online apps weren't cutting it. I found a local group online, signed up for a Sunday-meetup French group, and committed to attending three times a month.

I looked up mountain-getaway meditation retreats and discovered an amazing place in the Berkshire mountains. The retreat center was hosting a three-day, September yoga and meditation retreat for all-experience levels with mindful outdoor experiences and nutritious meals. I didn't care what the cost was; I was attending this. I booked a dorm-style, three-person room and decided to go all in and bunk with three complete strangers. I figured if we were all there for the same retreat, we'd have at least one thing in common. I broke a sweat when I clicked submit on the payment, but I didn't care. Come hell or high water, I was going and intended to love every damn minute of the experience. *Done. On to the next. Thank you, Lord.*

I found an Al-Anon at the local Presbyterian church in Downingtown. They held family support group meetings every Tuesday at 11 a.m. *I will attend tomorrow.*

I called my insurance company and researched area therapists online. I ran my fingers down the list of therapists and stopped on the one whose name resonated with my heart and soul. Her name was Kathy Moore, a therapist specializing in Cognitive-Behavioral Therapy. I selected two more as backup, called all three, left a voice-mail for each of them, and only received a response from Kathy's receptionist. I booked my September appointment and proceeded to book out the entire year of therapy on the spot, every Thursday at 10 a.m. Done. That's how I roll when I'm on a mission.

Al-Anon was life changing. I debated getting out of the car and sat in the church parking lot, watching the minutes tick down to 11 a.m. I finally dragged my butt inside and followed the signs to the meeting room. I grabbed some pamphlets from the table in the hall, walked into the small meeting room, and took a seat in the circle of chairs. It was a small group, with only five people, including the facilitator. I think there was a member's creed that everyone spoke before the meeting started. I don't remember. The whole experience felt out-of-body for me.

I introduced myself. People checked in, and when it was my turn to speak, I spilled my guts. Whatever memories surfaced about my dad freely flowed out of me. I don't remember what I said. I was shocked by the responses. Everyone related! I thought I was the only one who had memories and experiences like mine. The granular details and names might have been different, but the members in that group session shared experiences that resonated with mine. My heart was doing somersaults and was swollen with healing love. This was just what I needed. I left that meeting with a piece of my soul healed and never attended another one after that. I had received what I needed. *Done. On to the next. Thank you, Lord.*

The daily morning walks in the park soothed my soul and energized me for the day. I brought Arianna and Chad with me the first day and they taught me how to go across the monkey bars. I swear they grinned from ear to ear the entire time. They were so pumped to be teaching me how to do something. Chad made it look so easy.

I studied his technique and noted how he swung his body as he moved his arms to grip each subsequent bar. The swinging gave him momentum to get across the bars. I couldn't even advance to one bar, with each of them holding up one of my legs. LOL. Nonetheless, I showed up every day and practiced till my developing blisters started throbbing. I did not give a crap who saw me practicing. Yes, I was a grown-ass woman practicing how to go across a child's monkey bar set on a playground. But I tell you what, when I successfully crossed those monkey bars three weeks later, you couldn't tell me nothing!! *Done. On to the next. Thank you, Lord.*

I signed up for an outdoor yoga class at the local farm-to-table restaurant and brought Arianna with me for moral support. I hadn't allowed myself to attend a yoga class in over twenty years. For some reason, I had developed the limiting belief that Black girls with flabby bodies like mine didn't do yoga. I had my midriff-bearing sports bra on as I sat in the car rooted in fear, wrestling with my thoughts, watching the minutes tick by until the class started.

Arianna wanted to know what the holdup was. There was no way I was going to tell my impressionable, young daughter that I was too ashamed of my body to step outside and do yoga. I wanted to be a strong role model for her. I mustered everything I had, which amounted to nothing more than an ounce of courage and a drop of faith. I don't remember what happened next; I truly was out of my mind and body. The air felt so foreign on my stomach, which hadn't seen the light of day in almost a decade, minus last week's shore trip! I flowed through the yoga positions effortlessly, and I was in my zone.

My heart was swollen with so much healing love and gratitude. It was truly a Zen-like experience being outside with a view of the rolling hills of the Chester County countryside as I moved through the positions and released more of that stagnant grief. The class was about an hour, and I walked away in shock. I looked down at my body and breathed a sigh of relief. I was still alive; this experience hadn't killed me! No one laughed at me. No one pointed at my flabby belly. *What the hell!* For twenty years, I avoided *this*? I signed up for every outdoor class they offered for the remainder of the summer season and bought midriff-bearing sports bras in every color and style I could find. I practically floated back to the car with Arianna. I even made a video of the experience and posted it to the 'Gram. *Done. On to the next. Thank you, Lord.*

I attended one French meetup and was way out of my comfort zone. The café was run by a French native, and the croissants were amazing. The meetup group was a bunch of French expats, and I was no match for their conversational skills. I said a few words and just listened and tried to follow along as best I could. I stayed for about thirty minutes, then split. That was too much, too soon. But I did it! I signed up for a private, online, French tutor the minute I got back to my car. I also earmarked hotels for a trip to Paris and vowed to visit there in the spring of 2019. *Done. On to the next. Thank you, Lord.*

I started fixing up my resume and applied to Jenkins and Pearl Architecture Firm a few weeks later. They promptly replied with an email stating that my cover letter, resume, and work sample would be kept on file and reviewed when a position opened up. That was a good start. *Done. On to the next. Thank you, Lord.*

Last, but not least, I plucked up an ounce of courage and a drop of faith to call Rosanne about the outstanding electric bill. She answered immediately when I called her extension. I provided my case number and prayed for a positive response from her. Then she uttered some of the sweetest words I heard during this chapter of my life, "The account for Alec Miller has been closed, and the case associated with his account is also closed."

I blinked in silence. *Does this mean what I think it does? Is the debt forgiven?* I blurted out, "Thank you, Rosanne. Does this mean the debt is forgiven?"

She curtly replied, "Yes."

I exhaled a large sigh of relief and exclaimed, "Thank you! This means so much to me! You have no idea. I truly appreciate it. You've been so helpful. I appreciate you. Have a wonderful day."

We said our goodbyes, and I fell out of the dining chair onto my knees, bowed my head to the floor, and just sobbed and laughed. I was completely overcome with emotions, feelings of relief, shock, gratitude, satisfaction, exhaustion, and pure bliss mingled in my soul. Just like that, $17,000 worth of debt was erased! All my father's debts were now settled. He was free! I was free! This leg of the journey was officially finished. I had prayed for this moment and dared to believe it was possible. I was ignited with pure joy and a growing sense of blind faith that sustained me through many rough patches ahead. I was beginning to believe that despite challenging life events, wonderful outcomes were possible.

In between all these courage-building fear challenges, I made my routine trips to the Bristol house. Setting out to achieve these challenges filled my cup and gave me the resolve to finish cleaning out Dad's house. I cleared out all the papers in the bedroom. I rummaged through all his clothes and looked in every nook and cranny for hidden money, drugs, and weapons. I found nothing. The hall bathroom was practically knee high with empty beer cans and empty whisky bottles. The toilet was clogged, and the medicine cabinet was empty.

The kitchen just had crusty old dirty dishes and dead bugs. Thank God for that fogger. There was nothing in the dining room but piles and piles of empty beer cases. I brought the Mid-Century Modern console home from the living room and refinished it. It now has a place of honor in my home. I searched the files on the upstairs computer and found nothing but porn. I wiped the memory clean. There was nothing else of value upstairs: just old office furniture and an old bedroom set. There was nothing in the finished basement. The garage was Michael's domain; I was not setting foot in there after the exploding fridge incident. He cleared out all the tools, and we donated them to our local Habitat for Humanity.

After nearly three months of committing to relentlessly facing my fears daily and fighting through resistance, I finally made headway in clearing out all of Dad's clutter and sorted and sifted through all of his mail and personal belongings in the bedroom. Despite the frustration, grief, dread, and exhaustion, I consistently made the long and lonely drive to Bristol, stepped foot into that house, entered that bedroom, gathered those papers, and brought them home to sort. I closed out accounts, waited on hold for hours to speak with customer service representatives, and logged every mile and every expense.

I tracked down everything Harry asked me to and did my best to settle every outstanding debt my father had. The process was not pretty by a long shot, but it was effective. Every small and large act of courage boosted my confidence and expanded my capacity to take on increasingly larger challenges with ease. My grief was still there, but it was as if I had a larger capacity to contain it and sit with it without being all-consumed by it. I was ready for the next step. It was time to hire a company to clean out the contents of the house.

It was nearing the end of August, and I was ready to close this chapter, right on target as planned. I didn't think I'd ever see this day, but it came. My mom was there to help me, just like she promised. It took three large trucks to empty that tiny, 1200-square-foot Cape Cod, but it was finished in one day. I felt like my life was turning a corner and getting better. *Thank you, Lord.*

I also buried Dad at the end of August. His ashes were interred with my grandmother and grandfather at Beverly National Cemetery, in Beverly, New Jersey. The cemetery was minutes from Dad's Bristol house, practically just over the bridge. It was a small ceremony; just Michael, the kids, and I were in attendance. I was not able to locate Aunt Dix. Dad was buried with military honors by an Airforce Color Guard Team. He received a 21-gun salute. An airman played taps on the trumpet, and the American flag was ceremoniously folded and presented to me. *Done. On to the next. Thank you, Lord.*

CHAPTER 22

September felt like a fresh start. My grief was subsiding, the house was listed, the debts were settled, and the only thing left to do was check on the state and federal taxes. I felt like I had a new lease on life as I made the long, scenic drive through the Berkshire mountains to attend the yoga retreat. I was anxious about sharing a room with three strangers and was second-guessing myself as I wove through the winding roads and towering evergreens. This marked the third time in twenty years I was practicing yoga in public. *What would happen if everyone at the retreat was a master-level yogi? What was I getting myself into?* I was starting to think this was a ridiculous idea, but the trip was paid for, and I was not turning around after driving nearly 5 hours to get there.

Words can't begin to describe the experience. The wellness center was nestled in the woods about 5 miles off the beaten path. The winding road leading to the main buildings was flanked by towering, lush evergreens that shaded the road and created a sense of seclusion. Eventually the trees gave way to gently rolling, green hills and a grouping of several, brick buildings, that overlooked a lake and a lush forest. The lobby was grand and welcoming, with plush chairs, fresh flowers, and friendly receptionists. The space was bustling with attendees who were checking in and out. I checked in and made my way across the beautiful facility toward my room.

I noted the beautiful cafeteria; it was huge, and the buffet menu listed on the entry door sounded delicious. I appreciated the fact that all meals were silent meals. That immediately dropped my anxiety level down from a ten to a two. I didn't have to worry about where I sat or who I sat with for meals because there was no talking! The introvert in me loved this arrangement.

As I walked through the halls toward my room, I hoped that my roommates would be nice. I prayed that we'd get along well and maybe be lifelong friends. And just like that, when the student is ready to learn, the teacher appears. My teacher came in the form of Virginia Fernandez-Cuesta, and she was one of my roommates. Virginia was setting up her things on the top bunk closest to the door when I walked into the spacious, sparsely decorated room filled with two sets of bunk beds. She turned and greeted me with a dazzling smile and glittering, brown eyes. She tossed her long, brown hair to the side and said, "Hi, I'm Virginia. You must be one of my room-mates!" And the rest is history.

She and I were like kindred spirits, and we connected instantly. We talked and shared things about ourselves as if we had known each other for years and not hours. She lived in Virginia and was a loan officer for high-end residential real estate. She worked with interior designers and builders all the time. She was burnt out from work and was a recovering alcoholic. She was enrolled in the same yoga program as me.

The other two roommates were enrolled in different programs and our paths never really crossed except at nighttime to chat about our day and go to bed. I was on the top bunk, too, and the bed was the most comfortable mattress I'd ever slept on in my entire life. Our room overlooked the crystal-clear lake and the lush forest beyond. It was perfection.

When I told her about my dad and the recent events leading up to this trip, she had experienced a similar situation with her father two years prior. As we sat in Adirondacks overlooking the lake, I said to her, "Virginia, I just don't understand how my father could live in that hovel and sleep surrounded by trash. It was like he thought *he* was trash or something. Was he really a hoarder? If he was, why did he keep his keepsakes and photos of my family and me clean and neatly displayed in places of honor? Almost like a shrine. He did the same thing with the family Bible, boxes of old photos, and my grandmom's personal effects. I just don't get it! Why did he care so much about those things, yet neglect his own needs and lay down with trash? He died alone in a pile of garbage, of his own choosing! I just don't get it. Why wasn't his whole house a mess? He had rooms dedicated to his trash, and other rooms were pristine. The rooms dedicated to trash were the rooms he lived in."

Virginia looked out across the lake as she spoke, "I don't know why people do what they do. Listen to me, Momma. I wasn't a hoarder, but when I was in the depths of depression and tried to kill myself, I thought I was trash. Actually, less than trash, more like scum. During that time, the *only* thing that kept me alive and going was taking care of my kids. I may have looked like death warmed over, but out of my love for my kids, I dragged my sorry self out of bed and made sure they were fed and cared for. I may have thought I was scum, but they were precious to me, and I was going to show up for them and make sure they had what they needed, left the house looking good, and felt loved. I had none of that love, care, and respect for *myself*, but I had it to give to my children. Consider that a testament to how much your father truly *loved* you and your children. He kept his most prized possessions safe and sound, close to him, but not sullied by the wretched physical manifestation of his mental disorder."

She paused to wipe tears from her eyes and looked me square in the face to say, "You know, Momma, his bedroom was the epicenter of his biggest struggles, biggest regrets, and biggest loves. The love letters and the business card from the bar he owned. Your photos and the gifts you gave him. The artwork your children drew for him. His mother's Bible. His dad's military awards. His truck patent paperwork. That framed dollar bill. The drugs, the going-out clothes that he kept clean for trips to your house. All of it meant something to him. You meant something to him."

Tears streamed down my face as I spoke, "That is beautiful, Virginia; thank you for sharing your story, and it makes sense the way you explain it. But why didn't he care about his own life? Why did he think so lowly of himself? Why didn't he ask me for help? Why didn't he tell me what was going on sooner before the house began to look like a pig pen?"

Virginia shook her head, "Momma, I don't know. What I do know is that people tend to withhold the full truth from others for a variety of reasons. Mostly due to insecurity and fear of being ridiculed, or worse yet, outcast. They keep lies, instead of telling the truth and being set free. The lies we keep can be to save face and protect self-image or to protect loved ones. We avoid the messy, ugly, uncomfortable truth with pretty, little lies. The weight of that deceit takes a heavy toll. It always does more harm than good, in my opinion. I lied to myself and others for years. It drove me mad and nearly cost me my life. I was institutionalized for several months. I take medicine now and go to therapy weekly to work through my demons. I left my ex and take the time to pour into myself at retreats like this. Most of all, I tell the truth—to myself and to others. It truly has set me free. I am now married to a good man, and I am rebuilding my life. Keep talking about what you're going through. Go to counseling. Process this. Don't shove it down and try to fake being happy, Momma. You are doing good to come here, and you are doing good to talk to me and get things off your chest and cry it out. You are doing it, Momma."

I went to the retreat looking for a transformation and a fresh start. I wanted to challenge my fears and step into courage. And I got just that. I was more transformed by my talks with Virginia than by the yoga and massages. Having Virginia as a confidant, sounding board, and source of support was priceless. As we walked along the lake one final time before departing, I told her about the condition of the Bristol house and my concerns about it selling.

She quickly replied, "Momma, you just have to leap and trust. Do this. Sell the house. Trust me; there will be the perfect buyer for it. It could be a wild ride that puts you so far out of your comfort zone, Momma! But, so what? See what happens, Momma! Don't be like me and stress about stuff that never happens, anyway. Trust that it will all work out. And you've got me now; I will help you!"

As we said our goodbyes in the parking lot, we exchanged numbers and committed to talking every week. For the last five years and counting, we've done just that.

Her first text to me read, "Hello, beautiful Alexis, I am so infinitely grateful for being your new friend. Remember, it's not what happened; it's what you do afterward and what you make of it. Make it work to your advantage, Momma. Love and besitos, Virginia."

CHAPTER 23

September ushered in a new season of my life. I began seeing my therapist, Kathy. I had never been to a therapist before and had no idea what to expect. I checked into my appointment, equipped with an ounce of courage and a drop of faith. I prayed that she was a good fit for me. As we greeted each other at the reception station, I noticed that she was a short-statured woman with long, wavy, grey hair and a welcoming smile that made me feel at home. Her corner office was dimly lit and overlooked the main drive into the medical office complex. The room was filled with a desk, her chair, a comfy, plush, three-seater sofa, and a side table topped with a box of tissues.

As we sat in her cozy, corner office, she asked me why I came and what I was hoping to get from the sessions. I unloaded the events leading up to this moment as best I could without crying. I remember saying, "He was a hoarder, and he slept nestled alongside his own trash! Anything of importance to him was kept up for safekeeping away from the debris and litter—except himself; it was like he identified himself as having the same value as the very trash he slept in. And I'm afraid that I'm doing the same thing, but in different ways."

I paused to wipe away the tears and continued, "I am tolerating trashy situations. On the surface, my life looks great, but that's just a façade. The truth is, I've accepted trashy dead-end jobs with toxic leadership, trashy money management, trashy sleep habits, trashy time management, trashy boundaries, and trashy inner dialogue because, deep down, I don't believe I'm worthy of more. Somewhere along the way, I picked up the belief that I'm not good enough for better experiences. I haven't suffered enough and struggled enough to earn them. I haven't proven my worthiness enough; I haven't sacrificed enough. I'm not pretty enough; I'm not thin enough; I'm not smart enough; I'm not young enough. I'm not tall enough. The list goes on and on."

I paused to wipe away the tears and continued, "I want to learn how to become accustomed to believing that I already am good enough to receive all the best life has to offer, without thinking the other shoe is going to drop, and it's all going to go to hell. I'm done settling for the best of the bad. I don't think these behaviors are normal, and I don't want them to spiral out of control and leave me ending up like my dad. He had notebooks all over the place filled with ideas that he never acted on. I have Post-It Notes all over my house, filled with ideas I plan to do. I don't want to end up like him. Whatever you can do to help me to think better about myself and live to my fullest potential, I'd really appreciate it."

Kathy was most helpful during our first session and shared that she specialized in helping people overcome anxiety, depression, stress, limiting beliefs, people-pleasing, imposter syndrome, and grief. She also had personal experience with hoarding. Her late father's battle with depression and hoarding had inspired her to dedicate her professional career to helping others overcome and thrive. I breathed a sigh of relief when she said that, and I knew I'd be in good hands. In retrospect, it was nothing short of a miracle that I chose her, of all people. There were well over 25 providers in my area who I could have chosen to see, yet for some reason, I felt compelled to choose her. I thanked God that I had listened to my heart and chosen her.

I continued on with my personal history, "I recently returned from a yoga retreat in the Berkshires, and I swear it felt like I came home as a newer version of myself. I went there for healing and restoration, which happened, but the yoga actually had very little to do with my healing! Companionship changed everything for me. I had no idea I'd make a new friend. She was my roommate, and she was signed up for the same event as me! Talking with Virginia was so natural and effortless. It's like I've known her my entire life, and we just reconnected at the yoga retreat. We've talked once a week since and vowed to continue to do this. It's given me hope that things will start slowly turning around."

I wasn't sure what else to mention and randomly said, "I even dared to dream that my dad's house would be sold by Christmas, and I'd be finished managing his estate in the New Year. The house was listed this month, and some low-ball offers have trickled in. I decided to hold out for between $222,000 and $230,000. In the meantime, the thought of receiving that amount of money in a lump sum is freaking me out. What if I blow it foolishly? What if family comes out of the woodwork and tries to claim it? What if it triggers some tax? I'm scared to handle the money; I've never managed six-figures before."

Kathy briefly touched on money and mentioned my mindset and belief system. I wasn't sure what that meant, but we would cover it in later sessions. She continued, "I don't know why difficult things happen. But I do know that when we decide to embrace them, we have the opportunity to learn from them and develop new skill sets that will be to our advantage in the future. How might you choose to see some of the trials and setbacks you faced as defining moments? I invite you to reflect on any experiences that gave you a deeper gratitude for life, a sense of urgency, or a deeper empathy and compassion for others."

I paused for a moment and replied, "Well, I keep a gratitude journal now. I keep it on my nightstand and make an entry first thing when I wake up and last thing before I go to bed. I savor my breath more and all the little things like sunsets and ice cream. I can see how this could change me for the better, if I let it. I am starting to wake up grateful every day for the breath in my lungs and the opportunity to have another day on this earth. It's a privilege and a blessing that I don't take lightly or for granted anymore. I do my best to take care of my health, mind, body, and soul."

I paused for a moment to blot my tears and continued, "I do my best to savor every moment and let go of labeling persons and experiences as good or bad. Instead, I am trying to remember that they are just fleeting moments in time that will swoosh by in the blink of an eye and be nothing more than a 'was.' My father is now a 'was.' He was here, and now he's gone. All his hopes and dreams lost. I refuse to go out of this world like that. I will NOT go out like that. I want to show up as a woman who doesn't settle for trashy situations. I need practical tools to raise my standards and set boundaries in my relationships. I want to improve my relationship with myself, money, friends, family, work life, my mother, my mother-in-law, my sleep, and my sex life. Please teach me how to get out of my own way, and be my personal best in all these areas, Kathy."

Kathy replied, "From what I see so far, you are capable of displaying great courage in the face of adversity. The very fact that you are here in my office, willing to explore some of the shadowed parts of your inner world and bring them to the light, so to speak, is a prime example. Not many people are willing to do that. Some people choose to be the victim and blame others. It takes a strong person to ask for help. I will help you in any way I can."

I breathed a sigh of relief and felt my shoulders drop. I decided to trust her with the secrets of my soul. It was one of the best decisions I've ever made.

As summer gave way to fall, I continued to both meet with Kathy and talk to Virginia weekly. Three promising offers came in on the house in November, and in December, we received an offer that was in my price range. It was $228,000! We moved fast on it and closed on January 4th. What a great way to welcome in 2018. A pastor was buying the house. He flipped houses on the side, and he and his sons were going to gut the house and flip it. Talk about an answered prayer. He'd be able to do what I didn't have the heart to do. *Thank God.* I had hoped for a smooth closing, and it was, except for one thing.

It turned out that Dad had not filed his corporate taxes for several years. There were no state or federal taxes filed from 2010 to 2017, to be exact. Therefore, the title company would hold $80,000, from the sale of the house, in escrow until I rectified the situation. I would need to file the taxes, pay any monies owed and pay any penalties or late fees before the lien would be removed. Since the house wasn't owned by my father but by his corporation, Navco LLC, this added another layer of complexity to the tax filing process.

I thought I'd be walking away with $200,000 after fees and taxes were taken out. Instead, I left the closing with a $120,000 check in hand. I was practically trembling with all the mixed emotions simultaneously swirling through me. I was proud of myself for overcoming so many hurdles and facing my fears. I was grateful for the swift sale and professional services that Harry and Rob rendered. I was devastated by the news of the $80,000 lien and the unpaid taxes. If that wasn't enough, I'd also have to file the corporate and inheritance taxes for 2018 due to the sale of the house.

I was petrified to be in possession of $120,000. It was surreal to me that an hour ago, I didn't have $120,000, and now, after signing some papers and shaking some hands, I walked out $120,000 richer. I had no intention of cashing the $120,000 check anytime soon. I was actually afraid to go to the bank and deposit it. I needed to talk to my therapist first.

My mom was with me at the closing for support. As soon as the meeting was finished and we were in the car, she blurted out, "I knew it! That dirty, rotten bastard never liked to pay taxes when we were married. He ruined my credit! It took me years to restore it. That's classic Alec for you. Alexis, I bet you never thought to search the title *before* you decided to sell the house. Did you?"

I shook my head.

She replied, "Yes, based on your surprised expression at the closing, I thought not. He burned me years ago, and now he's burned you. I hate to say it, but I told you so, darling girl."

Chills ran down my spine when she said that to me; nothing like a cold, Carla comment to lighten the mood. There was nothing else to say but, "Yep, Mom, looks like you were right. I took a chance, and hopefully, this all works out for the best." Despite my outwardly cheery optimism, on the inside, I was secretly freaking out and wondering what I had just gotten myself into. We went out to lunch afterward, chatted about my kids, and made plans for the weekend.

I met with Harry the next day. He had specific instructions for me to follow. When we met in his office, he was swift and to the point. He reviewed how the filing process typically worked in situations like this. I'd file the federal taxes first using Form 1120. I'd have to file separately for each year from 2010 to 2018. Then I was to file the PA DOR corporate taxes using Form RCT-101, one form for each year spanning 2010–2018. I'd also have to submit a copy of the federal tax forms to the state. My head was spinning from all the information. This meant I'd need to go on a wild goose chase through all the paperwork I'd sorted in my garage. I had already shredded some papers and packed some papers away in bankers' boxes that were destined for the trash!

Harry's accountant was going to complete the forms and file them; I just needed to provide the requested information, sign on the dotted line, and provide payment if owed. Harry concluded the meeting by saying, "Alexis, until the tax situation is resolved and the lien is removed, you will need to safeguard the money you received yesterday. Its primary use during this time is for any additional fees or expenses that arise related to the estate or the business and to pay my legal fees.

"There are two accounts you must open. Place half the money in each account. Open a checking account for the Estate of Alec Benjamin Miller, III. This $60,000 will be used to pay any estate taxes or estate-related expenses. Open a second checking account in the business name, Navco LLC, of which you are now the acting president. This $60,000 will be used for expenses related to the administration of the business. Once the lien is removed, you may close both accounts and follow up with a status update to the Bucks County Register of Wills."

I blinked a long blink as I wrote all of this information down. I thanked Harry profusely and prayed to God that my newly grown, thick, shoulder-length hair wouldn't fall out from the stress of things.

I drove home in tears. For the next several days, I searched through paperwork and visited every bank my father had an account with. All I found were dead ends. There were no business expense lists, business files, records or ledgers, nothing. There was no evidence of any money being received or spent as related to running his Navco trucking business. His only source of income was his social security payment. That made filing the back taxes pretty quick and easy. Harry's accountant prepared all the paperwork, and I signed all the documents and mailed them back to Harry.

Whew, that took care of that. I expected to have that resolved quickly, the lien removed, and the $80,000 escrow check in my hand by June 2018.

I met with Kathy the following week. As I plopped down on her comfy sofa, I sighed and said, "I don't know what to do with the money I received from the sale of my dad's house; it scares me . I've never had this much money at one time, practically land in my lap. What if I mess this all up and waste it? I'm afraid to walk into the bank with this…what if they think I'm a fraud and stole the money? Seriously, how many people actually walk into the bank to deposit a $120,000 check?"

Kathy replied, "Okay, let's take a couple of deep breaths together, and then I invite you to start from the beginning and tell me what's going on."

After several deep breaths, I felt more relaxed and began to speak, "Well, I sold my dad's house last week for $228,000. I literally made six figures by walking into an office, sitting down, and signing some papers. Poof, just like that, I now have a six-figure check in this very purse I'm holding. Granted, $80,000 is in escrow until the back taxes are paid to the state. Turns out, Dad owed back taxes to the state and federal governments. The county took their money at the closing, but the state needs to be settled with the appropriate back tax forms and copies of the IRS federal filings from 2010 to 2018. It's all good, though! The main point is that I made six figures just like that. In my professional life, the most I've ever made in a year as an interior designer is $80,000. Yet, just like that, after all real estate fees were settled, I left that office in under an hour with a $120,000 check in hand."

I paused, and Kathy said, "Give yourself credit; surely you did *something* to earn that money."

I replied, "You're right, technically speaking; I worked my butt off for the past six months to clean out that mess in Dad's house, and the emotional trauma alone of going through his belongings was worth a million dollars. But still, for cleaning out a house and listing it with a realtor, I just made more money than I could by working for *two years* as an interior designer. I don't know how to process that. I never thought I could get that much money so fast, legally. I also don't know what to do with such a large sum of money. I am so confused. I've never been in a situation like this. I always thought you had to work a 9–5 to earn money. I didn't know I had other options."

Kathy took a sip of her tea and replied, "Yes, it sounds like your eyes were opened at the house closing."

I nodded and continued, "I also really liked the power surge I got while sitting at that table surrounded by lawyers, notaries, and realtors. I signed forms, and I got money. The transaction was fast and easy, and then I went out to lunch with my mom and went on with my day. No toiling away at the computer for hours to draw floor plans and quote furniture. It was rather easy, compared to working a 9–5. It showed me a glimpse into another way of living. And I liked it. And that scares me. I never considered myself rich and always thought of rich people as hoity-toity sinners. I almost don't want the money; that way, I don't have to deal with managing it and managing my perceptions. I also don't feel like I deserve this money or that I am worthy of having it. Is it wrong to have money if you believe in

God and go to church? I thought it was wrong to have lots of money and idolize it. I feel so conflicted by all these feelings. Is this normal?"

Kathy replied, "Very interesting observations, Alexis. Is there more you'd like to share?"

An idea came to me, and I said, "Now that you mention it, I felt like a triumphant, confident *Queen* for a hot second when my trembling hand accepted the check. My mom had come with me to the closing, and when we went to lunch afterward, it was surreal to think that I was holding six figures in my wallet. In some ways, I felt different, and in other ways, I felt exactly the same. I was no happier or smarter. Having all that money produced no immediate, radical change in my appearance, leaving me looking ravishing and radiant. In fact, despite the money, the same things still annoyed the heck out of me, like people turning at an intersection without using a turn signal; they just come to a complete stop, with no warning. That's so annoying to me! So, I guess a quick, take-home lesson learned was that more money doesn't make me happier or life less irritating. But I bet it sure can buy some nice creature comforts!"

Kathy replied, "Just to be clear; I'm not here to tell you what to do with the money or how to feel about it; that's your decision. What I am here to do is to help you uncover any limiting beliefs you have around money. I assure you that you are not alone in feeling this way and having these concerns. In my twenty years of practice, I have had the privilege of working with people from every walk of life and every economic level, and literally, every single person has expressed similar fears and beliefs around money.

"The amount of money that triggered them is relative. I've worked with millionaires who felt the same way as their business revenue approached the one-billion-dollar mark. I've worked with college students who felt that way about job offers paying $45,000 with a $400 sign-on bonus. They all wanted to know, 'Who am I to have that kind of money?' I tell you this to point out that in time, you may come to see that money is relative, and it's just a tool. It's neither good nor bad; it just helps you show up more fully as who you really are. I am here to help you talk this through and come to new conclusions about the way you perceive yourself and money."

Part of what Kathy said went in one ear and out the other; I don't think I was ready to hear what she had to say. I had to walk it out in my own experience to gather this wisdom firsthand. She wrapped up the session by saying, "I'm going to give you some exercises to work on before our next appointment. Feel free to try one that resonates with you, and we can talk about it next session. This will help you to step into new levels of worthiness around receiving $120,000.

"First, try to recall what your parental figures said about money when you were growing up. You can write them down if you like. And just ask yourself, are these statements absolute truth? Another exercise worth doing is to list all the ways that you are currently good with money. How have you successfully managed money in the past? This will help to dismantle doubts you have around successfully managing this relatively large sum of money. Lastly, if you are so inclined, I welcome you to look at money through the lens of spirituality. What do your beliefs say around wealth and spirituality? Can the two peacefully co-exist, or are they mutually exclusive? I invite you to make a list of all the people you know personally or in the public eye who are wealthy *and* spiritual. What are some of the ways that they make a positive difference in the world?"

These were all new concepts for me. I wasn't raised around a very positive language of money, so to speak. Money was usually *not* spoken about in a good way in my home. And certainly not in an empowering way. I was generally taught to scrape by on pennies in exchange for back-breaking work.

I paused and then said, "Yes, um, I kind of get what you mean. I was raised by a single mother who struggled at times to put food on the table, and although I don't recall her outwardly cursing rich people or saying mean things about them and their money, she definitely made it clear that we were not like them because they had it better off than us and lived an easier life, free of the struggles we had. She'd always tell me to stay in school and get a good education because then I could be wealthy too. She said it was my ticket out of being poor. I also went to Catholic school for twelve years, and I came to believe that money was the root of all evil, and that it was good to put others' needs above yours and show your respect to God by giving away your money to the church and to those less fortunate. I often felt a mixture of guilt and obligation around having money and donating it."

Kathy replied, "Alexis, that's brilliant; that's the kind of work I'm talking about! Beliefs are foundational to how we think and act in the world and how we think the world works. They help to form your perceived identity, and really, beliefs are nothing more than thoughts we've thought over and over and over again until they become absolute in our mind. But that is far from the truth; you can change your beliefs anytime by choosing to think new thoughts. So why not choose a better-feeling thought around this money? It may prove to be very empowering for you in more ways than one, as you learn how to use money to its full advantage."

I left that therapy session feeling bold and courageous. I decided to harness that powerful energy while I had it and deposit the check! I drove straight to one of my local bank branches and waited in line to speak to a financial representative. As I sat in the semi-private cubicle, my hands were sweaty, and I was so nervous. Jean waited on me that day, and I was so nervous about the transaction. What would she think of me when I produced the check? Would she think I stole it? Was she going to push some silent alarm button to have me escorted out of the bank and into a police car? *I'm being absolutely ridiculous!*

I took a few deep breaths and tried to clear my head as she processed both accounts and set them up. Luckily, I had been carrying all the documents with me that I needed. I was proud of myself for finally having the nerve to go through with this.

The entire process took about an hour, and I received a checkbook and debit cards for both accounts. I placed $60,000 in each, as Harry instructed. They weren't earning a whole heck of a lot of interest, but this was just a temporary liquid holding place for the money until the taxes were paid. Then I could safely transfer it to a high-yield savings account and earn more interest. Every time an anxious thought about the money popped into my head, I just repeated a couple of mantras over and over again to myself, "I am worthy of large sums of money. I am good with money. I am using my money wisely to support myself, my family, and my community."

Maybe one day, this would change my money story; today, it did very little to calm my fears. I left the bank giddy and trembling and needed to sit in my car for a couple of minutes to collect myself and calm my nerves. I texted Virginia to let her know I'd finally deposited the check. She sent back smiley face emojis and dollar signs. I vowed to complete all three exercises that Kathy had recommended.

Things appeared to be looking up for me, and I was on cloud nine when I received an email from Harry a couple of days later. I was in the office catching up on emails, and his was marked important. His accountant had filed all the back taxes, and he was confident we'd get a response in about six weeks, by mid-March at the latest. After I read that email, I leaned back in my chair with an air of contentment. This would finally be over soon, and I could put this all behind me and get back to my life. I was so relieved. I looked around the small home office with a satisfied smile on my face. *Damn, I went through hell and back and made it this far.* I could see the light at the end of the tunnel and savored this little victory.

As I looked around the room, my eyes landed on the black, alligator handbag dangling on the doorknob. It was my grandmother's handbag that I had taken from Dad's house when I was there securing everything after the police found his remains on Father's Day. So much had happened since last June, I had completely forgotten all about that handbag. I must have walked past it a thousand times since his death without giving it a second thought. Now that things had finally settled down, I decided to have a good look at it. It was in fairly good condition; I wondered if I could sell it online or at my favorite vintage shop in downtown West Chester.

It was a classic, mid-size, structured, black alligator bag with a small top handle. It looked like something the late, great Jackie O would have adorned her left forearm with. Seeing this handbag brought back fond memories of my childhood. This had been Mom's go-to handbag for any and every occasion. Mom carried it everywhere, no matter the season, and wore it with everything, even sweatpants. I was curious about its contents. Maybe a packet of Mom's old More cigarettes and one of her fancy, old lighters were inside? It would be nice to have mementos of her. Something inside the handbag that actually smelled like her would be the cherry on top. I missed my grandmom, and my heart had a twinge of pain as I looked at her handbag. It was so bittersweet. So much love I still had to give to her and Dad. I wished they were both still here with me so I could love up on them.

I set the handbag on the desk and inspected the outside. It was still in pretty good condition, for being over fifty years old. *I wonder why Dad saved it?* It's not like he was into handbags. Maybe he thought I'd like it? As I admired it, I noted that it had tight stitching, mildly scuffed gold hardware, and a slightly worn top handle. I decided to measure it and snap a few photos of it. Maybe I could consign it? It was about twelve inches wide, nine inches high, and about two inches wide. The top handle had a four-inch drop.

As long as the inside was intact with a recognizable name-brand label, I'd be set. When I gently turned the small, gold, twist-lock closure and opened the top flap, the black, cloth interior was worn and frayed, and several yellowed papers and envelopes were inside both narrow compartments. I scrunched up my face and turned away to sneeze. The papers smelled old and musty. This was definitely not what I was expecting to find inside, and I was intrigued.

I had a quiet afternoon, with the house to myself, until the kids came home from school. I decided to read through the papers instead of simply tossing them. It was so odd to find this handbag perched on top of a pile of trash in Dad's room that fateful night. He must have saved the handbag and its contents for a good reason. The least I could do was read the papers.

That chic, little, black, alligator handbag turned out to be like a ticking time-bomb. And it was about to explode in my face. The words that jumped off those pages practically blinded my eyes, damned near broke my soul, and shattered my sense of self. My budding sense of faith and optimism was tested with every page I read. Bad news was on the doorstep, and more than one home was wrecked that day.

CHAPTER 24

I looked at the papers in disbelief. At first, I had only casually gazed over them, out of morbid curiosity. The words didn't make sense to me. I thought I was reading about someone else, perhaps a distant relative with the same last name. But at some point, I recognized Dad's name and decided to take a closer look at these documents. The first, yellowed document was a typed investigation report from 1967, regarding a Cassandra T. Miller from Columbus, Ohio. I didn't even know I had relatives in Ohio. I was intrigued and read every word.

The grammar was so old school, stiff and antiquated. She was even referred to as "colored!" For some reason, she was under 48-hour surveillance, and her daily whereabouts were notated, down to the minute, from the moment she left her house in the morning until the moment she returned home for the evening. The report detailed what she was wearing, who she was with, where she went and what she was driving. She was mostly seen leaving and returning with "a young, colored girl, approximately three years of age, who was heavy-set and wearing a brown coat." *What was this?*

The investigator even reported on the contents of her mailbox and noted that the mail carrier confidently advised that the mail Cassandra received from 1801 Vine Street, Philadelphia, was a check, and she received them regularly from Philadelphia.

I was baffled. *Who was she, and who was this child? Why would my grandmother or dad keep these records? Why were they in Mom's handbag, and why did he set the handbag out for me to obviously find it? Was this some other unfinished family business? Was yet another shoe going to drop in my life? Because I already had my share, thank you very much!*

As I flipped back to the front page, I noticed that Cassandra's name was highlighted yellow, as was the phrase, "3-year-old colored girl." The highlighting looked recent as compared to the aged paper. Then it dawned on me—Miller was her *married* name. Her full name was Cassandra Tiffany Kelley-Miller. None of this made sense. She wasn't a Miller by blood, so who was she married to, who highlighted key points, and why was this document in my grandmother's handbag in my dad's bedroom? I skimmed the rest of the report and set it aside to read through the other papers.

The second piece of yellowed paper was a photocopy of a military employment record from 1964. It was for my father's record of employment at Mt. Home A.F.B, Idaho as a missile-facility technician from September 1960 – June 1964. The reason for terminating his employment stated that he left to live in Philadelphia. That letter didn't seem out of the ordinary. Dad was in the Air Force from 1960 to 1964; he enlisted at 18, did his four years, and left. This seemed right and made sense to me. I still wasn't sure why the document was worth keeping after all these years and in this handbag, of all places. *Maybe he was just hoarding things from the past?*

The next document I opened and read was a yellowed, legal-sized photocopy with a faded font that looked like the original was typed on a typewriter. It was labeled "County Court of Philadelphia; Domestic Relations Division," dated January 1965. It was regarding Cassandra T. Miller vs. Alec B. Miller, III. *This got my attention.* Their names were highlighted in yellow on the first page, as was the name

"Melissa." Alec was petitioning to have the child support he paid for Melissa reduced from $40.00 per week to $15.00 per week because he was only earning $90.26 per week at his new job at Honeywell.

It further added that the petitioner had no car and was unable to live elsewhere but at his mother's house because of the crushing effect of the child support he was ordered to provide for one of the two children. After reading this, I nearly lost my mind. I read the front page of that document over and over again and just sat at the desk and blinked multiple times. My brain simply could not process the information. I could not take this in and accept the weight of these words. I just sat there and stared at those papers and shook my head in disbelief, repeating over and over again, "I don't believe this; this cannot be happening." I was beyond dumbfounded and moving into a state of shock.

After what felt like eons, I gradually rose from the desk chair, walked over to the office closet, and looked on the top shelf for that leather-bound, black Bible I had brought home from Dad's house. I stood at the closet and flipped the book open; as I supported the Bible with one hand and turned the tissue-thin pages to the family tree, tears welled in my eyes. I knew what I was looking for, but didn't want to find it.

I flipped through the book and arrived at the middle, where the marriages, births, deaths, and family tree were recorded. Sure enough, plain as day, dutifully recorded in Mom's beautiful script, was all the supporting evidence I needed. Neatly listed under births was *Melissa – 1964*, and listed under marriages was *Alec B. Miller to Cassandra Kelley*. Directly under this entry stated, *"Alec divorced Cassandra in 1969 and became engaged to Carla – December 24th, 1969. Alec married Carla Williams on June 6th, 1970."* Carla was my mother, and she was the only living relative I could ask about this. The mere thought of broaching this subject with her gave me chills.

I sat at my desk blankly staring at the family information in that Bible for a very long time. The tears just streamed down my cheeks. I knew that my parents met at Honeywell. *Does this mean that as Dad was divorcing his first wife, Cassandra, he was courting his second wife, my mom? He possibly had two other children? I always wanted to have sisters; could this be true? Am I a sister? If this is true, I am going to recognize them as my sisters, not my half-sisters. I have a big sister named "Melissa"? I am not an only child, after all? I am a sister?*

I calculated the numbers to determine how old Dad was in 1964, the year Melissa was born; he was 22 years old. According to these documents and the discharge papers I found, that was also the year he left the Air Force and returned to Philadelphia. *He left his wife and infant? How old was the other child? Who was the other child? Why wasn't that child mentioned in the family Bible? Who else knew about this? Did my mom know?* I blurted out, "Oh, my dear God! Help me!" This was more than I could handle. I was supposed to be done with all of this. I cleaned out the house, sold the house, paid all the bills, and sorted out the taxes. That was all I had signed up for, nothing more and nothing less. *Now, this!!*

The room started spinning, and I blacked out. I regained consciousness some indescribable amount of time later. The kids weren't home from school yet, so I couldn't have been out for very long. I was slumped back in the chair, and my neck was stiff. I started gagging, and my throat was spasming. I took a couple of deep breaths and drank some water. My mind was racing, and I was trying not to panic. I had to get some answers. *Who was I? Who was my dad? Who was Cassandra? Who was Melissa? What was the other child's name?*

Were they alive? Did he abandon them? Why did they divorce? Could I really have siblings?

I wish he was still alive! I had so many questions and I needed help. But the only person I could call was my mom. I dreaded having to call her and tell her this news. I feared the shock would either kill her or crush what little bit of life was left in her hardened, bitter heart. I sat there staring at the Bible and the black handbag. They were both still there; it wasn't a bad dream. God, how I wished I had never sold that house. I should have just walked away from it all and let the house go to sheriff's sale. I began to cry.

I summoned my courage and looked through the rest of the papers in the black handbag. I recognized Mom's beautiful script. The paper was yellowed and smelled old and musty, like all the other papers. This was a handwritten tally of every $40.00 money order paid to the Clerk of the County Court from April 23rd, 1965, to August 2nd, 1965. This was the child support being contested. Was Mom paying this until Dad could earn more money? Or did she just log this information for him? I opened the next letter in the pile. It was from Dad's lawyer, and it was regarding Miller vs. Miller. Cassandra contested the child support being lowered to $15.00 per week. She wanted $25.00 per week and $2,000 in cash. Dad's lawyer was confident that she would accept less, and he recommended that Alec counter with a final proposal of $20.00 per week and $1,500 cash. This was dated 1968.

The next letter in the bunch was also from Dad's lawyer, and it was dated June 30th, 1969. Miller vs. Miller was coming to an end. This legal battle between the two of them had been going on for four years! Dad's lawyer was happy to advise that the Master appointed to hear his divorce action had filed his report recommending that a final decree of divorce be entered on the grounds of indignities to the person. I quote, "A final decree should be entered within the next two or three weeks, after which you will be free. Sincerely, Jerome Shannon."

What a crock! What indignities did he suffer? I was fuming. My emotions were all over the place. He lied to me! He probably lied to my mom, too. And my grandmother knew all this and never said a word! I briskly rose from my chair and practically knocked it out from under me as I wheeled it out of my way. I started pacing the office and was wringing my hands. I kept replaying the scenario I imagined these letters just painted. My dad left his wife and kids high and dry and started a new life without them. He left those kids the same way he left me. I wonder if they lived a good life growing up? I prayed that they were raised in a loving home and grew up to be blessed and prosperous. I couldn't make peace with my father and grandmother in that moment. *How could they lie? Why did they conceal his past? What was the big deal? Why were these documents kept for decades? Who highlighted them and neatly placed them in chronological order?* Plenty of people divorced and remarried! I had to talk to my lawyer about all of this.

I read through the next stack of papers; in the order they were in the handbag. There was a pink customer carbon copy of a J. E. Caldwell and Co. receipt marked CREDIT. The merchandise returned on December 20th, 1969, was two diamond rings, and Alec was credited $25.00 to his account. I bet they were his and Cassandra's! Why keep this information? Apparently, my father wasted no time. I rifled through all the papers I'd piled on the desk. Based on the chronologically arranged records, his divorce was finalized in June 1969, he returned the old diamond rings on December 20th, 1969, and four days later, he proposed to my mom. In a span of six months, he went from newly divorced to newly engaged. Oh, my poor mother, I bet she never knew any of this. *How would I tell my mom this?* I thought I was going to be sick.

The rest of the J. E. Caldwell and Co. thick, hand-written, white, cardstock receipts detailed the balance of $923.00 being paid off over a series of ten monthly installments from January 18th, 1970, to November 18th, 1970. I guessed it was for my mom's diamond ring. That 25-dollar credit, along with an additional $550 credit, had been applied to the first payment.

I recognized my mom's chicken scratch on several of the receipts dated in July and September. They were wed June 6th, 1970. She must have been getting involved in the household finances once they were married. Why else would she be writing the tally? The last of the J. E. Caldwell and Co. receipts was a blue, carbon copy, dated June 5th, 1970, and it was for two gold wedding bands, for a total of $95.70 paid in full. I guess they picked up their rings the day before they were due to be lawfully wed!

Oh, I dreaded the mere thought of calling her and rattling her dusty, old chains. I could only imagine what cold, Carla comments she'd have to say about this. But it had to be done. I jotted down some notes and made a quick timeline. The paper trail led me to the conclusion that Dad was a married man when he courted my mother. He ended his marriage with Cassandra in June of 1969 and entered into marriage with Carla the following June. Oh, my poor mother, I bet she never knew any of this. *How would I tell my mom this? Did she know he had a wife and kids when she met him?* I went for a walk to clear my head before calling her and emailing Harry for legal advice. I had about an hour before the kids came home, and I was hoping the chilly, March air would refresh my soul and give me a fresh perspective on things.

I steeled my nerves and called my mom. After some small talk, I went for it. "So, Ma, when were you and Dad married? I think it was in the summer, right?"

She promptly replied, "Yes, we were married in the summer, Alexis. It was June 6th, 1970, to be exact. The biggest mistake of my life, that I've regretted ever since. Why do you ask?"

I got chills as the words rolled out, "Well, I found some interesting paperwork today when I was going through Dad's things, and I need your help figuring it out. In fact, I found the paperwork in Mom's old, black, alligator handbag."

My mom replied, "What kind of papers did you find in her purse, and why was Alec still holding onto that old thing?"

I took a deep breath and replied, "Well, funny that you should mention that; it struck me as odd when I found the purse neatly perched on a pile of trash in his bedroom. Michael and I went over there to seal up the house after the police broke the door off the hinges, and her purse and a family Bible were the last things I was expecting to find in his room. I took them home and hadn't given them another thought until today. That purse has been hanging on the doorknob in my office since last June. I thought I'd find some of her old cigarettes inside. Maybe a lighter. But what I found were legal documents and receipts. Did Dad ever tell you about his romantic past? Like in terms of the kinds of serious relationships he'd been in before dating you?"

She promptly replied in an irritated tone, "No, he didn't, Alexis. What are you getting at?"

I continued on, "Well, I don't know how to tell you this, and I'm truly sorry to have to tell you this. I found divorce papers in the handbag pertaining to the divorce of Alec B. Miller III from a Cassandra Kelley-Miller. The divorce dragged out from 1965 to 1969 because of alimony and child support. It was finally settled in June of 1969. He was to pay his first wife $1500 and provide $20.00 per month in child support for his daughter, Melissa. He was married *when* he met you, and from what the papers say, he has two children."

I paused, and she said calmly, "Go on."

I took a deep breath and said, "I checked in Mom's Bible to see if there was any record of this, and there was. In the section under births, Melissa Miller is listed as being born in 1964. Listed under marriages was written Alec B. Miller to Cassandra Kelley. Directly under this entry stated, 'Alec divorced Cassandra in 1969 and became engaged to Carla – December 24th, 1969. Alec married Carla Williams on June 6th, 1970.' I'm so sorry, but there's more."

She said, "Go on."

"Well, there are also receipts from the jeweler, J. E. Caldwell and Co. One was dated December 20th, 1969, for the return of two old diamond rings, for which he received a $25.00 credit. And according to what Mom has in her Bible, he proposed to you four days later. In a span of twelve months, he basically divorced one woman and married another. The rest of the J. E. Caldwell and Co. receipts were installments of $34.80 that were paid monthly from January 1970 thru November 1970; I'm guessing for your diamond ring? Oh, and there was a receipt for two, gold wedding bands dated the day before your wedding. Does any of this ring a bell? Did you ever suspect *anything*?"

There was a long sigh, and I could sense the bitterness stirring as she formulated her sentence, "Well, I'll be damned. Yes, I did suspect something. When we met at Honeywell in 1964, he had just moved back to Philadelphia. He had just gotten out of the Air Force after being stationed in Idaho. We courted for about a year. He never really talked much about his time in the military or his life in Idaho. But I always suspected that he left for reasons that had nothing to do with his military career. I suspected it had to do with a woman. When we were first married, we lived in the upstairs apartment of his mother's duplex, and she was always intercepting our mail! I knew she was going through it before I could look through it. I always suspected she was hiding something. I questioned Alec about his mom's behaviors, and he just shrugged it off and said she was controlling. Call it a sixth sense, but something told me it had to do with another woman. I even asked him if he had any children or had ever been married before, and he said, 'No.' I'll tell you what, Alexis, that family is full of liars, deceit, and secrets. I don't know who to believe. This one says one thing, and this one says another. I also had my doubts before I married him. After we became engaged, a friend of a friend took me aside one day and warned me not to trust him. But love is blind. Well, let me tell you, I found out first-hand that you don't truly know someone until you've lived with them. Not until you've locked that front door."

I could feel the pain and anger in her voice as she spoke. I felt so sorry for her. Woman to woman, I would never wish this on anyone. She spoke again, "What are you going to do with this information, Alexis?"

I told her I was going to contact my lawyer for advice. She advised me otherwise, "Alexis, I don't think you should go digging around. Who knows what you'll find? Your father's side of the family had a lot of, shall we say, *unsavory characters* who I never felt safe around. Who knows what these people are like? It's best to let this remain in the past. But suit yourself, do what you feel you must. I shall say no more on the subject. He can rot in hell, as far as I'm concerned. Good riddance."

She was true to her word. She never asked me again about my quest to find my family. We spoke a while longer, and I could tell she was sad. It broke my heart to have to be the bearer of bad news. I emailed my lawyer next. Then, I called my therapist and Virginia. I needed support sorting this out.

CHAPTER 25

The duration of March and April was spent searching for Melissa Miller and my Aunt Vicks. According to Harry, legally, Melissa was next of kin, and as the executrix, it was my duty to notify next of kin of Alec's death. Since he only mentioned me in his will, I was not legally bound to share any part of my inheritance with any other siblings. I was grateful for this information, but frustrated nonetheless.

I searched for both Melissa and Aunt Vicks on every social media platform and found nothing. I searched on LinkedIn and found nothing. I looked in the White Pages and found nothing. I did a free, people search online and found nothing. It was as if the two of them didn't exist. I checked the obituaries and found nothing. Aunt Vicks was the only person who might be able to shed a clue on what happened all those years ago and where I might find Melissa. By the end of April, I was ready to give up and put this behind me, like my mom advised. Harry said I had done my due diligence as the executrix, and I was not required to search any further.

Virginia was a lifeline through all of this. Michael was on a six-month deployment, and I was on my own for another month. I don't know how I would have managed without her weekly calls and daily texts. After I was no longer legally responsible for searching for my family, I called her to vent. "I can't do this, Virginia. I can't have another thing come crashing down on me. I'm at my wit's end and about to lose my mind. I have to be strong for my kids, and I can't do this anymore. If one more thing goes wrong, I am going to lose my mind. Michael's not coming back from Fort Knox for another month!" *May can't get here fast enough!*

She replied loudly, "Listen to me, Momma, here is what you need to do. Keep calling me and texting me, as many times as you need. I am three hours away if you need me. Do you have friends who live close by? Reach out to them. You don't have to go into the details; just let them know you are feeling very out of sorts and your husband is deployed, and you may need to call on them at a moment's notice to watch your kids. Also, call your therapist and get an appointment right away. See her twice a week if you need to. When your husband comes home, after you've had time together to reconnect and do your thing, *leave!* Catch a cheap flight to someplace warm for a few days and just be. This has been a lot, and it sounds like you need to recharge. You are allowed to rest, Momma!"

She was right, and I needed to stop isolating myself and suffering in silence. I took a deep breath and said, "I feel like I'm losing all hope and my faith is being tested. I made a deal with God that I would do all of this so long as He helped me. And right now, I feel all alone and like I'm being pommeled by challenges. It's like I can't catch a break. I feel like my faith has been tested enough. I took care of my dad. I cleaned out the house after he died. I paid the overdue bills. I rummaged through mounds of disgusting garbage and piles of mail to find everything my lawyer asked for. I filed the taxes. I donated his tools. I donated his van. I even located his sports car at a local speed shop, paid for the repairs, and then donated the car! What more do I have to do to prove my faith to God and show that I'm worthy of having relief from this never-ending barrage of crap piling up on me? I thought He was a merciful God who was always by my side, even in the fiery storms? Well, where is God now?

"I just found out that I could have a sister, or possibly two! Somewhere out there, I could have sisters or a sister and a brother! And somewhere out there is my aunt, and she might hold the key to all of this! Yet, I can't find them. I just give up. I feel hopeless and ashamed for believing this would work out."

Virginia sighed and said, "I am sorry you feel this way, Momma. You have every right to, and I don't blame you or judge you for it. At some point, we all face challenges that rock us to our core and cause us to waiver and doubt. I believe we have two options: quit altogether or tap into reserves of faith we never knew we had and lean on God more to do the heavy lifting when we are weak. You can throw in the towel and walk away from all this. It's your choice. I nearly lost all faith in my dreams and in God when my third husband left me with three kids, no money, and I was pregnant with my fourth child.

"Who was going to want me? How was I going to provide for my kids? Who was going to hire a seven-months-pregnant woman with no college degree? I talked to God every day and asked Him to help me. My monies were running out, and I thought I'd have to move in with my sister and her family. I blindly trusted that God would reveal the next steps to me. And He did. People came into my life at just the right time to help me. It was nothing I could have ever planned or done on my own. It was like I was a magnet attracting what I didn't even know I needed, to me. It was nothing short of a miracle that I got a job with paid training in real estate and a mentor who taught me everything I know. Some people called them coincidences or synchronicities. I called them miracles from God. But I had to blindly trust Him and keep going. I believe that there are unseen forces working on our behalf behind the scenes, but we have to blindly trust and take action, *even* when, logically, it doesn't make any sense how things are going to work out. We have to look past what our eyes see and believe that something better is on the horizon and prepare accordingly for when it arrives. The heaviest lift isn't the action you take, it's the faith you muster and maintain despite it all."

I wiped my tears away and said, "Thank you for sharing that, Virginia. It makes me feel hopeful that this will eventually work out for the best. However, I am scared. What if things get worse? How am I going to handle it? I've already shed all the blood, sweat, and tears I can afford to give. How much more can I humanly give before I lose myself and implode?"

She replied, "Oh Momma, you are going to lose yourself. But not in the way you think. Let me tell you something, the scared Virginia with three kids, another one on the way, and no money; love her dearly, but she could have never gotten me to where I am today. The confident woman speaking with you today is the version of Virginia who got me this far and realized my dreams. You are going to have to release your old ways of thinking and being in order to step into the version of yourself, who's a sister. This experience is going to challenge you to dream bigger and be braver than you could have ever imagined possible. Didn't you say you always wanted to have sisters? As scary as it sounds, the best part of creating your dreams is who you must become to do so. Momma, I'm excited for you!"

I was stunned and tried to process her words. I had already faced so many challenges in caring for my father and managing his affairs. Now this? How many more challenges and transformations could my identity endure before I completely self-destructed? Is there even such a thing as changing yourself too much? Is there some golden rule dictating how many times a person can successfully undergo personal reinvention? *I'm about to find out and push the limits of possibility.*

Virginia continued on, "Momma, you can't possibly do this alone. I know you're strong, but you do not have the capacity as a human to figure this all out. The power I'm talking about comes from the Divine. This is the realm of miracles. God is going to provide what you need when it's needed, like He always does, but we take it for granted. Like the breaths we are taking right now and not even appreciating. This walk you are on is no different. He will provide, just like He provides the air we breathe. He provides in His perfect timing, not yours, though. That's why it's called blind faith, Momma. Do what you know how to do, and let Him handle the rest. During that time of waiting, focus your energies on preparing emotionally and mentally to meet your new family."

What she was saying made sense to me. I was so mentally and emotionally exhausted from trying to control all the outcomes. It would be nice to surrender control and rest my body and soul.

Virginia continued, "Be prepared. I believe you are going to get the help you are asking for. Keep talking to God, and keep being open to possibilities no matter how bleak and hopeless reality looks. Forget reality; focus on possibilities. It is possible that *someone* may be able to help you find your family. There are millions of people on this planet; someone is bound to know something. And when you look back on this, you will see how people and circumstances lined up to work it all out. But only in hindsight will you be able to see this. Not when you're in the thick of it.

"And in those moments when you rose to the challenges, and you were provided for, is when you are getting a glimpse of the Divine in action and a taste of your highest potential expressed. Get comfortable with the uncomfortable, Momma. Prepare to lose yourself and be transformed into something greater. You're not out of the woods yet, it probably will get worse before it gets better, and you will have help. I believe in you, Momma, and you got this. You are not alone. On the days when it gets tough, try to remember that it's best to do *something* in faith than to sit and do nothing in doubt. You just need faith the size of a mustard seed. Have you seen those things? They're tiny! You will live through this, and we will talk about this next year and reminisce. I love you, Momma."

After we hung up, I had a long cry and decided to pray for strength and help. I called my local girlfriends to ask for help and booked additional sessions with my therapist. A couple of days later, I received an odd DM from a second cousin on my mom's side of the family. Apparently, he was into genealogy and was compiling a Williams family tree online. He had come to my leg in the tree and wanted to touch base and learn about my family and the Miller side.

Once my mom confirmed his identity, he and I talked for over an hour. I told him about Melissa and Aunt Vicks. He offered to do a paid search to find them using his genealogy research contacts. *Praise the Lord! Talk about a miracle.* I shook my head, chuckled, and made a mental note to text Virginia about this.

Two weeks later, I had the results. He couldn't find Melissa, but he found Aunt Vicks' address and phone number. I mustered an ounce of courage and a drop of faith to write her a letter and leave her a voicemail. *Thank God she was still alive.* I prayed she returned my call and received my letter. I didn't tell her that her brother was dead; I just told her that something had happened to Alec and she needed to contact me ASAP. Life was too heavy for my soul, and I needed a release. I played the waiting game and tried to stay hopeful. It was time to blast my favorite club tracks and dance around the house. I needed to scream, shake, and wiggle these cares away.

Michael came home June 1st, which was a relief because the challenges did not let up. The taxes were rejected, federal and state. I had to refile them from scratch using a different accountant. Every time I had to dig through Dad's paperwork, it felt like tearing a scab off and scratching the tender raw skin with a sharp stick. Harry's accountant couldn't explain why the taxes were rejected, and thankfully, he didn't charge me for the service. Small miracle amongst the challenges. Thank you.

I had to set that down and come back to it because on the heels of Harry's email came a LinkedIn DM from someone claiming to be my niece, Meghan Miller-Smith, from Ohio. Was this a joke?

I emailed Harry about this new development, and legally, it was my duty as the executrix to reply. She might know Melissa. Should I request a DNA test? How did I know this wasn't a scam? I was so confused and bewildered. I shut my laptop down for the night and cried myself to sleep, telling myself, "It's almost over. You can do this. You can do this. You can do this! A little while longer. A little while longer. Come on. Hold on. Hold on. Trust God. Rest well. Tomorrow is a new day. Dance tomorrow before you reply to the DM."

The next morning, I courageously emailed Meghan and asked her how she found me. According to her, Melissa is her mother, and Alec is her grandfather. She was doing an online search to find out about her grandfather, Alec. She searched him and found his obituary; she found my name in the obituary as the surviving daughter and worked up the courage for the past year to contact me. She attached a photo of her mom and a couple of herself. Seeing the photos was all the proof I needed. Melissa looked like a carbon copy of my grandmother, down to the white lace-up Ked's sneakers and the long, skinny, brown More cigarette in her hand. Mom wore the same style sneakers and smoked the same style cigarettes. Oh, we were definitely related.

What next? I'm a sister, for sure! What did this mean for me? Harry advised me on how to proceed. Meghan and I exchanged personal emails and corresponded a couple of times per week. She sent me more family photos, and I sent her family photos. It turned out I had two sisters, Melissa and Martie. Martie was eleven months older than Melissa. When she sent me photos of Martie, I looked just like her. She was even lifting dumbbells in one of the photos. She liked working out, just like me! I literally have dumbbells strategically placed around my house so I can work my arms and core.

I wondered how much more we actually had in common and what it would be like to have sisters. I always wanted sisters. Could this dream be coming true? I explained to Meghan that I needed to send forms to Melissa to inform her of Alec's death. Meghan wanted me to mail them to her because she was Melissa's guardian and Melissa lived in a nursing home. *What? Why was a 54-year-old woman in a nursing home? Did I really want to know?* I had to ask; I was the executrix.

Meghan emailed me back one sentence that nearly made me faint when I read it. Melissa was cognitively impaired; she was born with a rare condition called Prader-Willi syndrome. I staggered back and had to sit down in my office chair before I fainted. I could not make this up if I tried. At this point, I was convinced that God truly had a twisted sense of humor.

I was speechless. It was like I was seeing my life flash before me. All the years I volunteered at Easter Seals, all the years I studied to become a physical therapist, ten years of treating special needs patients. All the life moments and interactions flashed before my eyes. I could accept that I had sisters. I could accept that my dad had a wife before my mom and kept all this hidden. But to find out that my sister had the exact *rare* syndrome that I had first-hand clinical experience with brought me to my knees. I was so overcome that I fell to the floor and wailed. That explained how Dad knew so much about special needs kids and institutions. I just thought he was an oddball, walking encyclopedia. He even tried to talk me out of becoming a pediatric physical therapist. He had so many misgivings about me working with special needs kids. Now, it was starting to make sense. He had his own special needs child! I couldn't believe this was happening. What were the odds that I would treat patients with Prader-Willi and my sister would have Prader-Willi? Even Mom was against me working with special needs kids. I remember showing her a newspaper article featuring me and some of the kids I worked with, and her only comment was that the kids were pitiful and should never have been born. Her shocking remark was so out of character from the Miller I knew, and I've never forgotten it.

All the years I dedicated to my medical career flashed across my mind. All the frustration. All the struggles. All the hurdles. All the caregiver burnout and compassion fatigue. All the guilt about changing careers and wondering why I became a physical therapist, in the first place. Had my ten-year career and eight years of higher education prepared me to receive *this* moment with grace? In all honesty, if I hadn't had that first-hand experience caring for special needs kids and adults, I might have deleted Meghan's message and refused to meet my sisters. But now, it was no big deal. I knew all I needed to know and wanted to meet them all in person this summer. Once I recovered from the shock, I emailed Meghan back and explained to her that I knew all about Prader-Willi syndrome. Before changing careers to become an interior designer, I was a pediatric physical

therapist working in institutions for special needs kids. We specialized in caring for children and adults with Prader-Willi syndrome.

Meghan was relieved that I had a medical background and knew
about Prader-Willi. She wanted to know if any other medical anom-
alies ran in the Miller family and if Alec or Mom had any medical
conditions that might impact Melissa's health. I told her everything
I knew.

When she and I FaceTimed for the first time, it was like talking
to my twin. We made plans for Michael, me, and the kids to visit
over the long July 4th weekend. Two weeks ago, I had no information on my sisters, and now I was planning on meeting them. I chose
to embrace them as my sisters, not my half-sisters. Life was moving
fast, and my sense of self was blossoming with each passing day. I
was asking everyone I knew what it was like having siblings. I had
no clue!

The week before our trip, Aunt Vicks called me, and instantly
my life changed yet again. I was confronted with realities I didn't
want to face and process. Old bones were coming out of closets, and
I was doing my best to embrace them with curiosity and grace under
pressure. When was the elephant going to be devoured? *Because I was
sick of eating small bites of elephant.* I didn't want any more elephant.

We made some pleasantries, and I told her about my kids, and
she told me about her grandkids, and then we dove into the details.
I told her about Dad and explained that he passed last June. I apologized for it taking me a year to track her down. She understood,
and I mailed her a copy of his funeral program when the phone
call was finished.

I explained to her that I had found my siblings, told her what I
knew about them, and told her about the contents of Mom's handbag.

Then I asked her to fill in the blanks. *What happened back then? Why did Alec and Cassandra divorce? Why was this such a big family secret?*

Aunt Vicks laughed a bitter laugh and said, "You and your mom were always kind to me and my kids. So, I'll help you. But after this conversation, do not ever try to find me again. I'm done with the Millers; they are dead to me. I can do bad on my own; I do not need their help. Understand?"

I agreed, and she continued on.

"Alec and I were a team growing up. I was his big sister and did my best to look out for him and shield him from Mom's wrath and madness. We always kept in touch, and he always knew how to find me when I had to get away from Mom and the Old Man's prying eyes. He did not keep those papers you found. Mom did. He confided in me that he wanted to come clean about all of it. It was Mom who kept all those papers and warped my poor brother's mind, ruined his life, and drove him to drink. He wanted to do right by Cassandra, but Mom wouldn't have it. Mom was a spoiled, trust-fund baby who could pass for white any time she wanted and was used to getting her way.

"She was *not* going to have the family name ruined by scandal. According to Mom, Cassandra was a trash-talking, opportunistic hussy. Mom wanted nothing to do with her or the children. Mom turned her back on her own grandchildren! She did not care. All she could see was that Cassandra had a high-school degree and came from humble beginnings. That was not good enough for Mom. Mom wanted someone better for Alec. Someone classy, educated, and most of all, light-skinned from a good family, not some low-class, dark-skinned Mexican.

"She didn't want them to get any child support. She got Alec believing all that BS and convinced him to see things her way. She kept him under her thumb with the lies she concocted. She'd dangle those documents over his head any time he got too independent and too far from her clutches. He was a grown man, and she did everything in her power to emasculate him and keep him her Momma's Boy. He just wanted to do right by her and felt obligated. I kept telling him to leave and never go back. But he couldn't turn his back on Mom after the Old Man died. Even though it cost him everything."

I was shocked, and chills ran down my spine as she talked. Things were starting to make more sense. I asked her if that's why he permanently moved back home after Mom had a small house fire in 1983. I was ten at the time and never forgot the heated argument I overheard between Mom and my dad.

"Oh, of course, that's exactly what happened. He called me so distraught. He came home to remodel her living room after her TV caught on fire. He was supposed to be there for the summer; that was it. He had a life in California. He was happy. He had a thriving business as a liquor store owner, and he was in love and wanted to get married. He had a life, and she took it from him! She tried everything in the book to get him to stay, and when all else failed, she pulled out those papers and threatened to tell your mom, you, and everyone in town about his past.

"He begged her to let him leave. He begged her not to do this to him. *He begged her!* And that heartless bitch did not relent. He lost everything and never went back to California. He gave up the next thirty-three years of life being chained to her. The prime of his life was ripped away from him for no damn good reason. I hate her for that. What mother does that to her child? She had money as a military widow. The Old Man's pension kept her well taken care of. She did not need Alec to drive her around and grocery shop and clean her house. I am positive that she ruined him and drove him to his addictions as a way to cope.

"When Mom dangled those divorce papers over his head and threatened to tell Carla, he was petrified of you finding out and hating him. He would have done anything to make you happy and have your love. He hadn't seen you in five years and wanted to make up for lost time. He truly regretted not being in your life when you were little and wanted to spend time getting to know you. The thought of never seeing you again broke his heart. So, he took great comfort in knowing that, at least by living in Philadelphia, he'd be closer to you. His sweetheart didn't want to leave California. She came to visit him once, and Mom didn't like her. Alec never talked to her again after that. He broke things off with her because of Mom. She had control over him, and he allowed it. She broke that man. I've never forgiven her for that. My brother was a good man. I loved my brother and wished I had done better by him."

She stopped to blow her nose and, I imagine, dab away tears. Then she continued.

"Mom was a pro at playing the role of the poor widow who expected her kids to take care of her. I wanted no part of that BS and left home as soon as I could. She made my life hell. She was on my ass like white on rice as soon as I hit puberty. Always wanting to know where I was going and who I was with. Always threatening to whip me to death if I put on too much weight, got bad grades, or was out past curfew. She was petrified I'd ruin Dad's precious military career or tarnish our good image. She was petrified I'd get knocked up. She literally tracked my monthly cycle and rummaged through my bathroom trash every month to visually inspect my sanitary napkins.

"She ruined my childhood with her controlling ways and tongue lashings. Meanwhile, Alec was running around town half-drunk with every prostitute he could get his 15-year-old hands on. And she'd cover for him, clean up his messes and keep it from the Old Man. She didn't care about Alec or me. She just cared about our good name and Dad's precious career as a Lieutenant Colonel. In the end, that's all she cared about. As a black family living in military officers' quarters, we had to maintain a certain image and could not create a spectacle. There weren't many high-ranking blacks at the time and she was going to make sure we set the standard for excellence. There was no room for error. She forced me to go to nursing school because she wanted me to be a nurse. I didn't want to be a nurse. She felt it would be good for the family name and would help me secure a good man with a good name. She didn't care that I hated nursing. She wanted the women in our family to be nurses. I quit that program before the first semester was over and made my own way. Of course, Mom never forgave me for it. Just like she never forgave me for putting on a hundred pounds of extra weight. But this is my body and my life, and I will do what I want. We didn't speak for years at a time when she was alive. But at least I was free of her and her clutches."

I didn't know what to say. I just listened as she continued to pour out her heart to me.

Aunt Vicks continued on, "Poor Alec wasn't so lucky. After Melissa was born, he'd call me crying. He was so confused. He wanted to do right by his wife and daughters. They were all so young. He and Melissa were practically babies themselves. To be 22 with two kids under the age of 2 was a lot for anyone, and layer on the fact that one had special needs? My heart ached for them. Mom wanted him to get a divorce and come take care of her. I happened to be visiting Mom during one of their heated telephone conversations, and I picked up the upstairs line to listen in. I will tell you everything I know, and then I never want to speak to you again. Do not try to contact me.

The Miller family has done me no favors, and I am only dredging up this past to pay homage to my brother and pay back a debt of kindness owed to you and your mom. She was kind to me in a moment of need, and I will repay her kindness.

"What I am about to tell you might change your opinion of your beloved grandmother. The Miller adored you and always called you her Angel Baby. Meanwhile, she gave me and my children the cold shoulder. She tried to ruin my life, and she outright ruined Alec's life. She was a nasty, vicious, calculating, conniving woman."

I didn't know what Aunt Vicks was about to say, and I braced myself for it. She said, "I can hear Mom and Alec talking like it was yesterday. Mom was furious, and her words were cold as ice as she said, 'Just tell them the baby's dead and leave that hussy. It's time you came back home, Alec.'"

"There's nothing for you there in Idaho. I bet you that first child isn't even yours. That hussy was probably pregnant when she met you, and she was just looking for a shiny, new, gullible GI like you, fresh out of boot camp, to sink her claws into. And now, eleven months after her first baby was born, you two newlyweds have welcomed a crippled child into the world! It serves your dumb ass, right! Didn't I tell you something like this would happen? When you lay down with dogs, you get fleas!"

Then she started shouting, "No son of mine would do this. I raised you better, Alec!! I *know* that you know better!! You grew up on military bases your entire life, boy. How could you be so dumb to fall for some local piece of ass hanging 'round the base? They're all just looking for health insurance and child support. Didn't you learn anything from your dad's Army buddies, Wilson and Carter? Both their lives ruined by wicked women like yours. Like I said, just tell everyone the baby was born crippled and died of complications. No one will be the wiser."

Alec calmly replied, "But, Mom, you don't understand; as far as I'm concerned, both kids are mine, and I love Cassandra. We'll be fine. We can move back to Philadelphia and live in your duplex. You don't have an upstairs tenant; we can move in! You'll see. That way, I'll be close to you. Right upstairs, literally, as your tenant. I know you've been struggling to do it all since the funeral last year. You and the Old Man had a great marriage, and I know this must be hard on you. With me there, I can easily help you and take care of my family. It doesn't have to be either-or. I can be there for you and my family. The Air Force has been good to me. I have good skills and can get a good engineering tech job, probably down at the naval shipyards." Unfortunately, his words fell on deaf ears.

"Look, Alec," she shouted, "Now's your chance to fix your situation and clean this all up, like it never happened, then get on with your life."

Mom pleaded, "Now that your father's passed away, I need your help here full-time. You're all I got, Alec," her tone was pathetic. "Your sister's good as gone; I can't depend on her for shit. She's visiting me now, but I'm sure it's only because she's broke and wants money. After all the Old Man and I did for her. We paid for her nursing school, and she threw it all away and got knocked up by a loser. All I wanted was for her to keep her legs shut and become a nurse. Was that too much to ask? That good-for-nothing hussy can go to hell, too," Mom finished with a bitter tone full of regret and remorse.

There was a pause as mom took a long drag on her cigarette, then, without missing a beat, she went back on her tirade, "You don't have time to raise a family and help me. And mark my words; a crippled child will bleed you dry in medical bills. The obstetrician should have told you two idiots that it was stillborn and secretly put that pitiful child in a home. How are two 22-year-old kids like you going to raise a 12-month-old baby and a crippled, 1-month-old baby? Alec, let me remind you, this is 1964, you're a Negro, and she's a Mexican. You're living on a military base in Idaho, literally in the middle of nowhere, surrounded by mountains, almost an hour outside of Boise. The odds are stacked against you, son. A light-skinned Negro like you and a dark-skinned, Mexican woman like her are just asking for trouble the minute you step foot off that base. What happens if you have to take that baby to specialists in Boise and your car breaks down in the middle of nowhere? The Old Man is dead and gone, and I'm in Philadelphia; what good does that do you? It's best for you to put this behind you and come back home," she spoke as if she were going to have the final say.

At this point, Alec lost his mind. He had been doing his best to remain calm, but that comment pushed him over the edge, and he let Mom have it. "I've listened to this crap long enough. Those are my daughters and wife you're talking about, and I won't have it! Stop calling my daughter pitiful and crippled. Do you hear me? Stop it! Her name is MELISSA. Did you get that, *Mom*? Her name is MELISSA!"

He yelled out, "I'm not your damn Momma's Boy. I'm not your doormat. I'm not your slave. I'm not your puppet. I don't answer to you. I don't need your damn help; I don't need your approval, and I don't need you!"

"Oh, well, well, now, is that so? You won't have it!" screamed Mom. "Well, son, you owe me. Remember all the times I covered for your drunken ass when you were in *high school*, running wild in Germany? Remember when that girl showed up at our front door saying she was pregnant with your child? I told her and her folks to get lost and that if they didn't get off our property, I'd have the MPs drag their asses off it. I slammed the front door in their lying faces! And who picked your ass up at the police station and covered it all up so the Old Man wouldn't find out that you were in a *whorehouse* at 15? I did!" screamed Mom into the phone receiver. "You. Owe. Me." There was a long pause in between those last three words, and Alec was sure his mom was lighting another cigarette to calm her nerves.

He fired back, "Leave the past in the past, Mom; I don't owe you anything, and I'm not going to be manipulated or threatened by you. That ship has sailed. Drop it."

Mom flatly stated, "Well, if that's how you want it, then I'm done sending you money every month to help your sorry ass pay the bills. Consider yourself cut off. See how long you last without me. Mark my words, you'll be crawling back home to your momma with your tail between your legs. So, like I said, finish your tour, divorce Cassandra, and go your separate ways. When you come back home, tell everyone the baby died, and the marriage ended. It's quite believable, especially since she was born with so many complications. If you want to give Cassandra child support, that's on you. As far as I'm concerned, Cassandra and her kids are dead to us. She can take care of herself and HER mess."

Alec nonchalantly replied, "Well, I guess this is where we part ways, then. I'm sick of your games, and I'm done caving into you. Goodbye, Mom." Alec slammed down the receiver. Mom just chuckled and said to herself, "Mark my words son, you're coming home for good."

"Sure enough, Alec moved back home. Those poor children and that woman were swept under the rug like nothing ever happened. Alec and Mom chose to keep that lie hidden for decades, and the ripple effect has ruined many lives. Now you know what I know, Alexis," said Aunt Vicks.

What a story; I could almost smell my grandmother's coffee and cigarette smoke as I listened to Aunt Vicks recount that horrific telephone conversation. Little did my grandmom know, on that fateful 1964 day, that Vicks had been upstairs eavesdropping on the entire conversation from the bedroom telephone. My head was spinning, and I thought I was going to be ill.

I was stunned. How could this be my grandmother? But part of me knew this was all true. Poignant points through the decades of my life began to flash before my eyes, and Aunt Vicks' story helped to connect so many decades' worth of scattered dots. I thought back to the heated argument I overheard between Mom and my dad. The home repairs were finished, and he planned to return to California. As a child, I didn't fully understand what was happening, but now the names made sense, and the powerful effect they had on him made sense. I also recalled Mom's repulsed reaction when I showed her and Dad newspaper clippings of me posing with some of the special needs kids who I assisted during a high school Special Olympics event. He just looked pained, and she said, "They are pitiful; they should have never been born."

I remember being shocked that my loving grandmother could say something so cruel. Now their reactions to the images made more sense to me. Flashes of my grad school internships came to mind. They must have both died a thousand deaths every time I paid them a visit and talked animatedly about the special-needs patients on my caseload.

Aunt Vicks continued, "As to why he left the handbag and Bible for you to find? Simple: he didn't have the courage to tell you the truth when he was alive. Not because he was ashamed of himself or his actions, but because he didn't want you to think less of him. He didn't want to lose you! You were his pride and joy. You were his greatest accomplishment. Alexis, he bragged about you and your family all the time, when we talked on the phone. It would have crushed him if you cut him out of your life and thought less of him. You were truly all the joy he had left in his life. He could not stand the thought of losing you and never seeing his grandchildren. It would have been like losing his first-born children and Cassandra all over again. It would have been like losing his California sweetheart all over again. He couldn't bear to lose another thing he cherished. He wanted you to know the truth, and he told you the only way he knew how. He was dying, Alexis. He didn't want to burden you with any of that, let alone the news of his past."

I just sat in a numbed, silent state of shock as she continued.

"We talked about it all. He truly never wanted to hurt you and hoped that you could forgive him. As for your mom, I'm sure it shocked her to hear this news. He caused her a lot of pain with the lies he told. Please don't feel like you have to take sides. You get to choose what happens next. This had nothing to do with you. Adults make mistakes in relationships and are horrible to each other. Children often get stuck in the awkward middle. You get to decide how you're going to process all this, move through it, and come to a place that feels right in your soul. You can support your mother and respect her and choose to meet your sisters and choose to forgive your dad. Do what you want, it's your life. Your mom needs time to grieve and heal. Give her space. She will move through this in her own time. All the best to you. I'm truly sorry. Goodbye."

I was devastated. She hung up, and that was it. I called Virginia, sobbing, and told her what had happened. I wanted to know why he lied. *Why didn't he stand up to Mom?* I said to her, "Nothing good comes from lies. Lies weigh you down. Look at the toll it took on my dad and my family! I'm not willing to pay that price. The cost of keeping a lie isn't worth it; look at what it cost him to keep this lie! He sacrificed a meaningful life with his wife and kids in exchange for a miserable life of numbing out on alcohol, sex, and drugs to forget his past and the family he left behind!"

Once I calmed down, Virginia spoke softly and slowly, "Listen to me, Momma, I would caution you about speaking in absolutes, jumping to conclusions, or passing judgements. In my experience, some lies are beautiful, and some truths are too ugly and painful to bear; give your father and Cassandra and your grandmother grace. You don't know what he and Cassandra went through as a young couple with two young kids. You don't know what it was like for them to try to raise a baby with special needs back then. You don't know what happened in their marriage and why they did what they did. You don't know what really happened between your dad and his mother. You don't know what Cassandra was like or what she went through. You don't have her side of the story. You only have a paper trail, your aunt's account and your mom's. You weren't there. You don't have the whole story."

I knew she was right.

She continued, "Is there anyone else who can shed light on this? Maybe ask your sisters what they know when you visit with them next week? Just hold space and see what comes from this. You know, there are things about me you don't know. I'm scared to tell you. It might change your opinion of me. I've shared them in the past with others, and it wrecked my career, love life, and reputation. But here it goes; I'm no angel. I was a broken, drug-addicted mess for several years after being molested by a babysitter and then later gang-raped as a teenager. I couldn't deal with the events and the trauma. My family made me feel like it was all my fault. My mom was so cold towards me. She told me to just get over it, because we all have sad sob stories. I was institutionalized on several occasions and placed in psyche wards as a teenager. You know, like padded rooms and all. No furniture, no shoes with laces, no items in the room I could kill myself with."

I listened in complete silence and shock.

"I have worked very hard to overcome that time in my life and become a stronger version of 'Virginia.' I am still working on my relationship with my mom, and I've been divorced and married more times than I care to tell. This time I think I've got myself a keeper. I don't tell that part of my story to just anyone. Has it changed your opinion of me? Do you not want to be my friend anymore? Does it repulse you? I don't share that with everyone because people judge, ghost, and act like their crap don't stink. Give your dad and grand-mom grace. I would bet there's a deeper story, and there are many sides to it. We all have skeletons, Alexis. Maybe they concealed the truth for a good reason. You will never know what really happened between him and Cassandra. Couples make unspoken agreements and come to an understanding about things. You don't have all the pieces; this happened over fifty years ago. Be easy about this, Momma."

EPILOGUE

Fourth of July weekend came quickly, and my family and I piled into the car and made the four-hour trek from Pennsylvania to Ohio. I was going to meet my sisters, Martie and Melissa, and my niece, Meghan, and her family. I hadn't spoken to either sister yet; I had only spoken to my niece, Melissa's daughter. After all my fruitless searching, how uncanny that she found me. I was so grateful that she reached out to me, and even more grateful that I opened her random DM.

As Michael drove, I wondered if my newfound family was as nervous as I was. *Would they like me? What if they hated me because Dad raised me and shut them out? What if they blamed my mom and me for their parents' divorce? Would we get along? Would we keep in touch? Would we become close over time?* There were so many unknowns, and I had such great anticipation. I brought along a small box filled with some of Dad's cherished mementos and some of the beautiful jewelry Mom had given me over the years. I planned to give it to them and hoped they liked it. I wasn't sure how much, if anything, they had of Alec's and Mom's. I hoped it would be well-received as a token of good faith.

I tried to calm my nerves on the ride by staring out the window at the scenery. The road looked like wide, flat ribbons undulating along the landscape at times. There were rolling hills, valleys, rocky, jagged hills, pine tree studded foot hills, and plenty of farms to occupy my time as we drove along the Pennsylvania Turnpike. The kids and I did our best to keep track of the long mountain tunnels we drove through: Blue Mountain Tunnel, Kittatinny Tunnel, and the Tuscarora Mountain Tunnel. Before I knew it, we were entering Ohio, and the next thing I knew, we were driving through Columbus and parking outside of Meghan's house.

As Michael and the kids were piling out of the car, I sat in the passenger seat and looked at Meghan's home. She had a beautiful, newly built, two-story modern farmhouse with smoky, gray-blue siding, dark, wood-paneled garage doors, and a luxe, black finish on all exterior hardware and lighting. Her yard was freshly mowed, with a thick welcoming green lawn. She lived in a beautiful, well-kept, cul-de-sac, suburban community. I was happy for her and the life she'd built. It was time to meet my family!

Before getting out, I texted my mom to let her know we had arrived safely, but she was ticked at me for visiting them and had been ignoring my calls and texts all week. She was still very bitter and hurt. Maybe one day, she'll have a change of heart.

As I made our way to the covered entrance, the front door swung open, and I heard a loud, "Hello, I'm so glad y'all made it! I'm Meghan!" And there she was; just like that, my heart did flip-flops in my chest and all my fears melted away. Meghan looked just like me, only shorter. She hugged us all and welcomed us into her home.

Meghan's two young boys ran to the entrance to greet us, hugged our kids, and dragged them off to play videos and games for the rest of the night. Michael and I made our way into the family room, where we were welcomed with big hugs. We met Melissa, Martie, and Reo, Meghan's husband. *There they were! It was like a dream come true!*

I was not prepared to see Melissa. She looked just like Mom, and it took my breath away and sent a twinge of nostalgic pain straight to my heart. It was like seeing a carbon copy. Mom passed over a decade ago, and seeing the uncanny resemblance was bittersweet. We all hugged and laughed and shed a tear and sat around talking about our lives and what we knew about our parents' past and tried to figure out why Cassandra and Alec split up and forever parted ways.

I did not have the heart to tell them about Aunt Vick's recent conversation with me. They did not need to know that. They had no living relatives on their side of the family who could fill in any of the blanks. Martie's only surviving uncle, Cassandra's brother, was a hundred years old, and his memory had faded. We all agreed that whatever happened between Alec, Cassandra, Mom, and Carla was in the past. We had nothing to do with their decisions, and we chose to wipe the slate clean and have a start fresh with no more secrets, anger, or resentment, just love.

We talked the night away and enjoyed a great dinner together. I couldn't help staring at my sisters and just marveling at the similarities they were oblivious to because they didn't know the Miller side of the family like I did. Melissa went by the name Mel; she had the same shuffling walk as Mom, and she carried her purse everywhere she went, just like Mom. She even clutched her purse the same. She was always announcing it was time for her cigarette break, the same way Mom used to! She even held her fork and sliced her food the same labored, intentional way Mom did. I was stunned.

Martie went by the name Piggy. Apparently, when she was a baby, she snorted like a little piggy when she laughed and the name stuck. Piggy moonlighted in a home décor store and wanted to become an interior designer. I am an interior designer. She and I both enjoyed working out and loved arm day! Piggy was a borderline hoarder and kept her collection of online finds in two storage units. Meghan and I both described ourselves as borderline narcoleptics. We could both sleep anywhere, anytime, at the drop of a dime. Neither of us cared where we set our heads down. Our husbands nodded, laughed in agreement, and swapped stories of our peculiar sleeping habits.

Fisher-Price Little People toys were always Piggy and Mel's favorite toys growing up. My dad always bought me Fisher-Price Little People toys and always bought my children vintage replicas of the very same Fisher-Price Little People toys.

The similarities ran even deeper and morphed from fascinating to bitterly ironic. Meghan and Piggy were both highly accomplished LPNs. Mom always wanted to have nurses in the family. She forced Aunt Vicks to be a nurse with disastrous results. Yet here were two nurses. Meghan's husband, Reo, was an Army vet with a background in logistics. He and Michael hit it off. Coincidently, my grandfather, the Old Man, specialized in logistics during his tour of duty. He wanted Alec to follow in his career footsteps, but Alec refused and joined the Air Force instead. It broke the Old Man's heart. Yet here was a logistician in the family. It turned out that Piggy's ex-husband, Ivan, was also an Army vet and specialized in logistics. What were the odds?

Mel was an accomplished artist and musician. Despite having a low IQ, she was very gifted in the arts. Her works were featured in local juried competitions, and she often won first or second place for her portraits and landscapes. She was accomplished in oil, watercolor, charcoal, and pen and ink. She was also a natural at the piano and was self-taught at age 6. She could read sheet music better than English. Mom always wanted Aunt Vicks to take up art and music, but Aunt Vicks refused. Yet here was the very prodigy that Mom had always wanted. She loved doing crosswords just like Mom, and she loved smoking More brand cigarettes back in the day, just like Mom. She lived in California for several years and worked at a local restaurant sorting the silverware and setting tables. I often wondered if she ever inadvertently crossed paths with our dad. I loved listening to her talk; her voice sounded just like Mom's. She even shared the same penchant for dropping F-bombs. I loved how she pronounced vacation as "bacation" and hospital as "hopital." She was instantaneously dear to me.

It saddened me to think of all the missed opportunities and unfulfilled dreams my grandmother experienced, simply because she refused to accept and love Cassandra, Melissa, and Martie. The very things she desperately wanted for her own family and regretted never having were manifested here in the very people she chose to turn her back on. All the qualities that ever mattered to her were embodied here in the people that didn't matter to her. Talk about bitter irony. She must be rolling in her grave right now. How sad for her and them. They never had the opportunity to know the woman I loved and knew as the Miller.

How sad that Dad never got to know and love these beautiful women. He loved children, and I know he would have been a great father to them. How sad I never got to know and love these women and have big sisters growing up. Since I was a little child, I had always wanted to have a big sister and be an aunt. They were here the whole time, less than four hours away. My heart swelled when I dwelled on them living so close by. How glad I was to be able to make up for lost time!

I put those thoughts out of my mind and continued to enjoy the weekend with my newfound family. We went to the zoo, toured Ohio State, and rode the roller coasters at Cedar Point. We all loved Mexican food and pizza and ate our fair share all weekend long. I hated to leave. They had folded my family and me into the mix like chocolate chips into batter. We all said our goodbyes, told each other that we loved each other, and vowed to keep in touch. We were sisters—not half-sisters. I left Ohio with a full heart.

All the pieces of my life just seemed to come together after that trip. It was as I if was coming to the last leg of a very long journey and everything was wrapping up and coming to a close. I learned many lessons on this journey—lessons on failure, loss, friendship, love, faith, and courage. I felt like I failed forward every step of the way and figured things out as I went, allowing God to make a way where there was none. I was tested in ways I could never have imagined and lived to tell the tale. I am stronger than I ever gave myself credit for. I am capable of so much more. Whenever I think that something isn't possible for me to accomplish, I remind myself, if I can become a sister in my adult years, then *anything* is possible.

After returning from my Ohio trip, I met with Kathy for my last therapy session. We unpacked a lot of things about my sisters, my father, and my grandmother. I accepted that I may never fully know what happened all those years ago and why people did what they did. And I decided to be okay with that! I decided to make peace with the past, love my family, forgive, and move on. I couldn't change the past; I could only move forward armed with new information, love, and a positive attitude.

I gave her an update on my money mindset shifts and how I was releasing issues around money and expanding my wealth consciousness. I began to see money as a neutral tool that could be used for creation or destruction. My feelings of guilt, fear, shame, tension, and scarcity around money were giving way to feelings of worthiness, confidence, safety, relaxation, fun, and abundance. I was getting comfortable receiving larger sums of money and using it to create experiences that benefitted me, my loved ones and the community on a larger scale. I came to know that we are all born inherently rich, despite the world's attempts to obscure that universal truth. We are here to be blessed and to be a blessing. I decided to accept life's blessings and pursue a high-paying, senior, interior design job. I accepted a role at my dream architecture firm, where I'd be heading up the design of hospitals and nursing homes. Throughout our sessions, Kathy had helped me to get clear on my boundaries, prioritize time to nourish myself, and embrace saying no. If I can't offer help from a place of love, why do it from a place of dread, guilt, obligation or resentment? Through my journey, I realized that I don't owe anyone anything. Regardless of what they've done for me in the past, I get to choose to do things for others from a full cup of abundance and love simply because I choose to and not because I *have* to. I've learned that loving others starts with loving *myself* first.

At the end of our last session, Kathy took off her glasses, leaned towards me, and declared, "In twenty years of practice, I have never met anyone like you or heard of a lived experience like yours. Your willingness to uncover the truth, face challenges, and bounce forward from trials is a rarity. You have a level of faith, courage, compassion, grace, tenacity, fortitude, and perseverance that few people ever realize in their entire lives. I am in awe of you, Alexis." I wasn't expecting this beautiful closure. I just assumed that what happened to me and how I chose to face it was commonplace. I accepted her generous outpouring with humility, and we parted ways. I drove past her office a couple of weeks later, and the space was vacant! The practice had moved, and that office space remained vacant for the next three years. It was as if she was there when I needed her and left when I could stand on my own.

Truth be told, when I reflect back on this journey, I was never truly alone. No matter how bleak the present circumstances looked, my eyes usually deceived me. More oft than not, there was always help on the horizon. I believe God works in mysterious ways and conspires to help us. Countless people came into my life when I needed them most, not just Kathy. Every time I demonstrated the smallest drop of faith to help Dad or settle his affairs, people with the information I needed appeared, right on time. Every time I blindly contacted someone, I had no way of knowing who would be picking up the other phone line or who would be on the other side of that office door or teller window. Yet time and time again, kind souls with big hearts revealed a bit of information to point me in the right direction until, eventually, I made my way through this winding journey, equipped with nothing more than an ounce of courage and a drop of faith. Even my mother came around and softened her tune and offered to help me in any way she could. In some ways, our relationship has deepened from this experience and I hope it continues to flourish.

I never imagined I'd find a best friend during this dark time in my life, yet that is exactly what Virginia became. We talk weekly, and we have been there for each other through all of life's ups and downs.

Harry was another kind soul who helped me immensely. It took me four years of due diligence to plow through red tape, resolve the back taxes, remove the lien, and receive the money held in escrow. It happened on an ordinary day at my kitchen table as I was preparing to make dinner. I received an email with the official tax documents and forwarded them to the title company while a pot of pasta boiled on the stove. That was it. It was finished in one, anticlimactic moment of sending an email. That was the last step to finally wrapping up everything. My duties as executrix were ending.

Shortly thereafter, I received a letter from Harry. To paraphrase, it read, "It truly was my pleasure being of service to you. I've never had a client like you and probably never will again. Your story touched my heart. I was always amazed when you arrived at my office, despite it all, with a smile on your face and a warm, encouraging word. Just so that you know, I only charged you a third of my full, hourly rate for all services rendered. Everyone loves a good Cinderella story. Have you considered writing a memoir? All the best, Harry."

In retrospect, I wouldn't change anything about the entire experience. It all just added up: the challenging times, the lovely moments, and the never-want-to-repeat moments. They all just added up to equip me for a time such as this. The totality of the experiences both broke me and made me whole. I'm so grateful for my life. What I've experienced, learned, and lived through. I am grateful for it all: the heartache, frustration, angst, confusion, pain, and joy—all of it. I wouldn't trade my lived experience for anything. Although it hurt like hell to go through it, I made it through alive. In the process, I witnessed miracles and uncovered gifts, talents, and qualities I never knew I possessed. I realized that God is stronger than I thought He was, He is bigger than my circumstances, and my strength is irrelevant. He is my supply and He does the heavy lifting. The experiences transformed me and enabled me to blossom into a greater version of myself. The lessons prepared me for the sweetest fruit of all: my sisters, niece, and nephews. Reflecting on where I came from helps me to appreciate what I have now. It is my hope that my story inspires you to give yourself permission to make peace with your past, love yourself unconditionally, and do something remarkable with your life while you're on this Earth.

The world has so much more to offer you, invisible offers are everywhere. Are you willing to let go of what you know in order to receive them? Faith is the substance of things hoped for; the evidence of things not seen. The secret to faith is action. May you choose to get in the arena of life daily and bravely accumulate as many firsts as possible while you still have the chance. Don't wait until catastrophe or loss strikes to test your faith and build your trust muscle. Each day offers a new beginning, a choice to be reborn and grow into your fullest potential. Dream big and be brave. The world is your buffet. Will you choose fear or faith today?

As for my sisters, me, and my niece, we've done many firsts together. We text nearly every day and FaceTime each other a couple of times per month. We've gone on vacation together; they went to the Jersey shore for the first time, with me. There are still awkward "getting to know you" moments, like when I didn't know Meghan's birthday, how many years she's been married, or what her favorite color is. In the end, I believe that love overcame all things and moved across space and time, to bring together two families separated by decades of lies and deceit. I believe in my heart that once I decided to go forward with saving the house from sheriff's sale and settling Dad's debts, every power in heaven and on earth conspired in my favor to bring our families together. My mom still hasn't decided to meet my sisters yet. Maybe one day, she will. I hope so.

I think my father would be pleased with the way things turned out.

I have faced adversity, loss, and grief and made my way through. May my life story inspire you during those times when you're facing your own trying chapter. Loss and grief come in many forms and levels and the lived experience is unique to each person. When you feel like you've hit rock bottom, show up as best you can, even if all you can muster is an ounce of courage and a drop of faith. Rock bottom is fertile ground for faith to flourish and identity to transform. Surrender to the circumstances and trust that a way will be made where there is no way. What if it's all coming together to reveal a new chapter, starring you as the person you most want to become? I am bearing witness to you and claiming your victory. I am passing my torch on to you. Share your story, it matters. Because, your victory over adversity is someone else's miracle.

MILLER FAMILY PHOTOS

From left to right: The Miller and The Old Man, military assignment, Germany, 1949

From left to right: Vicks, The Miller, and Alec, military assignment, Germany, 1949

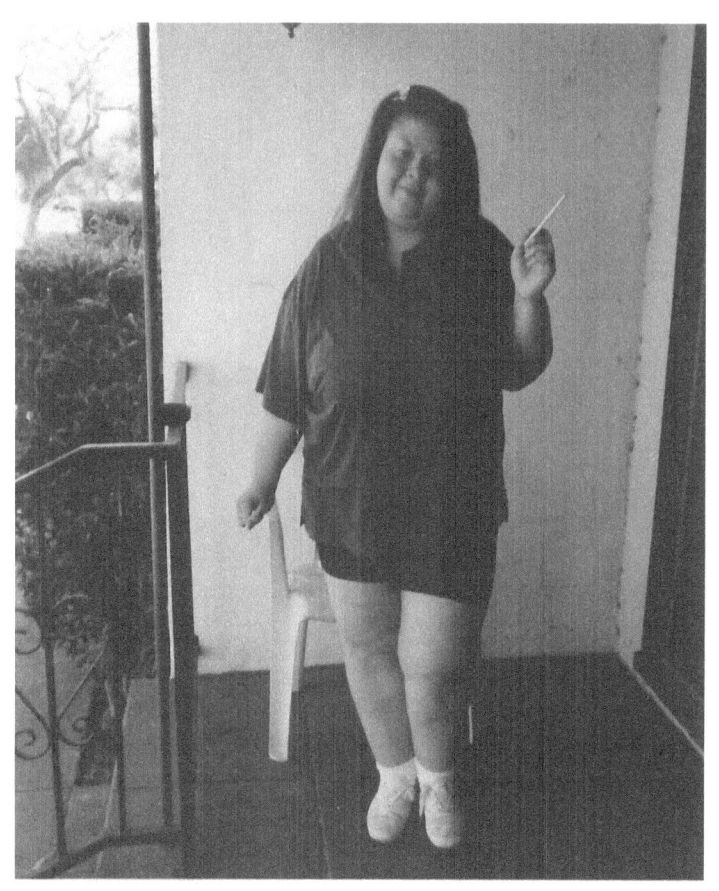

Mel, California, 1999

From left to right: Alexis and Alec, wedding day, Pennsylvania, 2000

From left to right: Alexis and Mel, first meeting, Ohio, 2018

From left to right: Piggy, Alexis, Mel, and Meghan, first meeting, Ohio, 2018

Thank You for Reading
The Miller's Angel Baby!

I hope my book has been helpful to you or someone you love. If you enjoyed this book, I would love to hear about it in a review. Your reviews are always welcome!

Thank You!

Remember to claim your free gift! Download your free copy of the empowering affirmations I developed over the past several years and compiled in one place for you. Your gift includes affirmations to help improve your mindset and outlook when facing daily struggles, grief, or setbacks. You can download your free gift today by visiting www.alexisrosebooks.com

Let's Connect

Website: www.alexisrosebooks.com

Instagram: @AlexisRoseBooks

Facebook: Alexis Rose Books

To keep up on the latest news and any upcoming books, I hope you'll connect with me today. I look forward to hearing from you.

All the best,

Alexis

ACKNOWLEDGMENTS

Writing a book is harder than I thought and more rewarding than I could have ever imagined. After reading countless acknowledgements in other books, I'm humbled, grateful, and honored to be writing my own. The life events that motivated me to share my story are bittersweet, and I knew it would be emotionally challenging to pour my heart out on the pages. The love and support I received along the way played a crucial role when I got stuck or scared. It truly took a village to make this memoir a reality.

First and foremost, I'd like to thank God; through Him all things are possible.

To my rock and favorite human, my husband Michael, thank you for always being my guiding North Star through it all. When I couldn't see a way, you guided me. Thank you for always having my best interest at heart, even when your brutal honesty stung, deepdown I appreciated your feedback. Thank you for modeling the values of commitment, integrity, courage, and humility. Thank you for reminding me that I can do anything I set my mind to.

Thanks Ma and Dad, I wouldn't have made it this far in life without you. Ma, you are incredible. I would not be who I am without your discipline, guidance, bitter truth bombs, and unconditional love. Thank you for the sacrifices you made to raise me. Thank you for encouraging me to pursue my dreams. Thank you for supporting my family as I turned my dreams into reality. Your commitment to my family gave me the comfort and confidence to spread my wings and fly, knowing that my kids were safe and loved at home. Dad, I wish we had been able to spend more time together. I feel like I barely knew you. Thank you for your generosity, support, unconditional love, and entertaining tall tales from your days on the road as a truck driver. Your practical pearls of wisdom, guided me as I wrote this memoir. You taught me that every life experience has its own value and purpose- even if it's not what you asked for- it still matters.

To my beloved sisters, Piggy and Mel, you are a miracle in my life. You are an answered prayer and have blessed me beyond my wildest dreams. The unconditional love, radical authenticity, instant acceptance, and big sister protection you generously showed me from day one, bursts my heart with grateful pangs of joy. I love you. Feisty Meghan, you were the missing key that unlocked everything. Thank you for finding me. This book would not have been written if it weren't for you. Meeting you was the catalyst that sparked my desire and fueled my will power to write this memoir. Thank you for your unrelenting pursuit of the truth. Your keen detective skills paid off!

To my grandmom, The Miller, you are the stuff of legends. Your grit, audacity, deep wisdom of the old ways, and unconditional love for me are indelibly etched in every fiber of my being. Writing this memoir doesn't change how I feel about you. I miss you and love you unconditionally. I think of you on rainy days, I know you're always looking out for me and seeing to it that I reach my destination safely. Thank you for being my guardian angel.

Virginia, my soul sister, my mirror, my teacher, my best friend. Words escape me. There are not enough adjectives to describe my feelings for you. You were a balm to my soul when my wounds were raw and exposed. You were there for every hurdle and victory, prodding me on and mending my heart. Thank you for being by my side and bearing witness to my journey. I couldn't have faced any of this without you. Thank you for your support and unconditional love.

Wendy, I miss you. Your hair salon was a place of refuge and replenishment during my darkest hours. Your life was taken from you, way too soon. Your memory shines on and this memoir is a small token of my appreciation to you and your amazing stylists. Your legacy continues and you will always be remembered for your generosity, warm smile and welcoming disposition. Thank you for many years of good conversation amongst the company of great women.

To Chandler Bolt, founder of Self-Publishing School, I am forever grateful that I stumbled across your podcast. Chandler, you've created a wonderful framework to help aspiring authors take their concepts and turn them into books that inspire and impact lives. Your team of coaches and community of authors was the glue that held me together and kept me accountable and encouraged. I knew there were other people across the globe just like me, staring at a blank screen and giving their all to the page during the wee hours and in the cracks of time during their busy lives. To the entire team of professionals at Self-Publishing School, thank you for helping me transform my raw ideas into polishing my raw ideas into a beautiful finished product. To my launch team, thank you for taking the time to read my memoir and promote it!

To the talented, Urban Fantasy Academy author, Barbara Hartzler, your guidance and accountability has been indispensable. I could not have asked for a better accountability coach and mentor. Your industry knowledge, guidance, encouragement, and tough love helped me cross the finish line. Thank you for pushing me. I appreciate you.

Then there is my editor, Jeannie Culbertson, whose profession-alism, creativity, and energy instantly drew me to her. Thank you for pouring yourself into this labor of love, honoring the spirit of my message, and amplifying it. You have a way with words, and I appreciate your talents.

To my marvelous proofreader, Tameka Brown, I believe we were destined to work together. You added the finishing touch and took this memoir across the finish line. Thank you for your keen eye and attention to detail.

To my talented photographer, Tracey Redford, you had me at Paris! I'm so glad our paths crossed. Your warm demeanor and charm, put me instantly at ease when I met you, and I knew I'd feel comfortable working with you. Your eye for style and composition is brilliant, thank you for the fun photoshoot and lovely talk about all things France!

About the Author

Alexis is a wife, mother, daughter, and, most recently, a sister! She is an avid reader, loves sci-fi, and is learning to speak and read French fluently. In addition, Alexis is a philanthropist and a servant-leader who enjoys inspiring others to live to their fullest potential. She lives with her family in Pennsylvania.

You can find Alexis online at www.AlexisRoseBooks.com

Resources

Books

The Alchemist – Paulo Coelho, 2014, 25th Anniversary Edition

The Bible

Love is Letting Go of Fear- Gerald G. Jampolsky, MD. 2011, 3rd Edition

The Four Agreements- Don Miguel Ruiz, 1997

The Illustrated Happiness Trap, How to Stop Struggling and Start Living.

The Mastery of Love, a Practical Guide to the Art of Relationship - Don Miguel Ruiz, 1999

The Miracle of Mindfulness, an Introduction to the Practice of Meditation- Thich Nhat Hanh, translated by Mobi Ho, 1987

The Miracle Morning, the Not-So-Obvious Secret Guaranteed to Transform Your Life Before 8 a.m.- Hal Elrod, 2016

Style Your Mind, a Workbook and Lifestyle Guide for Women Who Want to Design Their Thoughts, Empower Themselves, and Build a Beautiful Life- Cara Alwill Leyba, 2017

The Untethered Soul, the Journey Beyond Yourself – Michael A, Singer, 2007

Websites

Kripalu Center for Yoga & Health - Homepage | Kripalu

National Archives, Veterans Service Records. Request Military Service Records | National Archives

National Veterans Foundation; Life Line for Vets. How to Get a Copy of DD214 - Instructions to Receive (nvf.org)

www.ingramcontent.com/pod-product-compliance
Lightning Source LLC
Chambersburg PA
CBHW030908120626
46554CB00001B/54